RELIGION IN CONTEMPORARY JAPAN

DATE DUE

BRODART   Cat. No. 23-221

Religion in Contemporary Japan

by

Ian Reader

UNIVERSITY OF HAWAII PRESS
HONOLULU

Published in the United States by
University of Hawaii Press
2840 Kolowalu Street
Honolulu, Hawaii 96822

Published in Great Britain by
MACMILLAN ACADEMIC AND PROFESSIONAL LTD
Houndmills, Basingstoke,
Hampshire RG21 2XS
and London

Printed in Great Britain

Library of Congress Cataloging-in-Publication Data
Reader, Ian, 1949–
    Religion in contemporary Japan / by Ian Reader.
      p. cm.
    Includes bibliographical references and index.
    ISBN 0–8248–1353–7.—ISBN 0–8248–1354–5 (pbk.)
    1. Japan—Religion—1945–   I. Title.
BL2209.R42   1991   90–38407
291′.0952—dc20   CIP

For Rosemary

Contents

Acknowledgements   viii

Conventions   x

Introduction   xi

1 Turning to the Gods in Times of Trouble:
  The Place, Time and Structure of Japanese
  Religion   1

2 Unifying Traditions, Cosmological
  Perspectives and the Vitalistic Universe   23

3 'Born Shinto . . .': Community, Festivals,
  Production and Change   55

4 '. . . Die Buddhist': Zen, Death and the
  Ancestors   77

5 Individuals, Ascetics and the Expression of
  Power   107

6 Sites and Sights: Temples and Shrines as
  Centres of Power and Entertainment   134

7 Actions, Amulets and the Expression of
  Meaning: Reflections of Need and
  Statements of Desire   168

8 Spirits, Satellites and a User-Friendly
  Religion: Agonshū and the New Religions   194

  Conclusion: Mystery, Nostalgia and the
  Shifting Sands of Continuity   234

  Notes   244

  References Cited   260

  Index   268

Acknowledgements

I did the research for this book while living and teaching in Japan during April 1981–April 1982, and September 1983–January 1989. I would like to thank my colleagues, friends and students at the two universities where I worked, Kōbe University of Commerce and Kansai University of Foreign Studies, for making my stay enjoyable and for contributing in various ways to this book. Over the years I have also benefited immensely from countless conversations with friends, colleagues, acquaintances and people met casually in temple courtyards: I owe a large debt of gratitude to all of them. Special mention must be made of the Revd Oda Baisen of Tōganji in Nagoya for his friendship and constant support throughout these years and for making the temple a second home to both myself and my wife.

Many academic colleagues have added something, directly or indirectly, to this book as well. In particular I would like to thank Beth Harrison for many long conversations about all aspects of contemporary religion in Japan. I am grateful to the *Japanese Journal of Religious Studies* and its editor Dr Paul Swanson of Nanzan University for allowing me permission to reproduce, in slightly different form, the information on Agonshū in Chapter 8, which first appeared in the journal in 1988. My Japanese academic colleagues in the Shūkyō Shakaigaku no Kai in Osaka, especially Professors Shiobara Tsutomu of Osaka and Iida Takafumi of Toyama University, are also thanked for their contributions to my growing understanding of the overall subject.

I can do no more than extend a general thank-you to them, and to all the anonymous members of new religions, pilgrims, temple-goers and priests who spared the time to talk to me, and say that I hope this book is worthy of their help. Needless to say, what mistakes there are herein are mine alone.

There are three people to whom I have a special debt of gratitude. Professor Ian Gow, Director of the Scottish Centre for Japanese Studies at the University of Stirling, has actively supported the writing of this book by allowing me the time off other duties to work on and complete the manuscript: suffice it to say that without this generosity it would not have seen the light of day so readily. My wife Dorothy has given indispensable support throughout: she was an unflagging companion in forays to festivals and walks along pilgrimage routes and up to mountain temples, and a perceptive observer who helped in gathering information at temples and shrines and in interviewing priests. More than that she has constantly encouraged me and kept me going when I thought I would never finish the book, and deserves my deepest thanks.

The final thanks go to our daughter Rosemary who was born just about the time I started to put preliminary pen to paper on the topic, and was crawling enthusiastically as it came to completion. It is to her this book is dedicated, in the hope that she will grow to love and enjoy Japan as much as we have, and that she may enjoy one of the ideals central to the Japanese religious world – a happy, fruitful and productive life.

Conventions

Japanese names are given throughout this book in Japanese order, that is, family name followed by given name. Long vowel sounds in Japanese words and names have been indicated with a macron as, for example, in Sōtō Zen Buddhist sect. Following normal conventions I have omitted the macron in widely known words and geographical names (for example, Shinto, Tokyo, Osaka).

When Japanese words are used in the text they are printed in italics, with a general explanation of their meaning in English given the first time they occur. In a few instances I have continued to use the Japanese term throughout rather than use an English equivalent, because the potential equivalents are liable to convey nuances that are not quite applicable.

Two words that appear consistently throughout this book are 'shrine' and 'temple': the former is the standard word used in English to signify a Shinto institution, and the latter a Buddhist one. Thus when I speak of shrines I am referring to Shinto, and when temples to Buddhist institutions. I have reaffirmed this point in the first chapter, where I also suggest that in many ways there are not all that many differences between them anyway. I have also used the word 'sect' as a translation for *shū*, the suffix used for Buddhist organisations in Japan. This again is fairly standard: some people prefer 'school' but this gives, to my mind, too philosophical a slant that does not fit in with Japanese realities. All translations from Japanese sources are mine, and where they are from written sources I have given the reference in the notes.

Introduction

The major purpose of this book is to give the reader an overview of the contemporary nature of religion in Japan, in particular looking at religious behaviour and the ways in which religious themes are found in the lives of Japanese people. My focus is concerned with religion at ground level, in the actions people perform in religious contexts and with the extent to which social, cultural and personal behaviour manifests religious traits. In short, I am more interested in studying religiosity than the theoretical structures and philosophical frameworks of religion or, indeed, of religions. This is doubtless an approach conditioned by my own experiences and ways of working, for much of my study on religion has not only been from sociological and anthropological perspectives, starting with religion in Africa and then moving, via India, to the Far East and specifically to Japan, but has very much been involved with participant observation.

Before I first went to Japan I studied Zen Buddhist thought, but it did not take long living in and visiting Zen temples, talking to the people at them and watching what went on there, for me to realise that there was a profound difference between the ideals and theories espoused by Buddhism and what actually went on at Zen (and other) Buddhist temples. The year I spent at Zen temples helped me in my understanding of the problems facing religions as they attempt to deal with social situations and to work at ground level, trying to transmit religious ideas in a manner that can be understood by the ordinary Japanese looking through the lens of his or her socio-cultural experiences. Much of my earlier academic writing has looked from various angles at this problem, and it will surface periodically throughout this book, especially where I examine the social position and workings of contemporary Buddhism (Chapter 4).

After that initial period I returned to Japan and lived there for just over five years, during which time I taught courses about religion in Japan to both Japanese and Western students. Besides teaching and researching, I have talked extensively about religion to innumerable Japanese friends, colleagues and acquaintances, academic and non-academic, some religious and others avowing cynicism and lack of any religious feeling. I have interviewed religious officiants, worshippers, practitioners and other less devout participants in the religious process in many different situations – Buddhist temples, Shinto shrines, the centres of new religious movements, at pilgrimage sites and meditation centres, or at some of the innumerable little wayside shrines that dot the Japanese landscape.

It has been, wherever possible, a participatory, or at least an active, period of research. I love travel, and one of the delights of living in Japan was the ability to combine this love with my academic research. Sundays and other 'days off' were generally days to visit religious centres, while longer holidays were times to go off on one of the pilgrimages that make up Japan's rich pilgrimage tradition. All of this has, I feel, done far more than just back up the research I have done in libraries: it has conditioned much of my overall approach, may well have taught me more and certainly has given me more enjoyment! It has proved to be a most rewarding and entertaining, if at times exhausting and, occasionally, frustrating, experience which has shown me the immense energies, variety and richness inherent in the Japanese religious tapestry. If one major aim of this book is to demonstrate the workings and major themes of religion in Japan, another is to share some of the excitement and pleasure that I have derived from my studies.

Words like 'excitement' and 'entertaining' might not seem, at first glance, to be all that closely associated with common images of religion, but I use them here with emphasis. The immense varieties and constant developments within the Japanese religious world make it highly entertaining and stimulating to study and no one who is motivated to engage in study and research on religion in Japan is going to be bored or at a loose end. The ways that religious activities are carried out further heightens this sense of entertainment, as anyone who visits a crowded Buddhist temple or Shinto shrine on a Sunday, festival day or public holiday, when the religious centre might become a noisy marketplace of stalls, ringing bells and muttered prayers, will rapidly find out. The descriptions in Chapters 6 and 7, which are designed to highlight what may be seen at such places, will demonstrate just how the religious process in Japan is so often experienced not with any type of fear and trembling, but with friendliness and relaxed joy.

This is a theme encountered throughout the Japanese religious spectrum. I have travelled on buses with pilgrims visiting holy sites and with members of new religious movements journeying to the holy centres of their religions for a specially revered religious festival; invariably the atmosphere has been one of prayer and laughter. The manner in which 'religion is done' is infective, or at least it has been to this observer. Visually, too, Japanese religion is colourful and active, which makes it beguiling for participants and observers alike. It is also, to a great extent, celebratory, as subsequent discussions of festivals and rituals will try to demonstrate: there is, in the Japanese religious world in general, a major focus on, and commitment to, this world and the achievement and celebration of joy within it.

This is not to say, of course, that religion should only be viewed through the lens of entertainment. There are, naturally, times when a more sombre and serious face appears, as with the rituals that occur after death, with the rigours of the Zen meditation hall described in Chapter 4, with the austere and at times death-defying practices of ascetics described in Chapter 5, or with the problem-solving and exorcistic mechanisms of the new religious groups dealt with in Chapter 8. Throughout, though, there remains a powerful focus on pragmatic action, on ritual and expressive, externalised behaviour through which religious themes are given life and meaning: the focus that I have placed on praxis and action remains constant even where the themes that are expressed may vary.

In Chapters 1 and 2 I present a general overview of what I consider to be the major themes and frameworks of religion in Japan. Chapter 1 in particular discusses attitudes to and notions of religion in Japan by looking at some areas in which religious behaviour and belonging occur, and provides some contemporary perspectives and statistics concerning religious action, belief and belonging and the meanings and lessons that can be drawn from them. The second chapter follows on from this by discussing the major underlying and unifying themes and basic concepts as well as the cosmological orientations of the Japanese religious world. Chapters 3 and 4 look primarily at the social setting of religion in Japan, especially at the roles played by the two major established traditions of Shinto and Buddhism in social terms, the ways that they combine to provide Japanese people with a sense of social identity in the contexts of family, community, company and nation, and the changes that are occurring within them in the present day. Chapter 4 deals at the same time with the position of Buddhism in perhaps its best known Japanese form, by examining contemporary Zen temple life and how this relates to Buddhism's social position in Japan.

Chapter 5 looks at the position of the individual as a religious figure, and examines how the religious world has constantly been an arena for self-expression. It looks especially at the rich Japanese tradition of asceticism and the ways in which austere religious disciplines continue to exist and attract attention in contemporary Japan. The theme of self-expression is never far from the surface in Chapters 6 and 7 either, when I discuss why certain places become major religious sites that in turn frequently become tourist centres; what the visitor to such places may see; and what meanings can be read into what goes on at them. In Chapter 8 I look at the new religions of Japan, one of the most striking and commented-upon phenomena in recent religious history: my examination largely concentrates on Agonshū, one of a number of new religious movements that have sprung to prominence since the mid-1970s and that incorporate an interesting admixture of old cosmological themes and ultra-modern presentational techniques.

Throughout these eight chapters attention will be paid to contemporary changes and to the ways in which the rapidly changing face of Japanese society is influencing developments in religious terms in each of the areas under discussion. Issues such as Japan's economic wealth, the demographic shifts that have resulted from the country's transformation from an agricultural to an industrial society, and the overall processes of modernisation and internationalisation and the effects these are having on Japanese religiosity will also come under discussion. At the same time, the data introduced demonstrate that, whilst there is immense flux and change within the Japanese religious environment, there is equally a powerful tide of continuity, with many themes being constantly restated and reiterated in new and contemporary contexts. The conclusion attempts to sum up some of these themes and makes some overall comments on contemporary elements, changes and continuities in the Japanese religious picture at the beginning of the last decade of the century.

Ultimately, then, this book sets out to provide a comprehensive picture of the place, workings and perspectives of religion in contemporary Japanese society and in the lives of Japanese people, and also gives some indications of contemporary activities and developments within the Japanese religious world. Because it seeks to examine the contemporary situation, and because it takes, for the most part, an eye-level view, looking at religion through the ways it is carried out in daily life, there is minimal focus on historical and philosophical perspectives. Much literature exists in English and

Japanese to enable the reader to gain a background in these.[1] There is far less that deals with the overall contemporary situation, and it is this situation that this book attempts to rectify. I shall say no more for now, but will instead turn to the task of presenting the evidence on which I build my overall picture, in the hope that this will provoke further thought, discussions and enthusiasms on what is a fascinating and absorbing subject.

1 Turning to the Gods in Times of Trouble: The Place, Time and Structure of Japanese Religion

Not long after I first arrived in Japan in 1981 two Japanese friends, knowing my interest in religion, decided to take me out for the day to visit some Buddhist temples and Shinto shrines.* Before setting out they assured me that they were neither religious nor did they have any interest in religion: their participation in the trip was purely to show me some places that would be of interest to me in my studies. I have long since become inured to Japanese people telling me that they are not religious, even whilst performing acts of an overtly religious nature such as praying at a shrine or walking a pilgrimage route dressed in the traditional clothing of a Japanese pilgrim, so that nowadays I hardly take any notice of such protestations. At the time, however, I did, assuming that this meant my friends would act similarly to me at such places — interested, respectful but not worshipful.

It came as a surprise, then, that at the Shinto shrine we first visited, my friends both tossed a coin into the offertory box, clapped their hands twice — the standard way of greeting the *kami*, the deities of the Shinto tradition — and, bowing their heads, held their hands together in prayer. Next we visited a Buddhist temple, where they went through exactly the same performance, offering, bowing, clapping and praying earnestly. Technically one does not clap one's hands before praying at the Buddhist temple. Although the Shinto *kami* are conceived of as needing to be aroused or summoned

---

* Buddhist and Shinto places of worship are referred to by different words in Japanese. The most common for Buddhist places are *tera* and *jiin*, as well as the suffix *ji*, which is added to the temple name, while in Shinto the words most used are *jinja* and *jingū*. It is standard to translate the words relating to Buddhist institutions as 'temple', and for Shinto, 'shrine', and this is the convention I have used throughout this book. Thus, wherever the word 'temple' is used, I shall be talking of a Buddhist institution, and when 'shrine' is used, a Shinto one.

before one can direct a prayer at them, the Buddhist figures of worship — Buddhas and Bodhisattvas — are considered to be ever-vigilant. It is not, therefore, necessary to rouse them before praying. I have since become used to seeing Japanese people clapping before praying at Buddhist temples or praying at Shinto shrines without clapping, and no longer register surprise at this apparent transgression of the theoretical technicalities. At the time, however, I was taken aback and naïve enough to point out their mistake. They were mystified by my claim to know what they should have done, for each had imbibed this method of prayer from their parents, and had hardly considered that there might be any differentiation in the ways that one treated *kami* and Buddhas, at least on the level of encountering and making entreaties to them.

My friends' actions were a clear example of the ways in which, at grass roots level at least, Japanese people do not seem to differentiate much, if at all, between the two major religious traditions in Japan, Shinto and Buddhism. It also showed that the two are not at all exclusive: praying to one does not prevent one from praying to the other. The complementary nature of Shinto and Buddhism (and, indeed, of other Japanese religious currents and traditions) will be discussed more thoroughly later; for the moment this incident will suffice to show quite how naturally Japanese people may approach the two without any real discrimination or differentiation between the two.

There is plenty of empirical data available to confirm this, and I shall cite just one example here. In a survey conducted in 1983 by Japanese sociologists of religion amongst worshippers at Ishikiri shrine, a popular Shinto shrine in eastern Osaka, out of 153 respondents over one-third (55 in all) stated that they considered the *kami* and Buddhas to be the same; virtually the same number (58) felt they were different; while the rest were undecided, 19 answering that they did not know and 21 not responding. Of the 58 who said they were different, 45 were extremely unclear as to what differences there might be: in reality, according to the researchers, the degree to which those surveyed confused or glossed over differences between the *kami* and Buddhas was extremely high.[1] In fact, as will be seen in subsequent chapters, there is very little differentiation, especially at explicit levels of religious action, between apparently separate religious traditions in Japan, with Shinto and Buddhism in particular interpenetrating to form an amalgam in the eyes of the general populace.

Before I move on to deal with the perhaps more complex issue of why my friends both disavowed religious feelings and participated so openly in religious actions in not one but two traditions, I shall relate another favourite story, which I have used before in print[2] and in lectures but which bears telling once more. It concerns a conversation I had some years ago with two Japanese university professors, both highly literate and well versed in Western thought and culture: neither regarded himself as religious in any degree. However when, as is often the case when I am around, the conversation got on to matters concerning religion, one turned to the other and asked: 'What Buddhist sect do you belong to?' The other responded: 'I do not know: no one in our household has died yet.' He then added tht he also had no idea of the doctrines and beliefs of any Buddhist sect in Japan.

It should be noted that the first professor did not ask the second whether he was a member of a Buddhist sect: he took this for granted, a reasonably fair assumption in a country where, according to yearly religious statistics, some 92 million people, or over three-quarters of the population, are counted as Buddhist.[3] Nor did the second professor question whether he did or did not belong. He knew that, however little he might know about doctrine and the like, and however ignorant he might be at the moment about the name of his Buddhist sect, there did exist a sense of belonging and affiliation for him and his household. In particular there was a circumstance in which all would be known: the situation of death.

Buddhism has a history of over 1400 years in Japan and in that time has produced many great religious leaders and sects. There are several Buddhist universities and schools, and many noted Buddhist scholars. In addition, Buddhism has played a major part in the development of Japanese art and culture, while innumerable books on Buddhist thought and practice can be found in every bookstore. Yet, despite all this, my friend did not know either what sect he belonged to or any of its doctrines or beliefs. This ignorance, however, did not preclude affiliation or a latent sense of belonging which would materialise when the situation and circumstances demanded and required it.

Again, there is much relevant data to show that he was by no means alone in his ignorance. A depth survey carried out by the Sōtō Zen Buddhist sect, one of the largest and oldest Buddhist organisations in Japan, shows clearly how little people who are regarded as members of the sect actually knew about it even as they are involved in many of its rituals and ceremonies. Less than 10 per cent knew who had established the sect's main temples and who were its founding figures in Japan: only a similar number knew that the historical Buddha was the main object of worship in the sect. The survey in general showed a woeful lack of knowledge amongst members as to teachings, doctrines and facts about the sect, yet at the same time it showed extremely high levels of participation in memorial rites for the dead and various yearly rituals concerned with the dead that were carried out under its aegis.[4]

I have introduced these stories and related surveys not because they are out of the ordinary but because they so aptly sum up major themes encountered in the study of religion in Japan, especially in terms of everyday activity. My friends denying any religious beliefs yet praying at shrines and temples indiscriminately, or avowing a belonging to Buddhism without any knowledge of its principles and without knowing what sort of Buddhism it was, are very much the rule rather than the exception. Encapsulating the themes of both stories is the response made by one of my Japanese students to my question about her religious affiliations:

> I am not religious. My family belongs to the Zen sect but we did not know this until my grandfather died last year. We thought we were Jōdoshū [Pure Land Buddhist].

How, one might ask, can one be *not* religious *and* Buddhist at the same time, Buddhist yet ignorant of Buddhism, or, as with the first friends, *not* religious yet pray at different religious centres seemingly without discrimination? Should one see the couple as irreligious because of what they say, or religious because of what they do, or the professor (and those surveyed by the Sōtō sect) as Buddhist because of their recognised affiliation, or not because of their apparently total lack of understanding? How does one attempt to categorise the student, seemingly not religious and Buddhist in the same sentence?

These questions are pertinent, for in their answers can be found many basic guidelines to the understanding of Japanese religion at the very least, and also about the wider nature of religion in general. In order to begin to answer these questions, and to begin to draw some of the parameters that encompass the world of religion in Japan, I shall outline some of the empirical evidence that is available concerning the religious attitudes and behaviour of the Japanese: by analysing them, some perspectives on these apparently puzzling questions may emerge.

RELIGION IN JAPAN: SOME PRELIMINARY CONCEPTS AND STATISTICS

Japanese people in general are quick to say they are not religious and to describe their society as one where religion either does not exist or has in some way died out. Winston Davis writes of a conversation he had with a Japanese banker on a flight to Japan in 1971:

> When he learned that I was studying Japanese religion he shook his head and sadly assured me that there no longer was such a thing. I was later to hear the same thing from many other Japanese.[5]

In the 1980s I too have received similar assurances. It is almost as if many Japanese would like to convey the impression that Japan is a wholly secular society in which religion has to all intents and purposes disappeared. As this book will demonstrate, however, this is certainly not the case for, in reality, Japanese people in general exhibit extremely high levels of religious activity and behaviour, and Japanese society and culture are intricately interwoven with religious themes.

Admittedly, if one were to examine this issue from the angle of belief the picture of an irreligious society might hold some water, for the numerous surveys on religious affiliation and feelings that have been carried out by various official bodies, newspaper companies and academics in Japan (where data collection and analysis is something of a national pastime) invariably show the Japanese admitting to comparatively low levels of religious belief. A major survey carried out under the auspices of the Japanese public broadcasting system NHK in 1981 showed that only 33 per cent of Japanese respondents affirmed religious belief (compared to 93 per cent in a comparable American response), while 65 per cent stated that they 'had no religious belief(s)'.[6] In another survey carried out by Gallup and fondly quoted in support of the view that Japan is highly secularised, 14 per cent of the Japanese respondents considered religion to be very important, a far lower rate than in India, the USA and other countries surveyed,[7] while a 1978 survey carried out by the Japanese Prime Minister's office concerning religious attitudes amongst those under 30 showed approximately 20 per cent of the Japanese respondents affirming religious belief, in comparison to 57 per cent for France (the next lowest) and percentages well into the 80s for the USA and the UK, and of 95 per cent for West Germany.[8]

Further surveys carried out regularly on a five-yearly basis under the auspices of the Japanese Ministry of Education have produced fairly constant figures, with just over 30 per cent of respondents each time affirming that they have religious belief. The 1958 survey produced a figure of 35 per cent, while in 1963 and 1968 it fell to 31 per cent, going down to 25 per cent in 1973 before climbing back up to 34 per cent in 1978. In 1983 it had slipped a little to 32 per cent.[9] In all these surveys the numbers claiming no religious beliefs hovered around the 65 per cent mark.

In just about all the surveys that have been carried out in recent decades the numbers of those affirming religious belief have hovered somewhere around the 30 per cent mark and those saying that they have no religious belief somewhere around the 65 per cent mark. When, however, further questions are asked, it becomes clear that lack of belief does not mean lack of action, lack of concern or lack of relationship with religious issues. For example, when asked whether they consider religious feelings to be important, the Japanese are likely to respond positively, with on average around 70 per cent or more stating that they are important and somewhere between 10 and 15 per cent on average denying that they are.[10]

Levels of belonging also have traditionally been high in Japan and continue to be so. It is common for people, even while denying that they are religious, to state that they are affiliated to Shinto and Buddhism, the two major institutional religious structures in Japan. Every year, for example, the Japanese Agency for Cultural Affairs publishes a yearbook giving membership levels of religious organisations in Japan, and this invariably provides data to show that most people have a recognised sense of religious belonging, and that this belonging is often multiple in nature. In 1985 some 76 per cent of the population, over 92 million people, were classified as Buddhist, some 115 million as Shinto (almost 95 per cent of the population), just over 1 million as Christian and 14.4 million as belonging to 'other religions' (mostly new religious movements not counted under the Buddhist or Shinto rubric[11]) — a total of 223 million members of religious organisations. The population of Japan was, at the time, 121 million, which shows clearly that a very large number of people are registered as affiliated to more than one religion.[12]

The discrepancy is largely because of multiple affiliation, although there is the added problem that most religious organisations in

Japan in submitting their figures are liable to provide inflated and optimistic estimations of their strength. Common practices include counting every member of a household as a member when one person joins, and not removing from membership registers those who have long ceased their affiliation, which is particularly common among Buddhist temples.[13] New religions also have a penchant for signing on anyone who attends their events and meetings, whether they become active members or not: I found that I had become a member of one new religion some years ago because of my research and attendance at some of its ceremonies.

When there is multiple affiliation, it is usually Shinto – Buddhist: the phrase 'born Shinto, die Buddhist' reflects a general social and religious reality for many Japanese. It is customary to take new-born babies to Shinto shrines to receive the blessing and protection of the *kami*: at death it is the Buddhist temple to which one turns. The social aspects of religion, and the ways that these two religions in particular act in tandem, providing rites and ceremonies that frame the stages of life through which the individual passes as well as helping to integrate people into the overall social structure, will be dealt with at length in Chapters 3 and 4. This overlap is not just in terms of affiliation but in terms of action within the home. Figures show that approximately 61 per cent of households have a *butsudan* or family Buddhist altar at which the family ancestors are memorialised, and 60 per cent have a *kamidana*, the Shinto altar or god shelf which enshrines Shinto household deities. Only 24 per cent had neither, while 45 per cent of the households had both Shinto and Buddhist altars.[14]

Multiple belonging need not just involve Shinto and Buddhism, but can incorporate a third (or more) tradition besides. This is especially true of the Japanese new religions, which frequently encourage their members to fulfil their social obligations to the Shinto *kami* and to Buddhism as well as following their own individual beliefs through the new religious group. An excellent example of this is provided by Byron Earhart's study of Gedatsukai, a new religion with Buddhist roots: Gedatsukai members are taught not just to follow the religion's doctrines and practices but also to carry out and intensify their relationship to the Buddhist and Shinto structures as well, paying respect to each for their areas of import-ance, value and action. Indeed Earhart's research has indicated that those who join Gedatsukai tend to increase the levels of their religious participation in Shinto and Buddhist activities.[15]

This multiplicity of belonging has been a recurrent theme in Japanese religious history, with different religions traditions tending to be not so much divisive as inclusive, complementary rather than contradictory. In the next chapter I shall briefly outline the major traditions extant in Japan and how they have added to the overall picture but for the present I shall just suggest that in religious terms the Japanese have rarely been confronted with the type of 'this or that' dilemma that has led to so much bloodshed in other parts of the world. This does not mean that there have been no cases of religious strife in Japan, for in some respects the history of Buddhism in Japan could be seen as a long series of sectarian secessions and factional disputes, while there have been sporadic outbursts of persecution and suppression of religious groups. Notable among these have been the exclusion and persecution of Christianity from the seventeenth to the nineteenth centuries, the brief but severe repression of Buddhism in the 1870s and the proscription of several of the new religions in the period from 1925 to 1945.[16]

However, for the most part, especially in the ways in which the Japanese people have incorporated and assimilated these various religious traditions into their lives, there has been far less collision than cohesion. The enormous numbers of religious organisations in Japan — hundreds of Buddhist sects and sub-sects, scores of new religions, almost a hundred Shinto organisations, and many Christian churches as well as countless individuals who operate in some religious capacity, as diviners, spiritual healers and guides with small groups of followers — share a membership that has large areas of overlap.[17]

Religious organisations that demand single adherence have not, as a rule, got very far in Japan, at least until recent times.[18] Even where a religious movement does, by its doctrines, appear to prohibit activities outside its immediate sphere, evidence suggests that its members may not always take much notice, as the examples of Sōka Gakkai and Jōdo Shinshū (Pure Land Buddhism) demonstrate. Sōka Gakkai claims that it and its parent sect Nichiren Shōshū are the sole representatives of the absolute truth discovered by the thirteenth-century Japanese priest Nichiren and that all religious activities outside this tradition are heretical and should be avoided: thus Gakkai members should not, for example, acquire talismans from shrines or pray to the *kami* for good luck. In reality, though, many do so, with probably the majority, according to verbal estimates given to me by officials in the organisation, taking part in some religious activities outside the realms of the Gakkai.[19]

A recent survey shows a quantifiable and diverse degree of religious pluralism in the Jōdo Shinshū sect. This movement states that followers should place absolute faith in the salvific powers of the Buddha of the Pure Land, Amida, whose compassion will lead them to rebirth in the Pure Land after death. Followers should chant invocations of praise to him in the knowledge of his compassion: to perform other religious actions such as acquiring talismans or seeking help from other sources displays a lack of faith in this all-encompassing power and is thus to be avoided. Yet, as Kaneko Satoru reports, members do participate, if not at the same levels as other Japanese, in all the general socio-religious activities common to the Japanese spectrum, 43 per cent having a household Shinto altar, 17 per cent purchasing amulets and 13 per cent praying regularly for good luck.[20]

This multiplicity underlines what has aiready been implied in the statistics, that religious belonging and the practice of religion are not primarily conditioned by notions of belief. This is well recognised by many religious organisations in Japan, and has been confirmed quite strikingly by data produced by the Sōtō Zen Buddhist sect. In its report to the Ministry of Cultural Affairs it gives a membership of 6,885,000 people.[21] Yet, at the same time, it has published its own detailed research to show that it can only classify 287,000 people (a shade over 4 per cent of its apparent membership) as 'believers', people who study and express belief in the teachings of the sect and its priests.[22] One sees similar themes in Shinto: according to current figures, 115,600,000 people (95 per cent of the population) are affiliated to it through Shinto organisations and community shrines, a number that has risen steadily over the last 25 years.[23] It has, at the same time, extremely low 'belief ratings', somewhere around the 3–4 per cent mark.[24]

This picture of high levels of belonging and low levels of cognitive belief becomes a little clearer – or more obscure, depending on one's point of view! – when we look further at the data concerning religious activity and overt expressions of religiosity, such as visiting shrines, praying and participating in religious events. The Japanese score quite highly in surveys when questioned about such activities. The acquisition of charms and talismans of good luck at shrines, temples and other religious centres (an activity carried out by 34.4 per cent of the NHK respondents in 1978 and 36.2 per cent in

1983[25]), prayers to the *kami* and Buddhas for good fortune at specific times of crisis, and participation in local shrine and temple festivals and the various observances that occur throughout the year at religious centres are just some of the numerous activities that come up consistently in every survey on religious behaviour.[26]

There are certain times of the year, for instance, when Japan appears to produce an explosion of religious activity. The two most prominent and colourful are the period around New Year, when it is customary to visit shrines and temples to pray for good luck and happiness in the coming year, and the summer festival of *o-bon*, when the family comes together to venerate the souls of its ancestors and to visit the family temple. Both times are major holidays, with millions of people travelling to be with their families and going with them to religious centres.

It is estimated that over 80 per cent of the Japanese take part either regularly or occasionally in *hatsumōde*, the New Year's visit to shrines and temples: although this festival revolves primarily around the *kami* and shrines, popular and well-known Buddhist temples also attract large crowds. The numbers of those taking part in this annual festival have been rising more or less constantly over the last two or three decades: from around 30 million a year in the mid-1960s the figure had gone above 60 million by 1976.[27] This growth has continued and, according to a survey by the Yomiuri newspaper, 68 per cent or over 80 million people took part in this event in 1988.[28]

The vast crowds that take part in *hatsumōde* are more than matched by the numbers who participate in the various rites and festivals that centre around the memorialisation of the dead, a part of the religious structure which, as we have seen, falls into the Buddhist sphere in Japan. According to the NHK survey, 89 per cent of the Japanese take part either regularly (69 per cent) or occasionally (20 per cent) in the practice of *haka mairi*, visiting the graves of the departed to make offerings, pray to the dead (who are regarded as ancestors and protectors of the living) and to clean their graves.[29] Such visits are made especially at *o-bon*, but also at *higan*, the festival occuring at the spring and autumn equinoxes.

Hatsumōde and *o-bon* are but two in a round of activities, festivities and religious observances running throughout the year in Japan that will be dealt with more fully in later chapters. What is of relevance to the discussion in this chapter is the extent to which these mass participatory events incorporate social, cultural and religious themes at the same time. Many Japanese take part in *hatsumōde* because of its strong social and cultural nuances, because it is customary to visit shrines at this time of year with family and friends. The general holiday mood contributes to this: Japan is effectively a nation at play, and an air of joyous fun pervades the air as people don bright clothing — it is especially popular for young women to have their hair styled and to wear bright kimono — and go out and about with friends.

In fact many Japanese people I have talked to about *hatsumode* hardly consider it a religious festival at all, and are reluctant to view their participation in religious terms. However, they are going to religious centres (shrines) and they do take part in what are, for want of a better word, religious actions: anyone observing the New Year's crowds will quickly note that, no matter whether they are merely going along for social and cultural reasons, everyone does join their hands in prayer and make offerings. The majority also acquire talismans and amulets to safeguard them in the year ahead, and many will also collect *o-mikuji*, written oracles or divination lots, that are acquired for a nominal fee at shrines and which are believed to foretell one's fortunes.

The activities at *o-bon* reflect similar themes. It is customary to visit the graves of the ancestors at this time: it is also a time for family reunions, for returning to one's ancestral village and for a general escape from the cities that have in recent times become the home for most Japanese to the rural areas from which they originally came. But the holiday revolves around religious motifs, with the family uniting to pay their respects to the ancestors of the family and to hold a mutual celebration at the grave and at the Buddhist temple where the ancestors are venerated. Again, many Japanese state that this is a cultural and social event, revolving around family obligations and tradition: again, as at New Year, they will also go through overtly religious actions, in this case offering incense, flowers and food to the ancestors, as well as praying and receiving talismans for the benefit of the ancestors from Buddhist temples.

Much of what is done at New Year and *o-bon* does not require any prior or fixed religious commitment from the participants: it does not even seem to require belief in the existence or influence of the spiritual beings (*kami* or ancestors) to whom the prayers and offerings are directed. In stark contrast to the 75 per cent or more of the population who pray to the *kami* at New Year are the relatively small numbers who affirm belief in the existence of *kami*: only 21 per cent of respondents to the 1984 NHK survey did so, although another 15 per cent considered that they might exist.[30] This survey also showed 31 per cent of people believing in the existence of souls after death,[31] while according to an investigation conducted in 1979 by the Yomiuri newspaper 33 per cent of people felt that the souls of the dead watched over and protected the living.[32] While it is important to participate in *hatsumōde* and other such activities and while there is a broad and conscious awareness of some form of religious affiliation and belonging, this clearly does not imply the necessity of accepting the constraints of belief. In such terms it is clear that belief, or at least expressed belief, is hardly a reliable guide to religious behaviour in Japan.

THE IDEA AND SITUATION OF RELIGION

This all indicates the extent to which religious ideas, concepts and activities are socially and culturally imbibed without necessarily being explicitly recognised as religious by the performers. One major element here is the traditional role of social and group identifications in Japanese society, which has tended to define people less in individual terms than in terms of social identification and belonging. Some of the main social units of importance in defining the position, identity and sense of belonging of the individual have been the village, the local community, the household (in Japanese the *ie*), the nation and, especially prominent in modern times, the company or organisation one works for. The household has long been an especially prominent building block in the religious structure: it is the *ie* that is affiliated to a local Buddhist temple and Shinto shrine, with individuals being classified as Buddhist and/or Shinto not so much in their own right as through their belonging to the *ie*.

In recent decades, as the processes of modernisation and urbanisation have altered the Japanese social landscape, there have been shifts in the importance of some of these units with, for instance, a weakening of the overall influence of the extended household, along with a growth of individual volition, and this process will be given some attention in later chapters. Nevertheless, the household as a socio-religious unit still retains considerable strength and exerts influence over its members. Many 'non-religious'

religious activities (for instance, the veneration of the dead and the *o-bon* festival, and praying to the household deities at the *kamidana*) are socially imbibed through being a member of the household, children, for example, being taught by their mothers to bow to the deities and ancestors and to make offerings, without learning the meanings behind the actions.[33]

People participate in religious activities because of such socio-cultural belongings. *Hatsumōde* and *o-bon* are good examples of this: many Japanese people take part in the former because it is the thing to do at New Year and the latter because of household obligations. They can therefore pray to the deities and the ancestors because the situation and circumstance demand it, yet need not express belief in either. Participation thus cuts across religious boundaries: *hatsumōde* and *o-bon* are not so much Shinto and Buddhist as events with religious connotations identifying one as being part of the social culture of Japan. This can at times provide a convenient escape clause for Japanese who convert to religious belief systems that do not accept, for example, the existence of *kami* or the practice of ancestor worship. I once interviewed a young Japanese man who had converted to Mormonism: what, I asked, did he do at *o-bon*? The answer, of course, was that he went with his family to pray to the ancestors, satisfied that this was a cultural and social action and thus did not conflict with his religious beliefs. He could take part as a member of the family at *o-bon* and as a Japanese at *hatsumōde* without compromising his religious beliefs. In the same vein, people who are 'not religious' yet pray to the *kami* are not being contradictory.

A problem that occurs in all this is precisely what is understood when terms like 'religion' are used in Japan. The Japanese word generally used in surveys and elsewhere to denote 'religion' is *shūkyō*, a word made up of two ideograms, *shū*, meaning sect or denomination, and *kyō*, teaching or doctrine. It is a derived word that came into prominence in the nineteenth century as a result of Japanese encounters with the West and particularly with Christian missionaries, to denote a concept and view of religion commonplace in the realms of nineteenth-century Christian theology but at that time not found in Japan, of religion as a specific, belief-framed entity. The term *shūkyō* thus, in origin at least, implies a separation of that which is religious from other aspects of society and culture, and contains implications of belief and commitment to one order or movement — something that has not been traditionally a common factor in Japanese religious behaviour and something that tends to exclude many of the phenomena involved in the Japanese religious process.[34] When tied to questions of belief it does conjure up notions of narrow commitment to a particular teaching to the implicit exclusion and denial of others — something which goes against the general complementary nature of the Japanese religious tradition. In *shūkyō* and hence in the idea of 'religion' there is a hint of something committing, restrictive and even intrusive, and, as one Japanese scholar has recently remarked, for many Japanese the word conjures up bad images of being disturbed on Sunday mornings by ladies ringing one's doorbell and asking awkward questions.[35]

The general reticence of Japanese people to affirm religious belief in such terms is further compounded by the general image that organised religion has acquired in recent times in Japan. Buddhism, particularly because of its associations with the death process, has a rather gloomy and sombre image, while the new religions have, until recently at least, been portrayed in the media as manipulative and riddled with superstition. Shinto, too, has had its image tarnished because of its close associations with the nationalistic Fascism of the period leading up to the war defeat of 1945, while Christianity, because it cuts across vital social aspects of belonging, tends to be rather antithetical to Japanese feelings of identity. This lack of overall enthusiasm for *shūkyō* as organised religion is particularly strong amongst the young. Nishiyama Shigeru found, in a survey of 363 university students in Tokyo, that while they had high levels of interest in religious activities, they expressed extreme contempt for organised religion, with 92 per cent stating that they would not join any organised religious movement.[36]

Japanese sociologists of religion have long recognised that this general pattern of disdain, denial of belief and reluctance to affirm commitment to specific doctrinal systems does not prevent Japanese people from taking part in all sorts of religiously focused actions. Consequently their research and the surveys they have carried out, and on which I have drawn in this chapter, are directed far more towards what people do than to issues of belief. Ōmura Eishō, for example, has commented that the Japanese view organised, structuralised belief-orientated religion with suspicion even while having high levels of religious activity. He argues, from the statistics at hand, that the Japanese like religious events and activities but dislike organised and belief-centred religion. Thus, he asserts, a major theme of religion in Japan is its focus on action, custom and etiquette.[37]

It is such areas as these that need to be analysed in order to understand fully the scope and dimensions of religion in Japan. Quite clearly it is not viable just to analyse religion from the angle of belief and doctrine, for this not only overlooks the wider dimensions of socially inspired religious activity but can lead to rather erroneous conclusions. In subsequent chapters as I look at some of these issues in Japan, such as the roles of religion in terms of social bonding, as therapy for personal problems, as a way of celebration and as a means of self-expression and identification, amongst many others, it will become evident that, despite the opinion of the businessman quoted by Davis, there does exist a deep and continuing stream of religious motifs interwoven with (rather than separate from) other aspects of Japanese life and society. Just because they are deeply ingrained into the culture does not make them any less implicitly religious although, for reasons of terminology as much as anything else, this does mean that they are not always overtly recognised as such. What it does mean is that intensely religious dimensions still operate in Japanese society, permeating its structure and helping to frame the ways that people act and view the world.

THE PRIMACY OF ACTION

There is a deep relationship between situations, actions and religiosity in Japan. Situations demand actions that express a latent religiosity, as with the incidence of a death in the family. This necessitates actions: going to the temple, getting the Buddhist priest to perform certain rituals, enshrining the dead soul in the family *butsudan* and then performing acts of worship and making offerings before it. Certainly these actions are socially predetermined: the extent to which they are so structured and formalised can be seen by the fact that vast numbers of guidebooks are published by Buddhist sects and other religious groups detailing the correct procedures to be followed and the forms that such ritual processes should take.[38]

Such guidebooks do not just explain the ritual procedures and forms to be followed. They also outline the frame of mind in which they must be done, with a pure mind and with sincerity, both, as Helen Hardacre has noted, important religious ideals in Japan.[39]

Accordingly, when performed with purity and sincerity of mind, the traditional and socially prescribed reactions to the situation of death are not simply formalistic, but become vehicles of religious expression. Latent belongings to Buddhism are transformed into actualities, brought to life through ritual performances and acted out, even if only temporarily, with religious sincerity.

Thus Japanese people 'become' practising Buddhists in certain circumstances: when the immediate period of religious observances following a death is over (in the first instance, usually 49 days) their intense association with the Buddhist mode ends, to be reawakened at seasonal festivals of veneration for the dead, anniversaries of the death and other such situational occasions. One can see very similar patterns in events such as *hatsumōde*, shrine festivals and the birth of children: going to the shrine then is conditioned by socio-cultural themes. There one prays — again with sincerity — thereby entering into a Shintoesque orientation and expressing one's latent relationship with the *kami*.

The Japanese do not live in a system that demands full-blooded, belief-orientated and exclusive commitment that precludes any other. Rather, their orientations are situational and complementary: the necessity of dealing with the problem of death demands one set of responses and orientations while the time of year or the birth of a child requires another. All these fit into the overall framework of the social, cultural and environmental world within which the Japanese live to form a whole that conditions and underpins all their religious feelings.

This does not mean that belief is rejected or considered unimportant as a factor in Japanese religious life and, as will become clear later in this book, especially in the chapter on individual activities and asceticism, one at times encounters remarkable and even extreme levels of belief, devotion and commitment in Japan. In general, though, action precedes belief and is not in a religious sense dependent on it, although actions brought about by needs and situations may help in the awakening of a sense of religiosity that creates and nurtures the seeds of belief, leading to a fruition which may in itself become a commitment. The researchers whose survey at Ishikiri shrine in Osaka I cited earlier found that many of those who visited the shrine did so regularly and had done so for many years. Most had made their first visit for a specific reason (generally connected with the reputed healing propensities of the shrine's *kami*) and, because they felt that this had proved efficacious, had returned to thank the deity. This led to further and more regular visits, a deepening relationship between visitor and *kami*, and a movement from a situational and need-centred relationship to one based on belief and the repayment of gratitude.[40]

A former student of mine, a Japanese girl in her early twenties who was a member of Sōka Gakkai, told me that when she first became involved with this religious organisation she, like many Gakkai members, had continued to participate in other socio-religious events, going to the shrine at New Year, taking part in festivals and praying to the *kami* for good luck. As her involvement with Sōka Gakkai grew deeper, as she attended more of its meetings and became more dedicated in following the Sōka Gakkai religious practices, she gradually began to eschew other religious activities until eventually, after about two years, her commitment to the Gakkai was such that she would no longer take part in any non-Gakkai religious rites or actions at all.

This process, of action and practice, usually conditioned by circumstance, leading on to or at least opening the doors of committed belief is recognised by many in the Buddhist world. Certainly the Sōtō Zen sect is aware that the main avenue of contact between their members and temples is through the rituals and ceremonies connected with the ancestors and death. As a result, much of its religious literature centres on the social aspects and obligations of ancestor veneration and the religious links that exist between households, individuals and temples. This is designed to create a sense of empathy between participant and temple through which the formal relationship will develop into something deeper and, as one pamphlet produced by the sect puts it: 'We wish to make you, an affiliated member of the family temple, into a believer of that temple.'[41] Indeed, much of the strategy of the sect in recent times (and, I would argue, of Buddhism throughout its history in Japan) is based on the realisation that belief does develop through contact and action: ritualism may at times be formal but it can also progress in the right circumstances into committed participation and belief.[42]

The view that action is primary is seen nowhere more clearly than in the new religions of Japan. Davis shows how members of the new religious movement Mahikari, when speaking of the spiritual healing techniques they use to eradicate the evil spirits that they consider to be the cause of illnesses and other problems, exhort others to 'just try it and see!': there are no prior injunctions to believe first and then practice.[43]

The suspension of belief, or rather the injunction to do it and thus realise the inherent religious truth being propounded, is found elsewhere in the new religions. One of my students was a member of Shinnyoen, one of a wave of religious groups that have risen to prominence in Japan since the mid-1970s. The sons of the founder of Shinnyoen died whilst young. According to Shinnyoen cosmology these deaths were ordained, indeed sacrificial, in that they went across to the other shore, to the world of the dead, in order to guide the living when they die, to give them solace and to lead them to Buddhahood and enlightenment in the next world: much of the practice of Shinnyoen followers centres on these two figures and the guidance they offer.[44]

My student, in relating Shinnyoen's beliefs in this respect to me, remarked:

> I know this sounds strange and difficult to believe. I thought so too before I got involved and started to do the practice, but when I did it I began to realise its truth. If you do it you will understand too.

I have heard the same things from people in numerous new religious movements. Sōka Gakkai asserts that one can attain one's goals through the practice of reciting the *daimoku*, the invocation in the important Buddhist text, the Lotus Sūtra. As a goal-directed practice it does not demand prior belief: Gakkai members argue that performing the practice will demonstrate its validity. One member told me that when he first started he did not believe in Gakkai teachings, but through the practice (undertaken because of a particular need and situation and encouraged by the advice of a friend that it would work) his immediate goals were realised and, consequently, like my Shinnyoen student, he became a believer. Again, like my student, his advice to me was not to waste time delving into the theories and beliefs of the Gakkai but to 'do it and see — I did!'.

There is a very powerful experiential dimension to religion in Japan. To go beyond the circumstance-orientated frame of reference in which it operates, religion in general needs to produce experientially tangible results to validate itself and to inculcate belief. Many people, for example, are attracted to the new religions because they often offer solutions to personal problems, and a major barometer of whether they become believers is whether they can experience the results they seek. This is a major reason also why many new religions have high rates of turnover, for many do 'try it but not see'. Over 50 per cent of those who do the Mahikari training course, for example, drop out of the religion fairly soon afterwards.[45]

This does not always mean that the practice has not been efficacious: since people become involved because of needs, they may move out of the religious framework once that need no longer exists. Probably the most radical example of this that I have come across was a young man I interviewed some years ago on his religious attitudes and affiliations. He said that he had once been a member of Risshōkōseikai, a lay Buddhist new religion with a reputation for healing, because he had been troubled for years by headaches and nervous problems and had been persuaded by his brother-in-law to join this religion and try out its methods of spiritual counselling and healing. When I asked him why he was no longer a member, he replied simply: 'I got better.'

This does not necessarily suggest a flippant attitude towards religion: the young man in question was, at the time I interviewed him, living as a layman at a Zen Buddhist temple. He was a sincere practitioner intent on finding a spiritual meaning to life, and he was later ordained as a monk, finding Zen meditation the right outlet for his spiritual needs. His experience with Risshōkōseikai was a necessary step which helped with one problem and demonstrated just how possible it is in Japan to find a religious response to one's needs and worries in experiential terms.

Running throughout the Japanese religious world and overlapping the socially activated sense of religious action and expression is this strongly individual and strongly pragmatic dimension of experience. It is a basic reason why, in a religious culture where so many themes are shared, there are so many religious organisations and groups. Involvement with a religious group and its techniques can further lead on to new experiences, understandings and revelations which allow people to formulate their own interpretations and may even, in some cases, lead them to form a new religious group of their own. Mahikari, to cite just one example, developed as a result of the religious experiences and revelations received by its founder, Okada Kōtama in 1959. He was a member of the new religion Sekai Kyūseikyō at the time and when, after these revelations, he seceded to form his own religion, he incorporated into it many of the techniques and teachings of Sekai Kyūseikyō, which itself had imbibed many of them from another new religion, Oomoto, to which its founder had belonged before seceding to establish his own movement. Mahikari itself has, since the death of Okada, segmented into further groups, with Okada's adopted daughter, Okada Sachiko, and one of his chief disciples, Sekiguchi Sakae, each claiming to be his true successor and splitting the movement into two. Since then Sekiguchi's Mahikari organisation has split further, as one of his followers has now claimed a higher degree of revelation and has established another branch of Mahikari.[46]

This continued proliferation of religious groups, which has been a prominent feature of recent Japanese religious history, is only to be expected in a religious culture which affirms the value of 'doing it and seeing'. This emphasis on powerful individual religious figures who, through their own experiences, may reinterpret traditions, modify them, establish their own religious groups and gather followers — only to see some of them split off to form other groups because of what they have experienced — is a recurrent one in Japan and will surface in later chapters where I discuss powerful and charismatic religious figures and the new religions themselves.

TURNING TO THE GODS: THE FLUIDITY OF RELIGION

The strong sense of pragmatic functionalism manifested by the 'do it and see' attitude is inherent in all the relationships that the Japanese have with the religious world. When I asked a seminar group of twelve Japanese students that I was teaching to describe their religious orientations and to state when they last went to pray at a shrine or temple, eight of them responded that they were 'not religious'. All then went on to state that at the time of their university entrance examinations they had gone to various shrines and temples to pray for help. One student after another used the popular Japanese saying *kurushii toki no kamidanomi* (turn to the gods in times of trouble) to describe the sentiment they felt at such times.

It is a phrase commonly used, especially by the young. The education system in Japan places immense pressures on school-children in particular, especially during major examinations, and many feel the need to search for release valves and for solace and external support in such times of trial. Accordingly, students who might normally not see themselves as religiously active, but who are ready and able to make use of the religious world when they need to, are liable to petition deities of education for help in passing examinations and getting in to desired schools and colleges.

It is not just young people at examination times who so turn to the gods. As we have already seen, those who turn to the new religions may do so because of problems and situational needs, while in Chapter 7, when I describe the activities that occur at temples and shrines, it will become clear that much of what goes on at such religious institutions revolves around seeking help, protection and support in the face of worries and problems, and that these are issues of concern to people of all ages.

To conclude this chapter, however, I shall give one more example of the incidence of the idea of *kurushii toki no kamidanomi* in contemporary Japanese life in the context of the world of sport. It concerns one of my favourite Sumō wrestlers, the *yokuzuna* (Grand Champion) Hokutoumi. Having fought his way to the very highest levels of Sumō, an old back injury flared up again, putting him out of action for over eight months. During this time he missed three full tournaments and there were fears that he might never return to his previous prowess. At New Year 1989, just prior to his reappearance in the January wrestling tournament, he, along with most of the rest of Japan, took part in the custom of *hatsumōde*. Whereas, he later told reporters, he normally did not have much to pray for (in other words, normally he was just following a social custom), this year he did, and thus he made a special request to the *kami*.[47] One presumes that he asked for help in returning successfully to the ring: as it happens, he did so, winning his comeback tournament in powerful style!

Both Hokutoumi and the students I mentioned earlier are good examples of how situations lead people into religious behaviour and a relationship with the gods. Here, too, one can see the fluidity and responsiveness of the religious structure: the *kami* (and indeed the Buddhas) are there to be petitioned by those in need. Their existence is thus not so much a matter of cognitive belief (which, as we have seen, is comparatively low) but of cultural acceptance and requirement: when the situation calls for it they are 'there' to perform the role ascribed to them. In general terms, then, the religious world provides, for the Japanese, a psychological support system to uphold them in times of need, be called on when circumstances require it, provide answers and solutions when problems arise, yet not demand attention at other times. People may thus move into (and out of) religious modes according to requirements and circumstances. This is shown by the young man who 'got better' and then moved on to become a Zen monk as well as by the students who can seek solace at the shrine in the face of the pressures of Japanese education's 'examination hell' and then, afterwards, go back to being 'not religious' again — until, possibly, they find themselves in another situation where religious action is needed or called for, such as New Year or the death of a family member or some other crisis.

2 Unifying Traditions, Cosmological Perspectives and the Vitalistic Universe

UNIFYING TRADITIONS

Situation and circumstance are intrinsic elements in the Japanese religious world, amply demonstrating its populist, pragmatic and ethnic orientations relevant to the Japanese people, their life styles, needs and environment in this world. All these elements have their roots in the enduring Japanese folk religious tradition that was based originally in a primarily agricultural society in which such actions as cyclical observances and rituals, petitions to deities for good harvests, concern for the spirits of the dead and their potential for malevolent actions against the living, and beliefs in the powers of the spiritual world to help or hinder humans in their pursuit of happiness in this life were paramount, but which continues to exert its influences in contemporary, industrialised Japan. Over the centuries the folk tradition has provided what Miyake Hitoshi has termed the 'frame of reference' through which organised religious traditions have found their roots and grown in Japan,[1] providing a centralising dynamic through which all the religious traditions found in Japan have been interpreted and assimilated in such a way that each has added to the overall picture, contributing to a whole that is more than simply the sum of its parts.

Shinto is an ethnic religious tradition that, crystallising from and formalising many aspects of the folk tradition, is centred on the relationship between the Japanese people, the land and the *kami*, deities indigenous to Japan and specific to the Japanese context. The word Shinto itself means 'the way of the gods (*kami*)' and came into existence to differentiate what was native and specifically Japanese from the external religious traditions such as Buddhism that began to be assimilated into Japan from the sixth century AD onwards. The ethnic dimensions of Shinto are clearly manifested in the early Japanese texts the *Nihongi* and *Kojiki* that date from the eighth century AD.

Primarily written as legitimations of the Imperial rule that was spreading its influence across the country at the time, the *Nihongi* and *Kojiki* none the less express important foundation legends relevant to Japan and especially to Shinto as well as numerous religious themes extant in the folk religious culture of the time. Detailed lineages of *kami* are set out, seven generations of *kami* giving birth to a female and male deity, Izanami and Izanagi, who in turn created the land of Japan by thrusting a heavenly sword into the oceans. They then produced myriad other *kami* who inhabited and gave vitality to the land to which they had given birth.

In giving birth to the fire god, however, Izanami dies — a reminder that death may intrude on life, even that of a *kami*. This death, occurring while the processes of creative development are still extant, is clearly unnatural, a severance of natural order, and causes turmoil. Izanagi, displaying the grief of the living unable to accept the demise of a loved one, tries to follow her to the underworld where, in a scene of intense horror, he encounters her putrescent and decaying body, made the worse by her pursuing him angrily as if to drag him into the same state. He barely escapes, rolling a rock across the border between the worlds of living and dead. Izanami threatens that if the boulder remains in place she will wreak death upon 1000 persons in the land of the living each day, but Izanagi affirms the primacy of life over death by countering that these will be replaced and augmented by 1500 births each day. He then bathes in water, a process of purification that cleanses him of the pollutions of death and reintegrates him into this world, and gives birth to other *kami*, including Amaterasu, the Sun Goddess.

From the *kami* begat by Izanami and Izanagi and by Izanagi alone descended the Japanese people, with the Imperial line claiming descent (and hence the legitimation of its rule and ascendancy) from Amaterasu herself. The *kami* are thus directly present in the land of Japan, and there is continuity rather than separation between humans and *kami*: there is no overarching Creator figure but rather a combination of *kami*, a continuing process of reproduction leading to the creation of Japan. The purpose of the *kami*, and the relationship that exists between them and humans, is thus placed in this world, for the benefit of those who live in it.

At the same time the death, decay and malevolent anger of Izanami and the horrors that follow her premature death point to an intense feeling that death itself is, at least where it comes before its time, unnatural and disruptive, a radical threat to the productive processes of life. Izanagi's actions, once he has recovered from his humanesque grief and desire to follow Izanami, state the necessity of drawing firm boundaries between the worlds of the living and the dead so as to maintain the correct order and fertile balance of this world. His bathing bringing forth new and important *kami* indicates the validity, indeed primacy, of ritual and purificatory actions to eradicate the pollutions of death from this world, asserting that the disruptive influences of death may be overcome and enabling the living to return to a state of purity, reintegrated into this world and renewed. The avowal to produce more lives than the spectre of death can claim coupled with the birth of the new *kami* is a potent affirmation of the primacy of life over death and of its innate powers of renewal.

Many of the motifs that appear in these legends are recurrent in Japanese religious history and, remaining valid in the present day, will surface frequently throughout this book. The importance of purification, the innate powers of renewal within the world, and the disruptive influences of unnatural and premature death and its resultant pollutions are themes as vigorously extant in the contemporary age as they were when the *Nihongi* and *Kojiki* were compiled over a thousand years ago. Perhaps overriding all these is the view of this world and life as paramount and alive, with the inherent vitality of the *kami* as a spiritual force that permeates the world, giving life to it and upholding and protecting those that live in it.

The notion of quite what a *kami* is has always been hard to define. Traditionally anything that inspired a sense of awe (that is, which expressed through its nature some special quality or sense of vitality) could be seen as a *kami*, or as the abode of a *kami*. Thus rocks and trees, especially those of strange or striking shape, might be regarded as abodes or manifestations of the power of *kami*, a sentiment that still persists, for it is extremely common in contemporary Japan to see such natural objects demarcated by the straw rope insignia used in Shinto to signify the presence of *kami*.

They are not just expressions of natural force, however. The continuity between humans and *kami* means that human beings, too, can become *kami*, retaining an influence in this world, generally through a continuation of the qualities that marked them out in this life. A prime example of this is the great ninth century scholar Sugawara Michizane who fell victim to political intrigue and was sent into exile, where he died unhappily. Shortly after, a series of misfortunes struck the capital Kyoto: these were interpreted as being caused by his angry and vengeful spirit seeking recompense for the wrongs inflicted on him in life. Consequently the Court decided to appease him by building him a shrine and venerating him as a *kami*, thereby sacralising the malevolent and transforming it into something of benefit for the living. Because of his scholastic abilities it was natural that he should become a *kami* of learning and so Sugawara was enshrined as Tenjin, the *kami* of learning and education. Tenjin remains an immensely popular *kami*, with millions of school and university students flocking to Tenjin shrines across the country each year, especially prior to major examinations.

The living can clearly thus create *kami* or recognise that the importance of particular individuals is such that they should be recognised after death (or even very occasionally when still alive) as *kami*. Major ancestral figures that transcend localised divisions and pertain to the wider world of the Japanese are especially liable to become *kami*. The Japanese Emperor as a symbol of unity overriding all the local divisions of Japanese society is a case in point, with past Emperors, both real and legendary, being thus enshrined. In the centre of Tokyo, for example, is the vast Shinto shrine Meiji Jingū, dedicated to the veneration of Emperor Meiji, who died in 1912, while the Emperor Ōjin who, according to the *Nihongi*, reigned in the third century, is venerated at shrines throughout the country as the *kami* Hachiman.[2] Especially from the Meiji period onwards the Emperor was widely regarded as a *kami* during his lifetime, a view strongly promulgated with special vigour by the nationalistic government in the era leading up to and during the Second World War. This notion of the Emperor as a living *kami* was repudiated by the late Emperor Hirohito in 1946 and, although some Japanese conservatives still harbour illusions of restoring the Emperor to his former divine status, this denial of divinity is broadly accepted in contemporary Japan. The concept of the living *kami* (*ikigami*) is also found to some extent among the new religions, many of which revere their founders as such during their lifetimes.

The closeness of humans and *kami* has invested *kami* with many human traits and provided many religious messages that are relayed and constantly reiterated within the world of religious observances. They are not immune from the human pains of death and decay, as with Izanami, or the human emotions of grief and inability to accept loss, as with the bereaved Izanagi seeking his wife in the underworld. In the ensuing legends, Susanoo, the brother of Amaterasu, slighted because his sister acquires a more prominent role in the cosmology than he, behaves remarkably boorishly, insulting her and causing general mayhem in his rage. His sister in turn sulkingly retreats into a cave, casting the world into darkness until lured out by the other *kami*. The nature of *kami* can thus be seen to be somewhat dualistic: they represent a life force, a source and manifestation of energy found in the world and as such are benefactors of the benefits of that force, upholders of life and its goodness. However, just as nature itself, they are unpredictable and, just as humans, are prone to pique, jealousy, rage and other disruptive human habits which can disrupt the flow of life and cause problems.

They therefore need to be treated correctly: honoured, propitiated, venerated and thanked in order to maintain a balanced and productive relationship that can benefit the natural order (and hence human beings living in the world) and to direct their energies into creative rather than destructive directions. Shinto action and ritual largely centre on the development and maintenance of such relationships with the *kami*: purification rituals are performed to eradicate the pollutions of the mundane so as to symbolically bring humans closer to the realms of the *kami*, and rituals of respect, veneration, propitiation and offering seek to gain access to the life-giving powers of the *kami*. There is thus a strongly reciprocal element in the relationship between humans and *kami*, with the offerings and gifts of the one creating a sense of goodwill and beneficence in the other. This matrix of reciprocity, of creating obligations, receiving benevolence and responding with gratitude mirrors standard social relationships within Japanese society in general, where gift-giving and the creation and repayment of obligations have long been important.[3]

These elements are particularly directed towards the Japanese world, for Shinto carries within it profoundly ethnic dimensions. The legend of divine descent implies that both Japan and its people are unique, existing in a relationship with an ethnic array of spiritual beings special and relevant to their situation and existence. These distinctly ethnocentric orientations have given rise to underlying concepts of Japanese belonging and identity, and indeed exclusiveness, which retain implicitly religious connotations to this day. They have constantly given legitimation to the insularity and nationalism which have always lurked close to the surface in Japanese society, on occasion coming dramatically into the open, as with the period from the seventeenth to nineteenth centuries when Japan closed itself off from the rest of the world, and in the period of extreme nationalism and militarism that led Japan to war and subsequently to defeat in 1945. The importance of concepts of Japanese identity in a contemporary society that, straddling as it does a deep and strong cultural and traditional past and a rapidly changing present in which the values of the past are becoming challenged by new ideas, pressures and the cultural influences of westernisation, is faced with problems of identity and orientation will surface again in later chapters, but at present it is relevant to draw attention to the Japanocentric themes that have been present from the very beginnings of Japanese religious culture.

This Japanocentric dynamic is not Shinto's alone but permeates just about all the religious traditions extant in Japan. Even Buddhism, despite its apparent universalism as a world religion, has developed nationalistic themes in Japan, and it is not uncommon even in the contemporary age to hear Buddhist organisations asserting Japanese cultural values while denigrating those of other, especially Western, cultures quite fervently.[4] More radically still, many of the new religions of Japan have taken on strongly ethnocentric and nationalistic undertones, placing Japan at the centre of the world and positing it as the vehicle for world salvation. The new religion Byakkō Shinkōkai, for example, portrays Japan as the holy centre from which peace will emanate to the rest of the world, and similar views appear in the outlooks of various other new religions, including Agonshū, whose use of this idea will be discussed in Chapter 8.[5]

The ethnic dimensions of Japanese religious culture exemplified but not monopolised by the Shinto tradition show also its profoundly homogenising and centrifugal nature. External religious traditions have always been interpreted within a Japanese framework and have been absorbed and adapted wherever they can add to the human-centred ethos of the native folk tradition and Shinto. This indigenising process is itself Japanocentric, external entities frequently being Japanised as they are absorbed. We shall see this process in action in later discussions of Buddhism in Japan, but perhaps the most striking example of this dynamic can be seen in the way that Jesus, not perhaps the most readily apparent Japanese figure, has become assimilated into the cosmologies of many new religions. Mahikari, for example, states that Jesus came to Japan for religious training in the years before he began preaching and gathering disciples,[6] while Oomoto, a new religion that began in the last decade of the nineteenth century, has transformed him, along with others such as Moses, Buddha and Confucius, into Shinto (that is, Japanese) *kami*.[7]

Japanocentricism has not meant exclusion so much as absorption: Shinto has functioned in Japanese life along with external religious currents such as Buddhism, which was first introduced into Japan along with elements of Taoism, Confucianism and other aspects of continental, Chinese culture, from around the sixth century onwards. Although only Buddhism of these three has established itself in a formal sense as a religion with temples and priests, both Taoism and Confucianism have added their influence to the formation of Japanese religious culture.

Taoism brought with it methods of prediction and divination and ideas that fortunes are linked in some ways to the nature of time itself, with certain days and ages in the life cycle being more lucky than others, and hence suitable times for embarking on projects, and others being especially unlucky, and hence times to seek help from the spiritual world and refrain from new ventures. Such views were important in Imperial and aristocratic courts over a thousand years ago and were taken into consideration in the conduct of governmental affairs, but they continue today to have some influence on a broad and popular scale. Oracle lots (*o-mikuji*) predicting the future can be acquired at virtually any shrine or temple, and are especially popular at times of transition such as New Year. The concept of the individual life-cycle as involving lucky and unlucky years still merits some attention, especially in connection with the most prominent *yakudoshi* ('dangerous' or unlucky years), which are 33 for a woman and 42 for a man. In these years the person is considered to be especially at the mercy of bad luck, and consequently during that year they are especially likely to visit shrines and temples to seek the protection of the *kami* and Buddhas. It is still also extremely common for people to consult divination almanacs or visit a diviner when determining courses of action such as the most auspicious date for a wedding or the best position to build a house, for directions are themselves classified as lucky and unlucky. Days, too, are similarly categorised and are divided into six types, from the most to the least auspicious in a recurring cycle, and it is widely considered to be unlucky to embark on new undertakings or to hold weddings and parties on inauspicious days.

To a great extent, of course, the attention paid to such issues does not necessarily reflect an inherent belief in predetermination so much as a desire for emotional security and to be on the safe side. It is clearly seen as better to attain a sense of peace of mind by knowing that one has sought the help of the *kami* during one's *yakudoshi* or has married on a lucky day than to risk the potential anxiety and sense of guilt that could accrue if one did not. Certainly the Japanese in general continue to pay some attention to these questions, with 63 per cent of the respondents in the 1981 NHK survey stating they paid attention (18 per cent very much and 45 per cent somewhat) to the issue of lucky and unlucky days.[8] Perhaps the strongest evidence of the continued importance placed on auspicious and inauspicious days was seen at the death of the late Emperor Hirohito in January 1989. This event caused the postponement or cancellation of major celebratory events but, as a television news item reported from a sedate and darkened entertainment district in Osaka on that evening, there were not very many of these taking place on that day anyway: he had died on a *butsumetsu* (literally 'death of Buddha') day, the most inauspicious day in the cycle, and consequently virtually no weddings, parties and other such celebrations had been scheduled anyway.[9]

If the influences of Taoism may be seen mostly at the folk and populist levels, Confucianism's can be perceived running through much of Japanese society in general, instilling ideals of order and structuralising respect for one's elders and seniors both in family and social terms and asserting the importance of harmony as a social ideal.[10] These ideals have made their mark also in the religious sphere: harmony has become transformed into something of a religious ideal while Confucian ethical teachings and concepts of filial piety have underpinned the Japanese practice of ancestor veneration. Confucianist ideas have been expressed in religious terms largely through the medium of Buddhism, which itself had absorbed Confucian elements in its movement across Asia from India into China and beyond.

Buddhism, which has historically stood alongside Shinto as the major organised religious tradition in Japan, has its origins in India and in the enlightenment of the Buddha some 2600 years ago. Over the centuries, as it spread across Asia meeting and assimilating aspects of various indigenous cultures, it had developed beyond its early meditation-centred path to individual enlightenment and, by the time it reached Japan in the sixth century, it had become a broad-based religion encompassing the use of prayers and incantations, the veneration of innumerable figures of worship and all the other trappings of large-scale organised religions. Theoretically all of these are devices, aimed at leading people into the Buddhist sphere and hence towards the goal of enlightenment, rather than the main focus of Buddhism, but in reality they have become basic aspects of the religion for many people.[11]

All sentient beings, according to Mahāyāna Buddhism, can reach enlightenment: thus there is continuity between humans and Buddhas (an outlook which of course mirrors the sense of continuity between humans and *kami* in Japan). Thus the Buddhas and other figures of worship that have evolved in the Buddhist pantheon are those who have themselves trodden the path towards ultimate liberation and who have, in doing so, acquired spiritual powers, knowledge and wisdom that they can utilise to help others, by preaching, interceding to save them from suffering, and responding to earnest prayers. Having transformed themselves into Buddhas they are able to transform others.

These figures, the Buddhas and Bodhisattvas,[12] were powerful because they were enlightened, but inherent in that enlightenment was a compassion for the sufferings of all beings: through this compassion they could use their powers to intercede in the world to help those who called for it. They expressed a dual dynamic, expressed in the Japanese phrase *jōgū bodai geke shujō*, 'to strive for enlightenment while reaching down to help others'.[13] The ultimate aim was the realisation of the enlightenment that was inherent in all sentient beings, but interwoven into the path to enlightenment was the need to help others in their sufferings, worries and everyday problems. Thus Mahāyāna Buddhism combined its various teachings and techniques in the form of philosophical texts and meditation methods for guiding people along the path to enlightenment, with a host of figures of worship who personified powers and attributes more directly concerned with everyday needs.

The ethical and meditational dimensions of Buddhism also gradually took root in Japan but were never especially prominent either in its early Japanese foundations compared to the cults that developed around particular Buddhist figures of worship, or in its later widespread dissemination throughout the country.[14] The most attractive elements of Buddhism for the Japanese were its various figures of worship and the powers they were said to bestow, for Buddhism appeared to offer a further, broader extension of the this-world orientation of Shinto and the folk tradition, with new and perhaps more powerful spiritual entities who could be assimilated alongside the *kami*. Buddhism was initially adopted for such reasons at the Imperial Court which came to see the Buddhas as efficacious and magically powerful figures who could be utilised to uphold and enhance the power of the State and the prestige of the Court. Buddhism's subsequent popularity in Japan owes much to the apparent powers possessed by its figures of worship which have remained in the vanguard of general Buddhist development in Japan ever since. For instance, Yakushi, the Buddha of healing who offers succour to the sick, was the focus of a cult of worship especially in the seventh, eighth and ninth centuries, but continues to attract worshippers and supplicants today. Probably the most popular of all Buddhist figures of worship in Japan is Kannon, the embodiment of compassionate mercy who, in the important Buddhist text the Lotus Sūtra, vows to save all who call on her mercy and to adopt innumerable manifestations in order to do so.[15] By the ninth century tales of Kannon's miraculous powers of intercession and compassion had become widespread, contributing to both a literary genre and an oral tradition that have continued unabated to the present day.[16] Kannon is also the centre of a rich pilgrimage tradition that, developing from around the twelfth century onwards, has continued to be a thriving and active thread in the Japanese religious tapestry.

The compassionate response of Kannon and the other Buddhist figures to prayers, and hence the powers of their intercessionary grace and the benefits they are believed to transmit to people, are called, in Japanese, *riyaku* or, more formally, *go-riyaku*. Although originally the word *riyaku* had a Buddhist connotation, with its sources in Buddhist texts, referring to the benefits acquired through the response of Buddhist figures to prayers, it has become widely applied in Japan not just to the Buddhas but to the *kami* and all other parts of the spiritual world. People talk of receiving the *riyaku* of *kami* such as Tenjin as well as of Buddhist figures, while the new religions commonly speak of the *go-riyaku* of their charismatically powerful founders. Equally, many popular contemporary religious manuals speak of the *riyaku* to be attained at various temples and shrines and from *kami* and Buddhas, seemingly without differentiating between the entities concerned.[17]

Riyaku is not limited to this world or life, for one can pray for the benefit of the souls of the dead and for solace after death, but its primary focus, as befits the anthropocentric framework of the folk and Shinto world into which Buddhism was integrated, is very much in the present. Described in such terms as *genze riyaku* (*genze* meaning 'this world/life') it is within the sphere of this life that most of the prayers, requests and needs of the Japanese towards their *kami* and Buddhas are directed. This does not necessarily imply a primarily materialist ethic, however, for prayers may be directed towards the attainment of peace of mind and emotional solace every bit as much as they are towards material ends. Even the prayers said by students for educational success aim as much as anything to provide them with a sense of calm and solace in the worrying period prior to examinations. The notion of *genze riyaku* affirms the responsive and fluid nature of the spiritual world and its powers and abilities to give succour to the living in response to human petitions and needs, and the importance for humans of acquiring solace and reassurance as well as guidance for living peacefully and happily in this life. As such it is an intrinsic factor in the make-up of Japanese religion that will concern us throughout this book.[18]

Buddhism also brought with it the means through which this relationship with the Buddhas could be brought to life. In particular it introduced a vast liturgy of prayers, chants and sacred texts along with iconographic depictions such as statues and paintings of Buddhist figures of worship. Buddhism, by the time it reached Japan, had formulated a complex philosophical structure expounded in vast numbers of *sūtras* or sacred texts. However, it was not so much the texts themselves that became important for the Japanese as the implicit powers that they were believed to contain. While within the fields of academia and Buddhist scholasticism and in the temples of different Buddhist sects there has been some exegetical and textual study of Buddhist scriptures, this has rarely had an impact on the wider populace for whom texts have largely been seen as containers and liberators of spiritual power through the sounds and meanings contained within them.

By the time Buddhism had reached Japan it had developed a rich tradition of 'words of power' known as *mantra* and *dharani*, incantations that reproduced Sanskrit sounds believed to contain spiritual power, that could unlock or summon the powers of various Buddha figures and help the living. The efficacy of such prayers was heightened in the Japanese perception by the fact that, prior to the cultural influx from continental Asia of which Buddhism was a part, Japan had no writing system. The writing system introduced along with Buddhism, and in which its texts were set down, underlined the technological superiority of the incoming culture and hence appeared to reinforce the efficacious powers of the Buddhas and the texts associated with them.

From very early on, Buddhist texts and prayers were regarded as means of liberating and harnessing the powers of the Buddhas and were widely used in rituals for the benefit of the country as well as for the realisation of personal wishes and needs. This use of words as manifestations of and keys to power has been a continuing theme in the Japanese religious world ever since and may be found at almost every juncture. *Sūtras* are chanted at funerals and in the rites following death so as to purify the soul and to transform it into a state of enlightenment, while prayers and incantations are recited before Buddhist statues by people seeking to elicit the help of the Buddhas: every Buddhist ritual situation requires and incorporates the recitation of such texts and prayers, while individuals also may frequently have recourse to their use in times of stress and need.

Probably the most widely used of such texts, and certainly the one that is most likely to be heard recited at temples and other religious centres in Japan, is the *Hannya Shingyō*, or Heart Sūtra, a short text that is widely regarded as encapsulating the essence and power of all Buddhist teachings. It also ends with a short *mantra* of words of power, and this along with its brevity which makes it easily memorised — it consists of just 262 ideograms and can be recited in less than five minutes — has made it readily accessible and extremely popular in Japan.[19] People chant it in all sorts of situations, especially in times of stress: a Japanese friend told me she was so nervous prior to taking her driving test that she chanted the words of the *Hannya Shingyō* to calm herself. She also placed a copy of the text in the folds of her clothing when she got into the car, and this, she felt, helped settle her nerves and allowed her to pass.

In 1985 I attended a ritual at the Buddhist temple Kinpusenji in Yoshino, a small town in the hills south of Osaka, during the festival of *setsubun* that occurs in early February to denote what was, under the old Japanese calendar, the transition point between winter and spring. Rites are held at many temples and shrines at this time to drive away bad fortune and beckon good for the coming season: in this rite the invocation *fuku wa uchi, oni wa soto* ('good luck in, demons out') is chanted while dried beans are thrown to symbolically drive away the demons representing bad fortune. At Kinpusenji the rite has a slightly different nuance: rather than saying *oni wa soto* ('demons out'), the cry is *oni mo uchi* ('demons also in'), representing the Buddhist view that all existence can be transformed and made good.

At Kinpusenji, at the start of the rite, the temple hall was filled with priests and onlookers: the priests performed a Buddhist religious service, during which men dressed up as *oni*, or demons wearing fierce masks and carrying clubs, swords and axes, wandered through the temple. They disrupted the service playfully, much to the amusement of everyone there, especially the children, pulling at the priests' robes, pretending to chop people's heads off and generally being a thorough nuisance. At a given signal in the rite, however, an invocation was chanted to reform the demons and bring them into the fold: at this point the priests and everyone else in the temple took up the chant of the *Hannya Shingyō*, the priests throwing as they did so dried beans at the demons. As the powers of the words and sounds of the incantation resounded around the temple the demons one by one began to clutch their heads and fall to the ground, their evil subdued and destroyed, before rising again, revived and transformed into good beings who then helped the priests perform the next part of the ritual, carrying their implementa and generally being helpful where, moments before, they had caused obstructions.

The ritual was a vivid demonstration of the symbolic powers of the text, and indeed of any Buddhist text, able to transform bad to good, to eradicate evil and to purify all things. The powers of transformation, although embedded in the texts and chants, are, it should be emphasised, not conditional on an understanding of the inner philosophical meanings of the words themselves: it is the action of recitation itself that unleashes the powers inherent in the words.

The provision of such tools as texts and *mantra* that could be used to open up the path towards the achievement of human needs and to call into play the powers of the Buddhas was complemented by the statues and paintings that Buddhism introduced to put a form to the Buddhas and make them more graphically approachable and directly accessible in every physical sphere of life. It is interesting to note that whereas the *kami*, despite their humanesque nature, are not generally graphically represented in physical forms, Buddha figures – whose compassionate wisdom is non-discriminating and hence transcends humanesque limitations – invariably are. The first encounter between the Japanese and Buddhism was in the form of a statue sent by the ruler of Paekche in Korea to the Japanese court in the sixth century, and since that time the construction of Buddhist statues as objects of worship and manifestations of power of the Buddhas has been unrelenting.

Many are important as symbols of national prestige, such as the Great Buddha statue built at the then capital of Nara in the eighth century, or because of their intrinsic artistic value (as with the iconography of the temples of the former capitals Nara and Kyoto), but in religious terms their greatest importance has always been in expressing the all-pervasive and accessible nature of the power and compassion of those they depict and in providing a means through which people may enter into a relationship with and receive the power of the Buddhas. For instance, the writer of the eleventh-century classic of Japanese literature, the *Sarashina Nikki*, records how she had a statue of Yakushi made for her own worship, praying to him for assistance in the realisation of her ambitions.[20] The contemporary situation is no different, with statues built in great numbers and drawing large numbers of people who come to pray to or at them. For instance, in the 1970s the Sōtō Zen temple Chōkokuji in Tokyo erected a nine-metre-high wooden statue of Kannon whose *riyaku*, according to temple literature, eradicates all sufferings and grants all wishes: another Zen temple, Tōganji in Nagoya, has recently consecrated a bronze Buddha statue nearly eleven metres high that, according to the temple's head priest, is always accessible to the prayers of people seeking peace of mind.[21]

Sometimes such statues are widely publicised for their apparent powers and *riyaku*: there are regular advertisements in the Japanese press promoting a temple in Mie prefecture which has erected a giant 33-metre-high statue of Kannon that is claimed (somewhat spuriously) as the tallest figure of its kind in the world. It is but one of several giant statues of Kannon that have been built or planned in the last two decades in Japan: another that is 80 metres high has been recently built on the island of Awaji in the Inland Sea, while a 100-metre-high Kannon is planned for the island of Shodōshima. The advertisements for the Mie prefecture Kannon offer for sale a pendant which, on one side, depicts the statue of Kannon and, on the other, is inscribed with the *Hannya Shingyō*. The pendant has been sacralised through the power of the Mie Kannon, extending its power to those who, in purchasing the pendant, thus acquire Kannon's grace and protection.[22] This propensity for building large-scale Buddhist statues has become something of a fad in contemporary Japan, reflecting the country's growing economic wealth which enables more money to be put into such things combined with the streak of competitiveness that acts as a spur to those who want 'their' statue to be the biggest or to draw attention to their region or locality in some way. It is also illustrative of the continuing emphasis placed on Buddhist statues as objects of power in contemporary Japan.

The statues themselves are, in Buddhist terms, not simply objects but are graphic representations of the Buddhas themselves. A Buddhist ritual known as *kaigen* (literally 'eye opening') is performed, usually using Buddhist chants and prayers that summon up the powers of the Buddhas, through which the essence of the Buddha concerned is believed to enter the statue. Statues thus become the Buddha concerned, those of Kannon, for instance, being a combination of the physical form of the statue and her spiritual being. As manifestations of the compassion of the Buddhas, they are also a ready means through which relationships may be developed: by enabling people to perform a good deed such as making a donation, thus meriting the *riyaku* that the Buddhas can bestow, statues make the world of the Buddhas directly accessible to ordinary people without mediation, allowing them to enter when they choose into a relationship that may be casually temporary (as when a particular need surfaces) or more long-term, with gratitude being returned for previous help.

The friendly, relaxed, familiar nature of this relationship can be seen from the manner of offerings that are made – food, fruit, sweets, small bottles of sake and even cigarettes and packets of tissues may be placed before Buddhist statues. Statues of Jizō, the bald-headed Buddhist figure who guards travellers, children and the souls of the dead, are particularly well adorned with woolly hats, bibs and other articles of clothing. Jizō, in Buddhist folklore, is depicted as descending to the deepest hells to rescue the souls of dead children who have unwittingly fallen there: the hats and bibs are, depending on different sources, to remind him of the soul he is to save, to protect him in his arduous journey, as an offering in gratitude for his benevolence, or simply just to stop him getting cold.[23] At the bottom of all these reasons lie the feelings of warmth that his figure, with its kindly compassion towards children, evokes. Whilst walking across a snowy mountain pass on the island of Shikoku in 1984 I came across two Jizō statues standing guard: not only were they wearing woolly hats, but also each wore a new *hanten*, the traditional quilted cotton jacket worn by many Japanese in winter. Someone obviously felt that they deserved to keep warm during their compassionate vigil of protecting those along the way.

Quite clearly the Buddhist focus on compassionate figures who respond to the cries of all those in distress from the beginning fitted well with the pragmatic this-worldly orientations of the Japanese. It not only extended the numbers of those to whom one could turn in times of trouble but also broadened their scope, the infinite compassion and universalism of the Buddhas augmenting the more localised and capricious nature of the *kami*. Thus Buddhism, although originally resisted as a foreign import, was gradually welcomed, especially as it showed a readiness to fuse with the indigenous tradition. Buddhism has always had a tolerant dynamic, generally seeking accommodation with rather than subjugation of other, especially indigenous, religious currents it encounters. It was a trait that suited the assimilative Japanese religious climate very well, especially as many facets of Buddhism, such as the readiness of the Buddhas to be petitioned for help, and the continuity that existed between them and humans, matched indigenous views. As a result, Buddhism, while retaining its identity, merged into the Japanese religious milieu, working with rather than against Shinto and the folk tradition. The *kami* were seen from the Buddhist point of view as spiritual beings on the path to enlightenment and as localised versions of the universalism of Buddhism identifiable with figures in the Buddhist pantheon, Amaterasu, for example, being identified with Dainichi, the Cosmic or Sun Buddha of the esoteric Buddhism tradition that began to flourish from the late eighth century onwards in Japan.[24]

Many early religious institutions combined Buddhist and Shinto aspects, with both Buddhas and *kami* venerated and priests of both traditions officiating, the Buddhist priests chanting prayers that sought to lead the *kami* into enlightenment, compassion, conversion to Buddhism and, hence, extinction of the capricious sides of their nature. By so 'converting' the *kami*, of course, the Buddhist priests were also subtly converting the Japanese to Buddhism, but this process simultaneously helped to augment the powers of the *kami* to some extent. Inari, the fox deity who first came into prominence as a protector of the esoteric Buddhist temple Tōji in Kyoto, came to be regarded as a particularly powerful *kami* with heightened powers of *riyaku* because of this association with esoteric Buddhism, and subsequently came to be one of Japan's most widely venerated *kami*, with a network of shrines across the entire nation.[25]

However, this extension of Buddhist influence over the *kami* also threatened to overwhelm them and assimilate them, and hence Shinto, wholly under a Buddhist umbrella. As a response to this implicit absorption, to defend the identity of the *kami* and to safeguard their power in the face of Buddhist expansion, Shinto priests assimilated for the *kami* the role of defending the Buddhist images and temples standing on Japanese soil. The *kami*, because of their situation in the natural world, as manifested by rocks, trees and so on, and because of their very Japaneseness, have always had a geographical orientation connected to the land of Japan. As guardians of the physical space of Japan both in a broad national sense and in a narrower local one they have traditionally been involved and called into play on any occasion which concerns the land and the physical space of Japan. At local levels their protective help has traditionally been sought whenever any building has been erected, a function as prominent today in Japan as at any time in history. Shinto ground-breaking ceremonies invoking the support and protection of local *kami* are almost invariably held during the process of building, whether for new houses, office buildings, factories or other symbols of the modern rational world such as new university buildings.[26]

As guardians of the land itself it was logical that the *kami* should shoulder the responsibility of guarding Buddhist institutions, and it is a function still performed to this day. It is more common than not to find a small Shinto shrine dedicated to the local protective deity in the grounds of Buddhist temples. I stayed on two occasions at a rather austere Zen Buddhist temple in the mountains in central Japan: the temple had no running water or electricity, there was a strict meditation schedule and the monks went out regularly on the traditional begging round in search of food. I also went out with them on one occasion and noted that, as we filed down the mountainside, everyone bowed and performed an act of veneration at the little Shinto shrine dedicated to the guardian deity of the mountain. Even in the midst of the most stringent adherence to Buddhist monastic traditions the Shinto—Buddhist fusion remains strong.

One of the best-known and popular Shinto shrines in Japan is Toyokawa Inari, dedicated to Inari, the deity once venerated as a god of the rice harvest but now, symbolic of the shifting continuities of Japanese religion, equally popular as a god of business. The shrine dominates the small town of Toyokawa some 40 miles east of Nagoya in Aichi prefecture and draws huge crowds especially at New Year and other festival times when people come to seek Inari's help, praying especially for business prosperity and good fortune. The shrine itself is part of a wider religious complex which goes under the name Myōgonji, a Zen Buddhist temple affiliated to the Sōtō sect. The officiants who run the complex, including the Toyokawa Inari shrine itself, are Zen Buddhist monks who also practice Zen meditation and perform Buddhist rituals in the Buddhist sections of the complex: even the invocations they chant to Inari come from Buddhist texts.

No one at the temple seemed to see this as contradictory but as a natural expression of the Japanese religious situation aligned to local historical tradition. Locals and visitors alike refer to the whole complex as Toyokawa Inari, indicating its Shinto orientations, while finding no anomaly in the fact that it is run by shaven-headed priests with Buddhist robes.[27] The Buddhist priests of the temple Myōgonji directing prayers to the Shinto deity Inari for the folk-religious themes of pragmatic, this-worldly welfare in many ways symbolise the complementary nature of the Japanese religious world, bringing Buddhist, Shinto and folk themes together under one roof.

ANCESTORS, LIFE AND DEATH

Besides the *kami* and the Buddhas the most prominent spiritual entities of the Japanese religious pantheon are the ancestors (*senzo*) who act as guardians and protectors of the continuity and prosperity of the household lineage to which they belonged in life. Although, unlike the *kami* and Buddhas, their influence rarely extends further than this, they are the focus of a great deal of socio-religious activity including visits to their graves, the annual *o-bon* festival and rituals performed at the family *butsudan*.

Traditional Japanese cosmology considered that each person had a soul (*tama*) which invested the physical body with life: death was a result of the severance of the *tama* from the physical body.[28] The soul did not, however, cease with death but journeyed to the world of the dead while continuing to maintain an interest in this world, especially in its extant kin, looking over and protecting them as a guardian ancestral spirit. The journey to ancestorhood necessitated a series of rituals conferring a new role and status on the dead soul and ensuring that it adjusted to these happily and without resentment, and would thus look benevolently on the living. These rituals, which have long been carried out under the auspices of Buddhism, involve the household and the Buddhist temple in a relationship that has been crucial to the status of Buddhism in Japan and to the continuing role of the household as a religious centre in its own right, themes that will be discussed in Chapter 4.

The rituals themselves are believed to guide the dead soul not simply from this world to the next, but also to transform it into an enlightened being in its own right. The Japanese word for a departed soul, *hotoke*, also means a Buddha or enlightened being, and this dual meaning has produced a gloss between the two to the extent that for many in Japan the aims of Buddhism have become enlightenment not in life but after it. Buddhist rituals for the dead have strongly transformational and purificatory motifs, seeking to lead the soul to enlightenment by bestowing a Buddhist identity on it and eradicating the impurities of death, physically by cremating the corpse and metaphorically by chanting Buddhist texts and prayers that are believed to guide the soul away from this world, purify it of its shortcomings and transform it into an enlightened state. Attaining the state of peaceful rest after death (that is, completing the journey to ancestorhood) and attaining Buddhahood or enlightenment are also denoted by the same word, *jōbutsu*. Here again there is a sense of continuity between human and other states, the human progressing through death to become a *hotoke* and an ancestor.

The notion of who becomes an ancestor has always been rather vaguely defined: traditionally only certain people, generally patrilineal members of the family, usually male, who had procreated and helped extend the lineage would be regarded as ancestors. Not all dead (*hotoke*) would therefore, technically, be ancestors (*senzo*) although in common parlance people are more likely than not to gloss over any differences and see the two as very much the same.[29] It has however, certainly in recent decades, become more and more normal for other family members, including children, to be venerated as ancestors.[30] The household in Japan is not simply composed of its present, living members, but incorporates those who have given life to it from the past and those who will do so in the future. It is a continuing entity linking past, present and future, with its dead members, the ancestors who had provided it with life and vitality in their own lifetimes, continuing to contribute to it after death by offering it a sense of tradition and continuity and using their spiritual influence to oversee and affirm its continuing prosperity.

A poster I saw some years ago outside a Buddhist temple in the village of Nishijō in Nagano prefecture encapsulated the importance of the ancestors and the role played by Buddhism in this:

The prosperity of the family comes from worshipping the ancestors: let us meet them serenely before the statue of Buddha.[31]

The view that the ancestors are the transmitters of life and benefactors of the living is repeatedly emphasised in Buddhist writings. The Sōtō Zen priest Sakai Daigaku talks of the blood of the present generation as being bestowed to it by the ancestors[32] while Kamata Shigeo states that Buddhism itself is a gift passed on through the generations by the ancestors.[33] Beyond just giving life and a sense of continuity to the present and future generations, the ancestors act as guides and protectors, leading the living along the path to happiness, as these words, quoted by Davis, spoken at the beginning of a training course run by the new religion Mahikari, indicate: 'Your ancestors and guardian spirits have brought you to this training course.'[34]

Sometimes ancestral guidance may appear in the form of ostensible misfortunes containing inner messages for the living, an idea given form in the teaching of the Buddhistic new religious movement Reiyūkai, which tells its followers to cultivate their minds through spiritual discipline and obliges them to spread the religion's teaching to others. Rejections received while proselytising are, according to Reiyūkai, admonitions from the ancestors designed to draw attention to the faults of the living and to encourage them to make further efforts in the field of spiritual discipline. Hence apparent rebuffs are in reality benevolent guidance from the ancestors.[35]

The incidence of death and its spiritual repercussions may therefore be positive and affirmative. The life-affirming, optimistic and this-world focus of Japanese religion has never denied the reality of death as a natural process, the inevitable concomitant and end of life. Ideally, the separation of the spiritual life-giving force from the physical realm in which it existed can be transformed for the benefit of humanity, with the souls of the dead continuing to feel benevolence towards the living and assisting the process of renewal and continued prosperity through their benevolent guidance on the spiritual level. Ancestral influence is centred in this world, and there is little real concern, beyond the wish to be at peace after death, in what lies beyond it.[36] Although conceptualisations of other worlds have long existed in Japan, particularly in Buddhism which introduced the idea of other worlds, including hells and Pure Lands, to which the soul was destined depending on behaviour in this life, the Japanese have not, by and large, dwelt much on speculations about what lies beyond. Rather, like Izanagi rolling a rock across the gateway to the world of the dead, they have preferred to partition it off as long as it does not affect them adversely. Buddhism's perspective has also largely been this-worldly, not just in its rituals that transform the dead into ancestors who continue to exist in conjunction with this world but by its emphasis on the peace of mind (*anshin*) that may be attained through this union. This peaceful assurance is strengthened by the feeling that one will, in turn, not be forgotten after death, but will be memorialised by the living and so continue to exist in some form in this world.

Herein lies a major aspect of ancestor veneration: it is, like other relationships between humans and the spiritual world, a reciprocal one. The rituals that transform the dead soul into a peaceful ancestral spirit are set in motion by the survivors who continue to make offerings to the ancestors at the family *butsudan* and at the grave. These offerings provide sustenance to the ancestors, helping them to make the transition to peaceful ancestorhood, and affirm that the departed have not been forgotten. In return, the ancestors oversee family fortunes: it is, in effect, a reciprocal sharing of gratitude and benevolence which provides the living with a two-fold sense of assurance, first, that the ancestors are looking over them, and secondly, that they in turn will be cared for and not forgotten when they die. This at least is the ideal, and it presupposes that one will leave offspring: the religious ideal of ancestorhood and the social one of continuing the lineage reinforce each other. Dying after a long and fruitful life, with surviving kin who will memorialise and aid one to enlightenment, may be in tune with the natural rhythm of life.

Attitudes towards death, however, have always been somewhat more ambivalent than this. We have seen, in the legend of Izanami, the turbulence that comes when it occurs outside the apparently natural order, suddenly, violently or early, involving an abrupt rupture of the harmonious balance of the physical and spiritual. It can be a radical disruption in the flow of life, a threat to the existence and well-being of survivors. Izanagi's experience when confronted with his partner's death reflects the dilemma of the living: his desire not to be separated from her is offset by his terrified flight when he discovers the truth of what has happened. It shows the general fears and insecurities of the living when faced with this ultimate disruption to the enriching processes of life, torn between affection for the departed and the wish to distance themselves from the spectre of death that has come between them. More than that, though, it reflects a fundamental fear that malevolent spirits — particularly those who died angrily — might wreak damage on the living.

It has largely been through the medium of Buddhism that this threat has been countered in Japan: its powers have long been invoked not just to transform the dead soul into an ancestor but also to hem in and restrict the dangerous, polluting and angry repercussions of death. This dual role helped secure, over the centuries, a major social role for Buddhism, and one that endures to this day.[37] Pacifying the dead soul by memorial rites that directed its energies away from this world provided the means of neutralising such spirits: such rites were (and are) performed for those who have no kin or who died unhappily, in order to stave off the possibilities that their souls might cause problems to the living.[38]

Fears that the angry spirits of the dead might wreak trouble on the living, and the interpretations of misfortune as caused by the unhappy spirits, were common in earlier times, as the story of Sugawara Michizane, recounted earlier in this chapter, demonstrates. Such conceptions are by no means merely vestiges of the past, however, but continue to have credence among appreciable numbers of Japanese people in the contemporary age. Agonshū, one of a number of new religious movements that have become extremely prominent since the 1970s, contends that all misfortunes are the result of unhappy spirits that have not achieved Buddhahood because the correct rituals have not been done for them. They are therefore angry and unsettled, and as a result hinder the fortunes, health and happiness of the living, especially those of their family lineage.[39]

Agonshū members speak freely of the problems caused by unhappy spirits, and the benefits that accrue when these have been pacified. An Agonshū film *Reishō o toke* ('removing spiritual hindrances') shows a number of members narrating their experiences. One woman spoke of how, prior to her marriage, she and her fiancé had always had a pleasant and easy relationship. Afterwards they had nothing but fights and arguments. In despair she turned to Agonshū, one of whose trained spiritual counsellors diagnosed that the troubles were caused by an ancestor from her husband's family (women inherit the ancestors of the family they marry into) for whom the proper post-death services had not been done. The ancestral spirit had marked her out as an accessible means through which to express its unhappiness and get the recognition and rites it deserved. It had clearly chosen correctly, for the film showed her happily talking of how, once the problem had been diagnosed and various Agonshū rites had been performed to pacify the ancestor, her marriage was now blissful. Another woman in the same film talked about the problems — spiritual anguish and headaches — she had had after an abortion. These difficulties were interpreted as being caused by the distressed spirit of the aborted foetus, and she spoke of the respite she received when the appropriate rites were then performed to make it into a pacified spirit (*jōbutsu*).

The problem this woman faced is an increasingly common one in contemporary Japan: abortion is the major means of birth control, used increasingly as people wish to have smaller families. Many who do this later feel the need either to atone for this action or to make some reparation to the soul of the aborted child. Often, of course, both these factors are involved as people seek, through the religious framework, to deal with the psychological problems that accrue from abortion, and the growth in the practice of *mizuko kuyō*, memorial rites for the souls of aborted foetuses, that results from this is one of the most prominent phenomena of recent decades throughout the Japanese religious world, performed not just by Agonshū but by several other new religions and at many Buddhist temples as well.[40]

LIFE IN EVERYTHING: MEMORIALISING EELS, DOLLS AND OTHER THINGS

Memorial rites are not only performed for the souls of the human dead, however, for the idea that life is a coalition of the physical and the spiritual is not limited to the human realm alone. Animals and even apparently inanimate objects, especially when they have been of use to humans and hence part of the life-extending process and of the upholding of human happiness and well-being in this world, may also be seen in a similar vein. The first Zen Buddhist temple at which I lived in Japan used to perform a memorial service every year at the request of the Biology Department of one of the universities situated in its city. Attended by members of staff and students it memorialised and gave thanks to the animals who had perished in its experiments over the year.

Later I lived at a temple in northern Japan which regularly performed memorial services at the behest of the owner of a restaurant in the town that specialised in eels, a popular delicacy in Japan. The owner and her staff had the services done for the souls of the eels who, in yielding their lives, had contributed to the restaurant's prosperity. According to the priest, the owner felt that not to do this would invite retribution and threaten future success.[41]

Objects, rather than just being discarded when no longer usable, may also be memorialised for what they have given to humanity. The Buddhist newspaper *Chūgai Nippō* frequently carries reports of such services, and I shall just mention two here, one for dolls, the other for printing blocks. Similar themes were common to both. The service for the dolls is held annually on 17 September at Ōsu Kannon temple in Nagoya, sponsored by a number of doll-makers' unions and organisations: people bring along their discarded dolls which are ritually burnt by the temple priests after they have performed a memorial service for their souls. The service for printing blocks was held at a temple in Kyoto in September 1987 under the auspices of the Kyoto Advertisers Social Society (*Kyoto hōkoku konwakai*), an organisation uniting printing and advertising firms. Prayers were said and thanks were given to the blocks (which had been used to print advertisements and the like) prior to their being immolated. In both cases, words spoken at the services were remarkably similar: the chief lay-participant at the first and the head-priest at the second both used the term *jōbutsu*, the former stating: 'These dolls have always lived with us, and now, through this memorial service they will be able to attain Buddhahood peacefully',[42] and the latter: 'In Buddhism all life may attain Buddhahood: printing blocks also possess life and so can attain Buddhahood.'[43]

Objects are not just 'things' to be used and discarded with impunity: they contribute their 'life' to the present world and recognition should be made of this. This animistic view of the world places obligations on those who live in it: while human life is at the centre of the universe, it is not something that can be lived unthinkingly, without regard for the continuities of the past, for other realms of existence or for the consequences of one's actions. This does not prevent it from being exploitative when necessary for the benefit of the living: the eels are still killed and cooked for profit, the animals still give up their lives in the laboratory, and the dolls are still discarded. It does, though, introduce an obligation to make amends for actions taken, to express gratitude for things received and to recognise an inherent sense of the tragic in human life, which prospers in conjunction with the inevitability of death and destruction.

CAUSATION, KARMA, WELFARE AND MIRACLES

The recognition that physical events have spiritual causes is intrinsic to traditional Japanese views of the world but, as the example of the Agonshū film indicates, it still remains strong in contemporary Japan and forms a major element in religious behaviour and attitudes. The solutions posed by modern science and the contemporary world to the problems faced by humanity are not, in this light, full answers for they neglect to take stock of the influence of spiritual factors and impediments. Medicines and marriage counselling may be the prescribed modern means for dealing with headaches and marital ills but they are, in the eyes of many people in Japan today, not enough, for they do not deal with the underlying psychic elements of causation that are actually the source of the problems.

Problems develop when one fails to take heed of the spiritual repercussions of one's actions. The woman's abortion caused a premature rupture of the spiritual and the physical and unleashed an unhappy spirit that, because it was not properly cared for, caused hindrances and problems to its kin — in this case the mother — until some recognition of its plight was made and the necessary rituals were performed to pacify it. In the mother's case the effects of her failure to care for the soul properly were experienced almost immediately.

Karma (Japanese: *innen*), the notion that all events and actions have repercussions, often referred to in Buddhist terms as the law of cause and effect, may be immediate and direct, returning to the person most intimately associated with the actions that set the whole process in motion. It need not be, however: the other woman's problem came from an ancestral spirit she had inherited by marriage. Karma may thus be transmitted and shared — recognition, indeed, that people do not stand in isolation but are closely bound, especially through blood and familial ties, with each other, existing as a result of a series of interconnected causal relationships and defined through them, rather than in more individual terms.

Karma need not have negative connotations: the word *en* (affinity, karmic relations) which is frequently used in terms of relationships has distinctly positive nuances. When two people join their *en* together (*en o musubu*) they are getting married, and *en* may bring people into contact with each other, as I was told by a Buddhist priest who felt that the Buddha's *en* had guided me to his temple and us towards a lasting friendship. The whole field of relationships that develop between people and *kami*, Buddhas and ancestors is closely connected to the concept of *en*, to the process of creating it and causing it to continue for the benefit of the living. As such, also, there is a strong focus on the connections between people and on the interconnectedness of all who exist in the world.

When *en* is absent or when its flow has been broken or interrupted problems arise. The word for a spirit who has died without surviving kin or without anyone to look after his/her spirit, *butsudan* or grave after death is *muenbotoke*, a dead soul without any *en* or connections, and it is often such spirits, who are felt to be unhappy, angry and suffering because they have been neglected, that are seen as potential causes of problems and unrest for the living. It is when such problems arise that the issues of causation are most prominently encountered and when people feel the need to turn to spiritual solutions and to find where the causes of their problems may be located.

Since the root cause of physical events is located in the spiritual realm and in its influences, it follows that the way to deal with problems is to identify, in religious terms, the spiritual blockage or hindrance (*sawari*, *reishō*), source of psychic retribution (*tatari*) or the nature of the pollution (*kegare*) which may be impeding the productive powers of life. Even though it may be ritual neglect (for example, the failure to carry out the proper memorial services) that causes these spiritual impediments to develop this does not mean that there is no sense of moral guilt involved: ritual neglect is a result of the failure to live up to one's obligations or to atone for actions. Even when the problem may be identified as an ancestor of past generations (and hence the fault is placed, originally at least, with those in past ages who failed to carry out their duties correctly) this does not absolve the living from action or responsibility: karma is inherited and the obligations of interdependency need to be accepted. The alternative would be to ignore the spiritual impediment, thus allowing it to remain and perhaps threaten succeeding generations. a clear abdication of responsibility both to the past and future.

Since the fault is located in ritual neglect that allows pollutions and hindrances to develop, the process of ridding the living of these things involves ritual action with strongly purificatory and exorcistic themes. As has been seen, such motifs are central to Buddhist rites for the dead and are manifest in Izanagi's bathing after his flight, which purifies his body of the spiritual pollutions of death and opens the door to continued fertility.

The new religions, too, provide the means, via rituals and spiritual healing techniques, through which such hindrances may be removed and through which unhappy spirits may be soothed. Mahikari teaches its members a technique of spiritual healing, *o-kiyome*, which is believed to draw forth and identify possessing and malevolent spirits and either transforms them into peaceful and benevolent ones or exorcises them,[44] while Agonshū performs Buddhist fire rituals that, it asserts, can liberate unhappy ancestors and transform them into kind guardians. The spiritual malevolence of the distressed ancestral spirits is thus purified, and the transformation into benevolence provides an added motif of renewal and revitalisation, as the women in the Agonshū film made clear, stating that they were now existing in a new world from that experienced prior to the removal of their problems.[45]

Such solutions of problems through religious practices are regarded as miracles, manifestations of the direct hand of the spiritual in this world that have direct ameliorative results and effects in the lives of the beneficiaries in the present. Their miraculous content is very much in the eye of the beholder, and may range from direct and profound releases from suffering and illness to altogether more mundane things. Davis's survey of miracles experienced by Mahikari adherents showed not just a remarkable level of incidence of miracles (only 12 out of 688 adherents had not experienced any) but a wide degree of interpretation of what a miracle might involve, ranging from physical miracles such as repairing electrical gadgets by using Mahikari's technique of *okiyome* to such seemingly everyday events as catching a bus.[46] In this readiness to see even prosaic events such as catching a bus through a lens of miracles and spiritual influence there is a very definite reaffirmation of traditional Japanese views of causation and an assertion that these are still viable and relevant in modern society. It also affirms that the world of religious experience in Japan can be immediately and directly realised and interpreted within a framework relevant and specific to the individual concerned. It is, after all, those who experience the 'miracle' who interpret it as such, thus allowing themselves to transform such everyday actions into direct and valid personal religious experiences.

THE ENRICHING PROCESS, THE NEW RELIGIONS AND THE CASE OF CHRISTIANITY

This co-ordinated, affirmative cosmological outlook has provided the framework within which any religious tradition that seeks to be effective in Japan needs to operate. The new religious movements that have risen to prominence in Japan in the last century and a half have invariably drawn their major characteristics and cosmological outlooks, to say nothing of the deities that they worship, from the existing Japanese religious world. The new religions in general are perhaps more than anything renovations of traditional Japanese religious ideas and cosmological themes within a modern framework, presented in new contexts relevant for contemporary, especially urban, Japan. As a religious phenomenon they have been remarkably successful in this, attracting large numbers of Japanese because of a vigour and enthusiasm that often seems lacking in the older and more staid established religions, especially when they affirm the ability to solve problems through spiritual and religious means.[47]

Few new religions fail to emphasise the importance of the ancestors as a source of benevolence when correctly venerated and as potential causes of misfortune when neglected. All seek to provide the means whereby their members may receive benefits in this life, surmounting illness and achieving success, peace of mind and happiness. Often the this-worldly focus is given concrete doctrinal form: Tenrikyō emphasises this world as the location where humans have to find ultimate meaning and asserts the ideal of living a bright, happy life (*yōkigurashi*) in this world.[48] In such ways the new religions as a whole have fitted in with the basic cosmological orientations of Japanese religion, building on, reinforcing and augmenting rather than counteracting its general outlooks.

When a religion does not accept these basic orientations it has been far less likely to prosper, as is witnessed by the case of Christianity which has had a chequered and brief history in Japan: welcomed in the sixteenth century and shortly after proscribed and severely persecuted, and later grudgingly allowed back in the nineteenth century. Since then, immense amounts of missionary work and great educational efforts (many of Japan's best known schools and colleges are Christian) have failed to make Christianity more than a minority religious view, with little more than 1 per cent of the population as adherents.[49] Although Christianity has, in recent years, attained relatively high levels of empathy and admiration, especially among the young, because of its spiritual teachings[50] it has not yet really translated these into anything more solid in terms of adherents, primarily because being Christian can produce doctrinal problems *vis-à-vis* the ancestors and family obligations, and certainly involves some dichotomous problems concerning the this-worldly, causative and ethnic dimensions of Japanese religion.

Christianity has, however, added something to the overall picture. Jesus (along with Moses, Mary and other figures from the Christian tradition) has begun to take his place in the Japanese religious pantheon of the new religions, providing a channel whereby some Christian ideals at least may be translated into a Japanese context and expressed. On a more general level many Japanese recognise Christmas as a new focal point in the round of yearly events, perhaps by attending church, but more commonly through the rather more secular action of buying a cake. White Christian-style weddings have also become increasingly fashionable over the years and probably account for the majority of wedding ceremonies at present. Each occasion has entered the social calendar to the extent that, although Christianity remains very much a minority religion, aspects of its ritual and festive nature have entered the Japanese life cycle: one may now be born Shinto, marry Christian and die Buddhist, take part in *hatsumōde* and *o-bon* and buy a Christmas cake.

The ways in which all these religious currents have flowed alongside each other has made the Japanese religious world at one and the same time exceedingly rich, varied and unified. The core of shared actions and underlying cosmological attitudes is expressed through the medium of different religious traditions at different times, providing the Japanese with a sense of fluidity in which they can interact with different parts of the whole, depending on need. Each part of the whole also provides the ground for action according to different parts of the lifestyle of the community and individual: as Miyake has noted, the Japanese may pray at the *kamidana* and *butsudan*, go to the shrine at New Year, the temple at *o-bon*, the church at Christmas, and then during a life crisis may go to a new religious group.[51] As a Japanese student told me, her parents sent her to a Christian school because of its good academic reputation, bought her Buddhist amulets and prayed at Shinto shrines before her examinations, and celebrated New Year, *o-bon* and Christmas.

THE SPIRITUAL IN THE PHYSICAL WORLD: AN OMNIPRESENT FORCE

The diverse and numerous complexities of this composite whole are reflected vividly in Japanese spatial and physical geography: one does not have to look far in Japan to see evidence of the interpenetration of spiritual and physical worlds. Shrines and temples are everywhere, their courtyards full of sub-shrines or statues each venerating or housing some object of worship. Wayside shrines and stones depicting deities of all sorts are found along roadsides and footpaths. It is rare to walk along a mountain path that does not have one or more stone statues, most commonly of the popular Buddhist figure Jizō, the guardian of travellers and children, often adorned with small offerings testifying that they continue to be the focus of active relationships.

This is not just in the more traditional countryside, however, for the streets of Japanese cities have their fair share, with protective shrines and statues clustering around markets and shopping centres and in front of factories producing high-technology goods. The roofs of major buildings frequently house shrines to guardian deities and, sometimes, Buddhas, as is the case with the Mitsukoshi department store in central Tokyo. On its roof is a statue of Jizō, originally unearthed on the site during construction work in the previous century but now housed in a permanent shelter provided by the store, which attracts scores of worshippers who come to seek its intercessionary powers.[52]

At the heart of Minami, a bustling nightlife area of bars, eating houses, strip clubs and other places of raucous entertainment in the great business city of Osaka, is a small temple dedicated to the popular Buddhist figure Fudō. Many of the people going in and out of the bars and clubs around it pray, make a small offering or light a stick of incense as they go on their way, while those working at and running the bars around help in the support and upkeep of the temple, and Fudō is here venerated as a guardian and protector of the entertainment business. No one appears to find it anomalous that a religious place should be so integrated into an area devoted to apparently non-religious ends.[53]

The spiritual is innately present in the midst of life, not separate from it: there is a basic recognition that it may be encountered everywhere, that any setting is the potential location of a *kami*, Buddha or other spiritual entity. At times, especially when aligned to the pragmatically functional attitude to religion that is also characteristically Japanese, this leads to rather interesting and amusing results, as the following case shows.

On the street leading to Ishikiri shrine in Osaka are numerous shops selling herbal medicines, and many small shrines, temples and wayside statues. Many are, like the main shrine itself, connected with healing. At the side of one particular shop selling herbal remedies for ear problems was a piece of undeveloped ground commonly used by male passers-by as a place to urinate. In an attempt to stop this, the shop owner dug a small pond and placed in it two rocks joined by a straw Shinto rope, utilising Shinto symbols which he clearly believed no one would urinate on. He was correct, but people began to throw coins in, asking what the name of the *kami* was, and what *riyaku* it had. The owner then placed an offertory box to catch the coins and, in response to demand, designated the *kami* as one that could help those with ear problems. Over the years the site has developed into a small shrine in its own right, complementing the medicinal functions of the shop next door, satisfying the passers-by who have 'recognised' the presence of another deity in the area and are obviously happy to be able to call on its help. It has naturally also pleased the shop owner who not only solved a problem but found a supplementary source of support for his business — a clear case of the owner turning to the gods in his distress coupled with the force of popular will combining to produce another marker on the Japanese physical and religious landscape.[54]

The presence of spiritual entities is found indoors as well as out, as is shown by the widespread incidence of household altars, the *butsudan* and *kamidana* dedicated respectively to the ancestors who protect and watch over the family and to the guardian *kami* mentioned in Chapter 1. Inside shops, bars and restaurants there are often *kamidana* dedicated to deities such as Ebisu and Daikokuten who are associated with prosperity, while many business firms and even academic institutions may have a small shrine to a guardian deity on the premises. The presence of the *kami* and other spiritual entities, and of their protective influence, can be seen also on trains, buses, boats and other forms of transport. In summer 1984 when we were travelling from the southern island of Kyūshū up to Kōbe by the overnight ferry, my wife, a friend and I were invited on to the bridge by the crew. On the wall overlooking the wheel, the radar screens and all the other technological equipment was a small *kamidana* dedicated to Konpira, the guardian deity of sailors, complete with a number of religious talismans from Konpira's main shrine at Kotohira in Shikoku and various offerings, including a small bottle of sake. Offerings, we were told, were made every day.

This interrelationship of the modern technological world with spiritual protective entities is seen repeatedly in contemporary Japan. The Keihan Railway Company which carries millions of passengers on its commuter trains and buses in the Kyoto–Osaka region places in every train compartment and on every bus an amulet for safe travel. This comes from the Kōrien Naritasan Buddhist temple, a popular temple accessible from the Keihan line halfway between Kyoto and Osaka, whose main focus of worship, Fudō, has long been revered as a protector of travellers. The amulet representing Fudō's holy power and protection serves to assure passengers as they ride on the buses and trains that the Keihan company has taken every precaution to ensure them a safe ride, not just on the physical level but also by enlisting the help of the spiritual domain as well.

The omnipresence of religious motifs in the Japanese world shows the extent to which, even in this day and age, basic and traditional Japanese religious views of causation and of the interrelationship of the spiritual and physical continue to be important, underlying contemporary attitudes to existence in this world. It is a view which recognises a permeating vitality, an in-built religious content to all of life: its grounding is in this world, found in streets, trains and buses, and in shops, mountain passes and homes, just as much as it is in the temples, shrines and other more overtly religious places. The Japanese religious world is not separate from the general flow of life, but an intrinsic part thereof, upholding, strengthening and giving sustenance to it. This cosmological sense of unity is mirrored also by the ways that religious themes help to provide unity and coherence in social terms as well, and it is to this aspect of Japanese religion that I shall turn next.

3 'Born Shinto . . .': Community, Festivals, Production and Change

Religion has always had an intensely social nature in Japan, providing, and being used to provide, a sense of social cohesion, continuity, community and identity on many levels at once, from local and familial to regional and national. In national terms Shinto in particular has long had close ties to concepts of Japanese national unity and identity: the very creation of early writings such as the *Kojiki*, for instance, with their legitimations of Imperial rule and assertions of Japanese descent from the *kami*, testifies to this.

Indeed, until the post war era, one of the enduring themes of Japanese religious history has been the close relationship between the Japanese state and religious traditions. This has not been solely an issue concerning Shinto, however, for at various stages there have been close alliances between the forces of political control and Buddhism as well. The Imperial Court's adoption of Buddhism in the sixth century came about as much as anything, as was noted in the previous chapter, because it saw the Buddhas as providing a means of support for its rule, while in the Nara period (710–94) in particular Buddhism was patronised by and closely aligned with the state. As we shall see in the next chapter, the Tokugawa government which controlled Japan from the beginning of the seventeenth until the middle of the nineteenth century virtually used Buddhism as an arm of state to uphold and enforce many of its laws.

From the perspective of contemporary Japan, however, the most controversial and recent instance of fusion between religion, politics and the state has been the use made of Shinto by Japanese governments from the Meiji Restoration of 1868 onwards until the defeat and occupation of Japan at the end of the Second World War in 1945. This involved the creation of an overarching national ethic known as state Shinto, which involved government support of Shinto institutions, and the harnessing of the symbol of the Emperor (venerated during this period as a *kami* and as an ultimate symbol of unity), as a means of constructing a coherent national identity in a modern centralised nation-state, a process that led to the suppression of dissident religious organisations and to the development of the militant and fascistic nationalism that led Japan eventually to war.

Japan's defeat in 1945 and the collapse of state Shinto was followed by the adoption, in 1946, of a new Constitution, itself drawn up by the occupying American authorities, which guarantees religious freedom and affirms the principle of the separation of religion and the state. This has formally terminated the relationship between the Japanese state and any religious structure or organisation and is the situation that exists today, with civil authorities thus prohibited from supporting or patronising religious events and institutions. While sections of the nationalist right would like to breach this separation, especially by providing state support for Yasukuni shrine in Tokyo, which enshrines the souls of the Japanese killed in the war and which has long been a symbol of nationalism, they have invariably met with strong opposition from many liberal and left-wing political groups, and from many religious organisations, notably those with Christian orientations. Most Japanese regard such legal and constitutional wrangles with general indifference, though it is probably fair to say that the provision of a constitutional control that guards against the sorts of excesses that resulted from the fusion of state and religious themes in the earlier part of the century meets with general approval and consent.

In any event at the grassroots level the main functions and importance of both Shinto and Buddhism as they occur in the lives of ordinary Japanese people have for long been far more concerned with issues of social identity and belonging in terms of local community and household, and with the processes of change in individual and community life cycles, than they have with such political issues. It has already been stated, in Chapter 1, that the Japanese are 'born Shinto and die Buddhist', thus incorporating both traditions into their, and their families' lives. This cyclical process emphasises the importance of continuity and regeneration and indicates the vital role of the household as a continuing religious entity in its own right, central both to the individuals in it and to the continuity of the Shinto and Buddhist traditions.

Soon after birth babies are taken by their parents to the shrine to be placed under the care of the local *kami* and integrated into the local community: these same parents also venerate their ancestors who gave life to them, at the family temple and *butsudan*. In their turn — at least in the natural course of events — the babies will grow, produce their own offspring, take them to the shrine for a blessing and, along with their siblings, will see that the parents, at death, receive the correct mortuary rites at the Buddhist temple and become ancestors who will oversee the prosperity of the household and guard future offspring. In such ways there is a cycle of continuity relating the individual as child, parent, corpse and ancestor to the household, shrine, temple and community at large, and drawing them all together in one overall, coherent and ongoing entity.

Integrated into this continuity are the ways in which religious themes have worked on the temporal level to align human life to the passage of time. The various changes of season, transitions and changes in calendrical and personal cycles, and celebrations of joyous events, and reparations and adjustments of unhappy ones have been demarcated and ritually structuralised so that they are integrated into human life and placed in harmony with its natural rhythms. Just about all shrines and temples have their own yearly cycle of rituals, festivals and other calendrical events: these *nenjū gyōji* (regular yearly events) include activities that are celebrated throughout the country such as *hatsumōde* and *o-bon* along with special regional and local ones, providing a blend of national generalities and regional specialisations that has long been a characteristic feature of Japanese life.

The cyclical nature of the religious calendar and the cohesive social structure of religion have broadly been expressed through the two established religious traditions of Shinto and Buddhism. These have, through local shrines and temples and the rituals, festivals and individual rites of passage that take place there as well as through the altars (the *kamidana* and *butsudan*) enshrining protective deities and ancestors within the household, long formed the basic interlocking cornerstones in the religious life of Japanese people.

They were especially important in earlier ages when the local shrine and temple were major community centres at which a large proportion of the important events in personal, household and village community life took place. The yearly cycle of rites connected with crops, harvest and production chiefly centred on the shrine: the *kami* were invoked at important stages in this cycle of production that was so vital to the livelihood of rural communities, and were the focus of the celebrations and expressions of gratitude that marked the harvest. The Buddhist temple, also, often played a part in the cycle of production, symbolically protecting the growing crops through rites known as *mushi okuri* or *mushi kuyō* whose aim was to drive away pestilent insects.[1] Where agriculture was not the main source of economic support, as in areas that depended on fishing, forestry or hunting, the same patterns held true, with the religious world harmonised with the changing cycle of the seasons and invoked to uphold the means of production. Fishing villages would, for example, invoke the help of Ebisu, the major fishing deity, at optimal points in the year concerning the fishing season.[2]

Considering that the social dimensions of religion in Japan have their roots firmly established in a pre-modern agricultural society in which extended families and households were the social norm and the patterns of life depended on the cyclical nature of the agricultural calendar it follows that much has changed as Japan has become a predominantly urban, industrial society. Between 1950 and 1980 alone the percentage of the population living in cities increased from 37 per cent to 76 per cent and the numbers involved in agriculture declined from 30 per cent in 1960 to 10 per cent in 1980.[3] Rural areas have suffered from a continuing depopulation and local village shrines and temples – traditionally the heartland of Shinto's and Buddhism's support structure – have fallen into disuse along with many festivals and yearly rituals.[4] Although it is common for people to return, at festive times, to the villages from which they, or at least their ancestors, came, they have become less and less likely to help keep up such temples and shrines, switching their allegiances to religious establishments in the cities where they live. This trend is naturally increased by the passage of time, as more and more people have been born and grown up in, rather than just moved to, the cities. The move from a rural and agricultural economy to an urban, industrial one has also obviously diminished the importance of community and calendrical festivals centred on the relationship between the *kami* and the seasonal agricultural cycle of production. Urban life has resulted in the decline of the extended family (nowadays most Japanese live in nuclear units) and this has affected the traditional relationship between Buddhism, the ancestors and the living.

These changes have not, however, caused the collapse of the social parameters and functions of religion. Religion has never, in any sense, been a static and unchanging entity frozen within an unmoving system either in Japan or elsewhere: as the social structure within which it exists has changed so has it moved in tune with the shifting patterns of the times and kept pace with the fluctuations and shifts of the society around it. Contemporary social, economic and demographic changes, whilst they have deeply affected the social structure and position of Japanese religion, have not eradicated its influence so much as caused realignments in line with the changing circumstances of the age.

In this and the next chapter I shall look at the social position and roles of religion in Japan, beginning, as does life itself in Japan, with Shinto, the local shrine and the role of the *kami*, and moving on, in the next, to the end of life and the role of Buddhism. Both chapters will be concerned with the ritual and calendrical round of events in the life-cycles of households, individuals and communities, and with the implicit religiosity of these issues, as well as with the changes that have occurred, and are occurring, in the face of the rapid social and demographic changes of recent times.

Since Shinto and Buddhism, and the beginnings and ends of life, are so intricately related both in the individual's life and in the Japanese religious world in general it may seem somewhat artificial to deal with them in separate chapters. None the less I have chosen to deal with each in turn because, as well as outlining their social roles and the ways that people interact with them, this will enable me to present a case study of each in turn and to focus on some of the special elements within each tradition. In this chapter I shall, in looking at Shinto's celebrations of birth, production and fertility, also examine festivals, which are closely linked to the *kami* and are amongst the most visually demonstrative and entertaining parts of the entire Japanese religious spectrum, and the ways in which religious motifs, and especially the *kami*, are being utilised by contemporary business organisations and companies, many of which have 'turned to the gods' not so much in times of trouble but as a means of incorporating the socially bonding and production-orien-tated functions of religion, and especially of Shinto, into their own ethos. In the next chapter, the reasons why Buddhism has become so associated in Japanese minds with the image of death, and the ways it operates within this framework to provide a means of social and especially family unity even in the face of contemporary social change, will come under scrutiny.

Together these two chapters will make it clear that each tradition, despite being parts of one whole with many common features, and despite having so closely interacted with and influenced each other, also possesses its own identity, even in the images they give out, the one concerned with life and hence bright and joyous, and the other with death and thus dark and sombre. I shall also add that since the

Japanese do distinguish between them in terms of function ('born Shinto, die Buddhist'), it seems reasonable for me to do so too, and with no further ado I shall turn to Shinto and the beginnings of life.

BEGINNINGS, BIRTHS, FERTILITY AND FESTIVALS

There is a great emphasis in Shinto on beginnings, growth, fertility and celebration, and the events that occur in the lives of individuals, households and communities that bring them into a relationship with the *kami* and the shrine generally revolve around these themes. The ritual of *miyamairi*, in which the baby is taken shortly after birth to the local shrine to receive the blessing and be placed under the protection of the *kami* who is the guardian of the local community and area, integrates the child into the local community and also, because of Shinto's ethnic themes, into the wider community of Japan. Traditionally the household to which the child belonged was affiliated to the shrine: both individual and household were its *ujiko*, parishioners, under the protection of the *kami* and with various obligations to help in its upkeep and to participate in and contribute to the annual (or seasonal) festivals which helped to draw the community together and provide a sense of social bonding.[5] The shrine often served (and still does in some places) as a community centre, the setting for meetings and recreational activities as well as various religious events. In such terms the local shrine stood as a regional and territorial entity, a focus of the community of identity and belonging. It also formed, especially in earlier times when communications were not so highly developed, a link between the village and the wider Japanese world. Local shrines were often branch shrines of nationally known ones, enshrining *kami* of nationwide repute such as Hachiman, Tenjin, Inari or the *kami* venerated at the shrines of Ise: in fact two-thirds of Shinto shrines today enshrine one of these *kami*.[6] The shrine thus, besides symbolising regional community, acted as a conduit uniting the village and its people with the wider social world of the Japanese nation.[7]

In many respects Shinto has been, especially at local levels, more of an amorphous tradition of shrines related to local communities, identities and life cycles, and concerned with the maintenance of a continuing and productive relationship with the *kami* than anything else, and it is these themes that will concern us most here.

Although demographic changes have altered the religious land-scape in recent years one can still find shrines that perform a centralising role in their local communities: contemporary change does not always sweep away all vestiges of earlier times. In order to illustrate the workings of Shinto in social terms and shed light on the major events that take place at shrines throughout the country I shall here describe one such shrine. Whether one could call it 'typical' is a difficult question: with approximately 80,000 registered shrines[8] in Japan there is probably no such place. However, the events celebrated and the times when people visit it are standard enough to make it as reasonable a microcosm of the overall as is possible. It is a shrine I came to know well not through academic research but because my wife and I lived near it for two years during which time we came to regard it as 'our' local shrine (in a way that we never had with shrines in other places we had lived in Japan), announcing it as such to those who came to stay with us and making it our first port of call during the New Year's celebrations.

The area in which Katano shrine stands is situated halfway between the cities of Kyoto and Osaka, in an old rice-farming area that has, due to its proximity to both cities, become commuter territory, its fields built over as the population has increased dramatically in recent years. The whole area is a juxtaposition of new housing, old farmhouses, rice fields, apartment blocks, bars, *pachinko*[9] parlours, electrical stores and rice merchants, of frantic businessmen and office girls rushing for trains to the city in the morning, of housewives visiting the local market to buy food, and schoolgirls clustering in the music shop for posters and cassettes of the current idols — in short, the rather typical mixture of old and new, and the crowded jumble of buildings, telegraph wires, narrow streets and level-crossings that may be found virtually anywhere in contemporary urban Japan.

The shrine clearly benefited from the remaining local community of farmers and from the influx of new faces, for it managed to support a full-time priest who could call on the services of a number of assistants, especially *miko* or shrine maidens, at festivals. Although part of the shrine dated to the sixteenth century and was deemed a prefectural cultural asset it was hardly known outside the local region. Nor was it especially large, the whole area of the shrine, surrounded by an old mud and brick wall, being approx-imately 60 metres long and 50 wide.

While not attracting people from further afield the shrine was certainly an active centre for the local community. I used to go by it every day on my way to and from work and frequently saw people passing through the shrine and paying their respects to the *kami*. On Sundays there were often several babies being taken on the *miyamairi*, clad in a bright baby *kimono* with several lucky amulets attached to it: the priest would chant Shinto prayers while one of the shrine maidens performed a sacred dance and gave a symbolic purificatory blessing to the baby. The reason that Sundays are the most common day for such activities (and indeed for most shrine and temple visiting) is a pragmatic rather than a religious one: it is the only day most people in Japan have off work and hence the most convenient for such things.

Besides the general flow of passers-by, regular worshippers, babies receiving the *kami*'s blessing, people coming to pray for safety because it was their unlucky year (*yakudoshi*), and the occasional wedding that might be celebrated there, the shrine had a number of regular yearly events (*nenjū gyōji*) that punctuated the year. In November the shrine, along with most others in Japan, came alive with the *shichigosan* (7–5–3) festival, in which girls of three and seven and boys of five are taken to the shrine to be further placed under the protective blessings of the *kami*. The chief day for this is 15 November (or, more commonly, the Sunday nearest that date) but the blessings are, as at most shrines, dispensed throughout the month. As with *miyamairi* and New Year it is an occasion for dressing up and for overt display: the children are dressed formally, usually in a bright kimono but sometimes in formal Western-style dress. Their parents also dress up for the occasion, usually in Western style. More and more frequently, in line with the growing economic wealth of the country, the parents are liable, both at *shichigosan* and *miyamairi*, to be carrying expensive cameras or, a prominent feature in the last few years, video cameras to capture the event for posterity. It may not be unreasonable to suggest that events such as these provide an interesting barometer of Japan's economic prowess, with the progression from ordinary cameras to video recorders, and the growing numbers who own the latter, manifesting a continuing display of economic power.

Probably the two most active times at the shrine were the *hatsumōde* period in January and the annual shrine festival in mid October, and at these two periods the shrine and the surrounding area became alive and active. The former is a nationwide and the latter a local festival specific to the shrine, although it has wider connotations for its roots are in the harvest celebrations that are still celebrated at countless other festivals throughout Japan at this time. There are festivals all the year round in Japan, and it is possible to find one occurring somewhere on virtually every day of the year, but certain periods, such as the beginning of the year, the traditional planting season of spring, the hot months of the summer which are eminently suited to relaxed evening festivals, and the period in mid October are definitely peak times for festivals across the country.

The New Year's festival is both a national holiday, a time for celebration and relaxation, and a religious event with themes of regeneration, purification and renewal as the old year and whatever bad luck it contained are swept aside in a tide of noisy enjoyment. It is traditional to clean one's house thoroughly and to pay off all debts before the end of the year (indeed I have seen, in the national newspapers, reminders during the last days of the old year that this is the time to clean one's house), thus clearing away physically and metaphorically the residue of the past year so as to allow one to start again new. Throughout January there are numerous 'first' festivals, such as the *hatsu Ebisu* ('first Ebisu') widely celebrated especially in the Kyoto–Osaka region from 9–11 January, which is the first festive day of the year of the popular deity Ebisu. All such festivals reiterate the theme of transition from old to new, of the sweeping away of the hindrances of the past and of fresh beginnings, expressing optimistic hopes for good fortune.

The New Year's festival is the largest of all these, and at this time it is customary to visit shrines (and some of the better-known temples as well) to pay one's respects to the *kami*, to ask for good luck and help in the coming year and to make resolutions fortified by the general mood of optimistic renewal. This is accompanied by a great changeover in religious amulets and talismans as new ones representing the power and benevolence of the *kami* and Buddhas are acquired and old ones are dispensed with. The most commonly procured of these at New Year is the *hamaya* (literally 'evil-destroying arrow'), a symbolic arrow that is placed in the home as a protective talisman to drive away or absorb bad luck. Other lucky charms, talismans and amulets (whose meanings will be discussed at greater length in Chapter 7) are also on sale at the shrines and temples, the income this produces often making an important contribution to the upkeep of the institutions. Often the talismans that are purchased are placed in the household *kamidana*, thereby creating a further link between shrine and household, with the *kamidana* itself operating as a localised shrine in its own right sacralising the house itself.

At the same time the old amulets and talismans from the previous year are jettisoned, and most shrines and temples at this time designate a special place where these can be left. Some time later, usually in mid-January, these will be formally burnt in a purificatory rite, generally to the accompaniment of priests chanting prayers whose powers, along with the exorcistic nature of the fire, transform the impurities and eradicate the bad luck that have been absorbed by the amulets and talismans. The pollutions and hindrances of the past are thus dispensed with and the way is opened up, symbolised by the acquisition of new charms, for regeneration. Naturally, too, in the process of cyclical transition, those same, new talismans, will be brought back the next year to be burnt, in a continuing round of change and renewal.

On the evening of 31 December it is customary for families to eat a special seasonal feast together: it has also become something of a custom to watch the television, where a number of musical spectaculars, particularly the *Kōhaku*, a song contest between teams of leading female and male stars that is broadcast by NHK, have become integrated parts of the New Year's Eve ritual. The *Kōhaku* programme ends a little before midnight, giving people enough time to get to their local shrine before the bells chime in the coming year. In both years that I went to Katano shrine a long line of people, most of them in family groups, stood waiting just before midnight in front of a straw ring of purification erected before the shrine. The act of passing through this ring prior to worshipping symbolically removes past pollutions and allows them to greet the *kami* anew. The shrine itself and the houses around it were brightly lit with lanterns, and the crowd numbering around 500 or so bubbled with conversation and anticipation as the priest turned on the radio. This broadcast the sound of the bells of Chionin, a famous Buddhist temple in Kyoto, whose great bell tolls, as do the bells of innumerable Buddhist temples throughout the country, 108 times just before midnight. The number 108 is symbolic for the numerous ills, unhappinesses and evil passions inherent, according to Buddhism, in the world, and the tolling symbolically eradicates them one by one. As the year ends, then, the Buddhist temple plays its part in purifying the past and realigning the world, complementing the shrine through which the coming year is greeted.

As the tolling ended and the time signal chimed midnight people began to flow through the arch, clapping their hands in prayer,

tossing coins into the offertory box and praying. After this they
went across to the shrine office where all manner of religious
talismans were on sale, including the special *hamaya* of the shrine
and wooden votive tablets (*ema*) on which petitions to the *kami* may
be written. In the Sino-Japanese system there is a twelve-yearly
cycle somewhat akin to the zodiacal system, with each year represented by a different animal, and at this shrine as at many others, the
ema depicted the year-animal of the coming year. As 1988 was the
year of the dragon, the *ema* bore dragon insignia and, in 1989,
snakes.

Soon the entire shrine area was crowded, and everyone, or at
least every group, appeared to have a *hamaya* and several other
talismans besides. Money was spent freely, as is common at festive
times when the economic constraints of everyday life are commonly
laid aside in favour of the freedoms of the moment. Much of this
was at the instigation of children who, in their excitement at staying
up so late, were particularly insistent that their parents buy them
charms and divination slips. The latter are usually read aloud, with
one's friends and family, invariably in a light-hearted manner, and
then tied up on the trees or fences in the shrine precincts. The
action of tying up the paper strips is done, depending on one's
informant, so as to allow the bad luck predicted in the oracle to be
blown away by the wind, to share out good luck predicted and thus
balance out other people's bad luck or, more prosaically, simply
because this is what everyone else does! Whatever explanation may
be given, the trees and fences at the shrine, as at any shrine in Japan
at New Year, were rapidly festooned with strips of white paper.

Inside the main hall of the shrine the priest chanted sacred Shinto
prayers to the accompaniment of shrine music played by assistants
while shrine maidens wearing the traditional apparel of a red
hakama, or split skirt, and white blouse performed *kagura*, sacred
dances designed to please the *kami* and facilitate the transfer of the
kami's benevolence to the people. Other shrine maidens helped run
the office, sell talismans and impart purificatory blessings. Not all of
these were trained officiants, for the sheer tide of visitors means that
virtually every religious institution needs to take on part-time help
in order to cope at this time, and one year I found myself in the
crowd being blessed by one of my students performing her temporary job as a shrine maiden!

In the shrine various donations were arrayed from the community
and local businesses thanking the *kami* for past support and seeking

its continuation. Where feasible it seemed that the neighbourhood shops sent offerings connected with their trade, the rice merchants for instance sending sacks of rice, but when this was not possible the most common offerings were food and sake (rice wine). The gifts were not just from the older and more traditional establishments but also from the newer ones: one of the local beauty salons which catered to the fashionable young of the district, for example, sent two bottles of sake. Sake is a popular offering that can be swiftly recycled after it has been placed on the altar and thus sacralised: thereafter partaking of it becomes a pleasant act of communion with the *kami* that helps one enter further into the spirit of the festival. A stall was set up in the precincts where small cups of shrine sake could be quaffed free: it should be added that no one appeared to indulge in much more than one symbolic cup.

After the first night the shrine became gradually quieter and quieter, returning to normality on 4 January: the *hatsumōde* period really lasts until 3 January at all but the most major shrines. At Katano most people came at or soon after midnight: by 1 a.m. they were moving off elsewhere, either back home or to catch trains to Kyoto or Osaka to visit the larger and more famous shrines and temples there. The trains, which run all night at this period, were packed with revellers either going home clutching *hamaya* or on their way to get them. It was interesting that most of the people in the area made their visit to Katano before going on to the more nationally known centres nearby, a sign perhaps of the continued importance of the shrine to its surrounding community, indicating that local loyalties may still take precedence over wider ones.

The annual festival, spread over two days in mid-October, was similar in many respects, and also very much resembled most other festivals that take place throughout the year in Japan: at the same time, though, it was clearly a local, community affair specific to that area, its people and shrine. The shrine grounds became an evening market with stalls selling snacks, drinks and toys or offering the chance to win small prizes at various games while, amidst the general entertainment, people found time to ring the shrine bell and pray to the *kami*. A stall manned by helpers dispensed sake liberally and with a little more abandon than at New Year, and on one evening a community film show of children's cartoons took place. At one point during the festival a *mikoshi* or portable shrine into which the *kami* is temporarily transferred was carried around the area by local men. This activity, in which the *kami* passes by the houses of those in the district that uphold the shrine and venerate the *kami*, is a common feature of such festivals and emphasises the relationship between the *kami* and the local community and the *kami*'s continuing protection of the community.[10] To carry or draw the *mikoshi* along requires that the men pull together and in harmony, and is thus also a symbolic reminder to all in the community of the necessity to co-operate and work together for the communal good.

The festival was not solely, however, a ludic affair, for it also involved a solemn rite with offerings to and actions performed on behalf of the *kami*. The Japanese word for festival, *matsuri*, in essence contains within it implications of prayer, worship and offering as well as the more overt sense of communal festivities, and in such terms a *matsuri* contains a solemn centre of religious ritual held in order to commune with the *kami*.[11] On the second morning of this festival the mood, for the only time, became noticeably reserved and quiet as a ritual known as *yutate* (literally, 'immersion in hot water') took place.

In this rite an area of the shrine precincts was cordoned off to create a specially sacred space within which a fire was kindled under two cauldrons of water. When the water was hot the fires were extinguished and a group of people comprising four priests, two *miko* (shrine maidens) and a group of dark-suited men (patrons of the shrine and representatives of the community) were ritually purified by the head priest who waved over their heads a branch of *sakaki*, a tree that is sacred in Shinto as a symbol of life, which had strips of white paper (which symbolise the presence of a *kami*) tied to it. A short prayer to the *kami* was followed by a sacred dance by the *miko* to invoke the presence of and entertain the deity, after which one of the *miko*, dressed wholly in white, the symbolic colour of purity, performed the central rite itself.

She tossed salt, a traditional purifying agent, on to the ground around the cauldrons and then added to them rice and sake, two foodstuffs basic to pre-modern Japanese society and still highly important today, one by one in a series of formal, slow and rhythmic movements. The *miko* then took a wooden scoop and bowl and symbolically scooped, from above her head, nectar from the land of the *kami*, into the bowl, and then 'poured' this into the cauldrons. After this she filled the bowl from the cauldrons and passed it to one of the priests who took it into the inner shrine and offered it at the altar to the *kami*. When the water is thus offered it becomes sacred, endowed with the presence of the *kami* whose essence is considered to pass into it.

At this point the *miko* took two bunches of bamboo leaves and with them began, after a short invocation, to churn the sacred water containing the protective powers of the *kami*, spraying copiously for several minutes so that droplets of hot water showered all around her and on the heads of those watching the rite. As this is done people and *kami* are symbolically united and become one through the medium of the water, a communion that is, at many other shrines that perform this rite, further intensified as the water left in the cauldron is later handed out to the onlookers to drink.[12] The rite ended with the *miko* taking a *suzu*, a cluster of bells which are sacred ritual implements of purification, and waving them over the heads of all present, including a large group of children from a number of local kindergartens who had been shepherded into the shrine by their teachers. The rite ended with a short prayer to the *kami*, after which the kindergarten children were led by the priests into the shrine hall for a further blessing.

Rituals and festivals such as these provide a visual and dramatic demonstration of the implicit religious meanings of Shinto. Sonoda Minoru has noted that the essential motif of festivals is the 'renewal of life-power among the *kami* and human beings in a given life-space'.[13] This rite which, with slight variations, may be seen at many Shinto shrines, expresses the basic Shinto values of purification and regeneration along with expressions of gratitude and veneration to and entertainment of the *kami*, all leading to a sense of communion in which the powers of the *kami* are harnessed for the continued benefit and life of the human world and, in this case, the local community.[14] It thus posits the creation and maintenance of harmony, between *kami* and community and in this world, as a basic ideal leading to the continued and fertile development of human life. Purification (as was seen in Chapter 2 in the discussion of Izanagi's flight) is central, an intrinsic aspect of all Shinto (and most other Japanese religious) ritual, transforming and eradicating the impure, removing spiritual obstructions and opening the way to regeneration. The process of ritual purification and regeneration makes ideal statements about what belongs and is desired, and what is not, separating the one from the other and creating the ideal state through which the living may most efficaciously pursue the goals of life free of spiritual hindrances.

Pleasing the *kami* and expressing gratitude for its continued support enable the priest and community to enter into a symbolic communion with the *kami* which reaffirms social cohesion and unity, expressing the desire that this may continue for the benefit of the living community. The ultimate goal, then, is based not so much in the veneration of the *kami* as in the positive maintainance of a harmonious relationship that will benefit the community and provide further help in this world, *genze riyaku*, for future growth and prosperity.

The relationship between the shrine and the community shown in this festival was not limited just to specific shrine events or even to the site of the shrine itself. The priest was often called out to perform various rites in the community, particularly ground-breaking rituals (*jichinsai*) when new houses were to be built, a frequent occurrence in the area. On at least one occasion also he officiated at a ceremony commemorating the completion of a new library and lecture room complex at the university where I worked, which was about a kilometre from the shrine. In this rite an altar for the protective *kami* of the site was temporarily erected in the new building, before which the university president, other university officials and representatives of the staff and students made offerings and prayed for the successful growth of the university. After this rite, the priest, president, university staff and local residents' association representatives gathered together for a communal meal and celebration.

The local shrine in such ways may continue to play a role in the community, providing a good example of the meanings of Shinto and its calendrical activities as a force of social cohesion.[15] This picture is not, however, found uniformly in contemporary Japan. This is not just because the move to the cities has frequently denuded rural shrines of their traditional means of support and left many of them unable to support a priest. Especially in areas which have been developed as commuter belts for the major cities there frequently is not the same form of community infrastructure, including the community shrine, as existed in the villages, and many who have moved to the cities have been faced with problems of social disorientation and loss of identity because of this. The more people commute from their areas of residence to the workplace, and the less their economic means of existence is connected to the area immediately around them and their local community, the more their focus of loyalty and belonging moves from their community of residence to that of their work or, in the case of the young, of school or college. This also naturally has repercussions on the traditional shrine–community network and relationship, and it is probably safe to say that few Japanese who have moved to the cities have developed strong ties to local community shrines. The vacuum thus created has been one influential factor in the growing importance of the new religions which, with their active networks of support groups and community activities, have been very successful in attracting support in urban areas. This question will be given more attention in Chapter 8 when I examine the new religions themselves, but at present I wish to draw attention to changes more directly concerning the social aspects of Shinto and the festivals that are perhaps its most visible expression.

NEW EVENTS, OLD MODELS: CHANGING PATTERNS AND ENDURING THEMES

The festivals and life-cycle events celebrated at shrines serve as 'punctuation marks'[16] in the calendar, helping to structuralise and define changes in season and situation while providing times of celebration, entertainment and enjoyment, when the troubles of the everyday are set aside. In serving to renew and invigorate ordinary life they express a lasting quality and importance that is not eradicated by contemporary change, even when the agricultural rhythms on which they were founded no longer govern the tempo of modern society and even though the traditional community nature of Shinto appears to be in decline. Instead, festivals and other such occasions for letting off steam and stepping outside the normal patterns of life have become perhaps ever more prominent, especially as counterweights to the increasing tensions and pressures of contemporary city life.

Because they appear to thus represent aspects of a rural, traditional society that have been lost in the processes of modernisation their popularity is frequently tinged with elements of nostalgia. Kurehayashi Shōji has written that one major element in the contemporary popularity of festivals is that they represent Japanese cultural and spiritual roots that stand as a counterweight to the turbulent changes of modern society. He describes festivals as representing the Japanese 'spiritual homeland' (*kokoro no furusato*),[17] a phrase pregnant with emotional connotations that is widely used in contemporary Japan to represent and denote a sense of spiritual belonging and cultural heritage special to the Japanese experience. The word *furusato* means 'one's native village/place of origin' and is generally used to denote the place or village from which one (or one's family) originally hails, while *kokoro* (mind, heart, spirit), when linked to it, transposes it to a spiritual rather than purely physical level.[18]

The use of emotional imagery connected to a sense of Japanese cultural belonging and identity is itself prevalent in much contemporary Japanese religious literature and will be encountered again. The force of nostalgia has certainly come to be associated with festivals in contemporary Japan and has become a factor in their enduring and indeed growing incidence and popularity. This has been further fortified by economic growth which has increased the celebration of many religious occasions, with events such as *hatsumōde, shichigosan, miyamairi* and festivals being celebrated in probably greater numbers and more lavishly than at any previous time in history. The increase of wealth brought about by contemporary Japanese economic growth has been a causal factor in the increased incidence and opulence of all such festivals and events both by providing greater scope for their planning and enactment and by stimulating the wish for more opulent, and more frequent, celebrations.

This does not mean that the traditional cycles and patterns of festivals and shrine visiting have remained constant, however. When I described the *hatsumōde* festivities at Katano shrine I noted that most people went on to other, more famous shrines and temples in the nearby cities. In many areas the pattern is to go just to famous centres: the growth in *hatsumōde* participants has not been mirrored by an increase in worshippers at local shrines. It is the big, well-known shrines such as Meiji shrine in Tokyo, Sumiyoshi in Osaka, Atsuta in Nagoya and Fushimi Inari in Kyoto, to name but a few, that benefit, attracting increasingly large crowds running into several millions every year. Visiting Fushimi Inari on 1 January 1988 we shuffled along in a densely packed crowd, taking 45 minutes to reach the shrine from the nearby station, a walk that on normal days took only three or four minutes.

Better transport facilities have contributed to this pattern, making the 'name' shrines more and more accessible to people from outlying areas while the transport companies and railway lines that cater to them have stimulated this trend further through their own publicity campaigns. Before New Year, for example, all private railway lines and the nationwide Japanese Railways put up posters of the well-known shrines and temples that *their* lines go to, encouraging their passengers to visit them at New Year. This tendency is followed also by the media: many newspapers publish lists of important shrines and the numbers expected at them at New Year, and this further helps to create a sense of excitement around the larger centres and to draw people away from smaller, local shrines and to them.[19]

This growing focus on events and places has come about as social change has divorced people from the traditional settings of their local shrines, communities and loyalties. This has perhaps encouraged a deeper national awareness, with the move towards prominent centres at *hatsumōde* implying participation in a quite definitively *national* rather than local event. It also reflects the continuing growth of choice that was not present in earlier eras when community pressures, economic circumstances and the lack of transport facilities virtually forced people to go to the local shrine. These constraints are no longer relevant: as a result of the erosion of local and regional ties that committed each person and family to a relationship with a shrine, temple and community, a large section of the Japanese populace has become, in the words of Fujii Masao, a 'religiously floating population'.[20]

These shifting patterns are seen clearly within the contemporary world of urban festivals. The older city communities and districts have long had their own festivals, many of which have been strongly promoted in recent years in order to develop local community feelings anew, and many newly developed areas and housing estates have instituted their own festivals in order to create a sense of belonging and co-operation where previously there was none.[21] More commonly still, many city, town and regional authorities have inaugurated festivals with little or no religious content in order to stimulate the local economy, trade and tourism, often with the co-operation and assistance of local chambers of commerce and tourist boards.[22] Traditionally a festival involved both social mobilisation (drawing the *ujiko* and neighbourhood associations together in a spirit of co-operation) and religious action: modern festivals in emphasising economic motivations have focused on the former while playing down the latter.[23]

As the 1946 Constitution insists on complete separation of politics and religion, such events, when funded by local authorities, of necessity have to eschew overtly religious activities of the type normally implied by the concept of *matsuri*. Some get around this by having the civil festival coincide with, and thus incorporate, the festival of an important shrine in the town, as was the case with the city festival of Naze in the Amami islands in southern Japan, but even in this festival the religious content has become increasingly peripheral to the issue of promoting commerce and tourism.[24] Such 'kamiless' festivals have become quite numerous in contemporary Japan and appear, as in the case of the Kōbe Festival (Kōbe matsuri), to assert an open secularism. This festival, sponsored by the civil authorities, is intended to create a sense of civic pride and community feeling in the city and consists of pageantry, parades and spectacular street events which have little or no religious content.[25]

As festivals marginalise or even omit religious symbols and themes it could be argued that they become less overtly relevant to discussions of the contemporary religious situation, yet it is worth noting that many of the traditional themes of the *matsuri* continue to be important even in this apparently more secularised form. Modern urban *matsuri* provide, as did traditional shrine *matsuri*, the means of stepping temporarily outside the everyday routines of life to regenerate energies as well as offering the legitimation to do so. These are themes that are particularly underlined by the association of modern festivals with the imagery of tradition and nostalgia which affirms their identification, in a modern setting, with the festivals of the past. Their use in building community consciousness is a direct continuation of the traditional role of the *matsuri* while the economic motivations behind contemporary festivals show close parallels to the ways in which the shrine and *kami* have been harnessed to generate the cycles of production and renewal. One might even suggest that civil authorities and tourist boards seeking to strengthen or create a local economic infrastructure or counteract a lack of community feeling have, in their assimilation of the framework of the *matsuri*, in their own way 'turned to the gods', even if, simultaneously, they have had to keep them out of the picture.

RELIGION AND BUSINESS: NEW COMMUNITIES AND RENEWED CONTINUITIES

It is not only civil authorities that have made use of traditional religious forms, albeit in a contemporary mode, to promote unity and economic growth: the modern world of business and commerce has long done likewise. Japanese companies and business concerns are well known for their efforts at creating harmony and cohesion, with their social welfare schemes, company housing and leisure facilities as well as the various activities, from company songs to organised outings, that provide for their employees and instil in them a feeling of loyalty and belonging.[26] These are important factors in the trend mentioned earlier of people shifting their loyalties from their local community to their place of work. Various rituals that replicate or mirror the socially cohesive and calendrically ordering patterns of shrines occur within the company framework, including induction ceremonies in which new employees are initiated into the firm by making oaths of loyalty and allegiance, and various celebratory parties at the end of the year (*bōnenkai*) to get rid of the year's frustrations, and at its beginning (*shinnenkai*), to express hopes for the future.

Many companies have gone further still by actively adopting religious institutions and forms to reinforce the sense of devoted discipline they seek from their employees. It has long been common for companies to send groups of employees, especially new ones, to Zen Buddhist temples to take part in periods of monastic training that are aimed at strengthening their resolve and formulating a sense of disciplined obedience to rules of etiquette and action. When I first stayed at Eiheiji, one of the Sōtō Zen sect's two main temples and famed throughout Japan as an austere meditation centre, I met a group of twelve new employees of a company in the city of Fukui. They had been sent to the temple for a five-day training period in which they participated in the temple life, getting up at 4 a.m. to meditate: the aim, as one of them informed me, was to give them a sense of discipline that would make them into better workers. It also made them rather disgruntled: none of them appeared to be enjoying the experience![27]

Many companies also sponsor communal memorial rites at Buddhist temples for their employees who die: the Keihan railway company sponsors such a rite every three years at the Kōrien temple which supplies the safety amulets for its trains and buses, while the famous graveyard at the Shingon Buddhist centre at Mount Kōya contains many communal company graves and memorials commemorating their dead employees. Such rites and memorials, which supplement rather than replace ordinary household mortuary rituals, are further affirmations of the caring nature of the company as a community in its own right, looking after its members not just in life but beyond.

It is, however, the *kami* and Shinto structures that are most widely co-opted for the benefit of business concerns because of their traditional involvement with fertility, production and the support of the community. This in turn perhaps reflects a tacit recognition in the Japanese commercial world of traditional views of causation: even the creation of wealth may need co-operation on the spiritual plane from the *kami*, while the uncertainties and insecurities involved in the business world may make their psychological reassurances and support especially attractive. Changing economic patterns have not eradicated the influence and role of the *kami* here, but have seen it continue anew, expressed in modern guises, as with Inari, the rice god who has, as was noted earlier, also become a god of business. It is common to see at Inari shrines such as Fushimi Inari in Kyoto, the greatest of all Inari shrines in Japan, the *meishi*, or business cards, of company directors and businessmen affixed to the doors and railings of the shrine to attract Inari's attention and help.

The contemporary influence of Inari was commented upon recently in an interesting article in the Mainichi newspaper of 12 December 1987 which examined Inari's following amongst contemporary business companies. It appears that this following is especially high among firms dealing in shares, equities and securities. In Kitahama, a district of Osaka where many stock and share dealing companies and securities firms are located, an association of 67 such firms organises regular seasonal visits to various religious centres in the Kyoto—Osaka region, including an annual visit by approximately 700 employees and their families to Fushimi Inari on 25 October every year to pray for prosperity and for Inari's continued support for their companies. Some companies have their own Inari shrines on their premises and hold regular rites before them. Some even have a priest from Fushimi Inari visit them every month to hold an Inari *matsuri* at the company shrine: a spokesman at Fushimi Inari reported that thirteen companies in the Kyoto—Osaka region, including nine securities firms, had similar monthly Inari festivals to which a priest from the shrine was summoned.[28]

The sponsorship of festivals and the patronage of special shrines has, according to Uno Masato, become a growing phenomenon in the Japanese business world.[29] Some companies have even adopted or built their own shrines, as is the case of the Toyota car company, whose shrine is located close by the company's head office in the town of Toyota near Nagoya.[30] Shiseidō, a leading cosmetics firm, has a shrine on the roof of its headquarters in Tokyo's Ginza district, enshrining two *kami*, including *Seikō Inari* (literally 'success Inari'), a branch deity of the Toyokawa Inari shrine, before which various company related rites are performed: it is also open to the public during the Ginza festival every October.[31]

The use of shrines and *kami* has been carried abroad as well: Japanese companies building factories and offices outside Japan often have a shrine placed on the premises and a *kami* installed there to help in the process of affirming Japanese identity while symbolically upholding and stimulating unity and production.[32] At least one Japanese company, Kibun, has extended this use of religious symbols to support the promotion of the needs of business enterprise further by presenting its newly opened factory in Scotland with a *mikoshi* as a symbol of the importance of co-operation, harmony and pulling together. The portable shrine at the factory is intended as a reminder to its employees there of these ideals, so necessary in Japan's traditional farming communities and intrinsic also to the world of its business success.[33]

Even if Shinto has suffered structural weaknesses as a result of contemporary change, and even though many of the modern manifestations of its traditional themes, such as urban festivals, have been less reliant on overt religious symbolisms, it is clear that many of its underlying functions and outlooks continue to be relevant today, adapted to the new conditions of the age and manifested in new guises relevant to contemporary circumstances. The ways in which the *kami* have been embraced by contemporary business is evidence that the relationship between the Japanese and the *kami* is a continuing and continually changing one, but that it is still constantly centred around the generation and celebration of life and production in ways that are beneficial to the living and that provide harmonious social bonding. This concern with beginnings, growth, identity and communities of belonging has always been a prime focus of Shinto and the *kami*, and remains at the heart of its social role in Japan. This is, however, but part of the overall social perspective of religion in Japan, and in order to view the whole it is next necessary to examine what might be described as the other half of the picture, in which the Japanese 'die Buddhist', and it is this issue and its implications in the contemporary age that will be discussed in the next chapter.

4 ' . . . Die Buddhist': Zen, Death and the Ancestors

On the surface at least it might appear rather ironic that the religion that started when the Buddha left his family in order to seek awakening and enlightenment in his own lifetime, a religion that has evolved an immense depth of scriptural teaching, philosophical erudition and spiritual practice, should be seen by the vast majority of Japanese as something associated with the rites of death, with social bonding and the preservation of the household. As was noted in Chapter 1, most Japanese, even if they have no other or prior contact with, knowledge of or belief in Buddhism, 'die Buddhist'. Buddhism is both the agency for dealing with death and the religion of the household, supporting the community of lineage that provides its individual members with a sense of identity and continuity in generational and historical terms, its social roles interlocking with the support and structure given to the community of belonging in geographical and regional terms by the Shinto shrine and its cycle of rites and festivals.

Buddhism's concerns, however, are not just with social belonging and the rituals of death: the pursuit of individual awareness and liberation have never ceased to be part of its dynamic in Japan, and these have in fact contributed to and stimulated, rather than been antithetical to, its social roles. The dual dynamic of Buddhism, aimed simultaneously at enlightenment and the alleviation of the everyday problems of people in this world, has already been discussed in Chapter 2 and need not be reiterated here except to remark that this has been a basic factor in Buddhism's assimilation of its social role in Japan. This chapter will seek to give a comprehensive picture of the position of Buddhism in Japan by looking at it both as a path of enlightenment and as a social religion. Since both these aspects are closely related and necessary elements in its overall make-up they will be taken together. I shall first discuss Buddhism as a way of personal liberation, after which I shall go on to discuss the ways in which Buddhism became the religion of the household and of death. This in turn will lead to a description of the rites, implements, procedures and meanings involved in the process of 'dying Buddhist' and, at the end of the chapter, an examination of the effects of contemporary social change on all of this.

SAKE, ANCESTORS AND MEDITATION: A VISIT TO A ZEN TEMPLE

Some years ago I spent a few days at a Sōtō Zen Buddhist temple in Nagano prefecture in the mountains of central Japan. It was one of the sect's recognised training centres where those who had taken a Buddhist monastic ordination could spend time studying Buddhist thought, rituals and meditation, either as training for further meditative practice or — as is most common — as a step on the path of qualifying as a fully trained Buddhist priest able to take over and run a Buddhist temple and perform all the rituals associated with it, including the death rituals and memorial services for the ancestors. I had been staying at various Sōtō Zen temples during that year in the course of my research and had been invited to this one by the head-priest, a noted scholar and teacher, so that I could, at first-hand, study the workings of the temple, talk to the trainees and talk over some questions concerning my research.

Arriving late on a cold December afternoon I almost immediately found myself in a car with the head-priest and three young trainees. As it was the death anniversary of a member of one of the households that had long been affiliated to the temple, the priests were going to perform a memorial service at the family *butsudan* and I was being taken along to see what went on. When we arrived at the house, the head-priest explained to the family who I was and that I was going to participate in the service: by then I had already had various items of Buddhist regalia draped about my person and had had a book of Buddhist chants thrust in my hand. The family did not seem at all taken aback, accepting my presence in the open way to which I have become accustomed in the Japanese religious world.

We all knelt before the *butsudan* and chanted for perhaps an hour. The older members of the family sat with us the whole time, mostly keeping up with the chants, while the younger members, including a couple of children, seemed to drift in and out, putting in an appearance rather than participating. It was a typical Japanese memorial service in that those most overtly involved were the older generation (presumably those who best remembered the deceased), while those ostensibly farthest removed from the processes of death, the young, were the least interested. After the service a splendid meal was laid out for us, along with plenty of sake (Buddhist priests in Japan are not forbidden to drink alcohol), and we all ate and drank while sharing in a general conversation about all manner of things, from local gossip to aspects of Buddhism. It was late before we returned to the temple and went to sleep.

Traditionally, Zen temple life starts very early with one or more periods of meditation, and we were all in the meditation hall the next day at 4 a.m., doing *zazen*, seated Zen meditation, in which the legs are crossed in the lotus* position, the back is kept straight, the hands are rested one on the other just below the navel with the thumbs lightly touching, the eyes half open, the mouth firmly closed, and the breath inhaled and exhaled slowly and deeply through the nose. The meditation hall was unheated, lit only by candles, and we sat still and silent in the freezing cold of the early morning, each exhalation of breath turning into a stream of mist, for 90 minutes — two periods of seated meditation of 40 minutes and a short walking period in between, in which we walked slowly in single file, allowing our legs some respite but maintaining our deep breathing and meditative state.

From the meditation hall we proceeded to the main hall of the temple where, kneeling on the floor, we chanted prayers and Buddhist texts for half an hour, followed by a round of the temple complex, chanting at various Buddhist images. After this we gathered buckets and cloths and washed the cold wooden floors rigorously. One monk prepared breakfast, a sparse meal of rice gruel, pickles and green tea that we finally ate, after a long prayer, in silence at around 7.30 a.m. A short rest period after breakfast was followed by a long talk by the head-priest on points of Buddhist thought and action, after which there was a longer period of work in which we swept the temple grounds, cleaned parts of the graveyard, chopped some logs for fuel and carried out other physical tasks. The rest of the day continued along similar lines, with more meditation and chanting, some periods of relaxation and a question and answer session with the head-priest about Buddhism. Later on, two of the

---

* In this posture the legs are crossed, with the right foot placed on the inside of the left thigh and the left foot on the right thigh. The half lotus, in which only one of the legs is placed on the opposite thigh, and the other tucked under it, is also a common meditation posture.

young trainee priests went out to chant prayers at the altar of another of the temple's affiliated households while the rest of us went back to the meditation hall for another 90-minute session in the evening.

The life of the temple thus encompassed austere meditation and rites for the dead, striving for self-awareness and pastoral care for others. Seeking for enlightenment in life, which is the focus of the whole of Zen temple life and practice, operates in tandem with the aim of caring for others, including the spirits of the dead, and transferring the spiritually enlightening powers of Buddhism to others, including the ancestors, to enable them to attain peace and enlightenment after death. As a training centre for Zen priests the daily routine at this particular temple contained far more in the way of meditation and spiritual training than would most temples, the vast majority of which are run by one priest and his family (maarriage has been the norm for Japanese Buddhist priests since the Meiji Restoration) and deal almost entirely with the issue of death and the ancestors, but it is a good example of the ways in which Zen in Japan operates within the two-fold dynamic mentioned above.

This is not something limited to Zen, which is by no means the only form of Buddhism to have taken root and flourished in Japan. Others include Tendai Buddhism, with its combination of scholastic and textual learning with esoteric rituals and various spiritual and ascetic practices, Shingon Buddhism, focused specifically on esoteric practices, the various branches of Pure Land Buddhism, with their focus on devotion, faith and salvation, and the militantly nationalist and salvationist Nichiren Buddhism with its devotion to the major Buddhist text the Lotus Sūtra.[1] All encompass similar themes in that they have their own spiritual disciplines that combine with various ritual practices concerning death and the ancestors: Zen is no different from any of the others in this. I shall focus on Zen here because it is almost certainly the best known of all these, especially in the West, due to the numerous books that have been produced about it and due to the growing numbers of Zen meditation centres that have developed in North America and Europe. It is well known, too, not only for its profound focus on meditation and spiritual discipline but also for its contributions to the development of Japanese art and culture, including its close relationship with the tea ceremony, calligraphy and various martial arts.[2] None the less despite these aspects it is, like all other forms of Japanese Buddhism, primarily encountered by the Japanese as a religion of death, and this, along with the fact that it is also the form of Buddhism with which I have had most personal contact and experience,[3] makes it a suitable topic for discussion here.

The word Zen itself means meditation, and is the Japanese pronounciation of the Chinese word *Ch'an*, itself derived from the Sanskrit *dhyana*, meditation. Zen is the generic name of a branch of Buddhism that, developing in China, sought to re-emphasise meditation at a time when many felt Buddhism was becoming too ritualistic and scholastic, and moving too far away from its original focus on meditation and enlightenment. At the core of the Zen view of the world is the notion that all beings possess the Buddha nature, the ability to become enlightened: this state of enlightenment or Buddhahood is intrinsic to existence rather than something special and separate from the normal and natural state of life. The prime way to realise this innate enlightenment is to do as Shakyamuni the historical Buddha had done, to sit in meditation (and the posture and form of Zen meditation is viewed in Zen as a re-enactment of the meditation and enlightenment of the Buddha), letting go of all dualities between body and mind. Meditation is not simply the gateway to enlightenment but, as is especially strongly stated in the Sōtō tradition, the grounding and manifestation of enlightenment itself.

Zen was transmitted to Japan from the thirteenth century onwards by Eisai, a Japanese monk who went to China, studied and brought back the teachings of Rinzai (in Chinese: *Lin chi*) Zen Buddhism, and Dōgen, who brought back the teachings of Sōtō (in Chinese: *Tsao-tung*) Zen. Both Sōtō and Rinzai emphasise the centrality of seated meditation, although with slightly different nuances. Rinzai focuses on the use of *kōan*, seemingly illogical problems, which the meditator grapples with mentally and uses as a tool to break down the logical barriers that, in Zen terms, prevent the intuitive realisation of enlightenment that is contained within all beings, while Sōtō concentrates on silent concentrated meditation. Both emphasise rigorous and austere monastic discipline, the meditator living in a community of like-minded seekers who meditate, study and work together under the guidance of a teacher whose own religious awareness learnt through Zen practice enables him (like Buddhism in general and all branches of it in Japan, Zen remains very much a male-dominated affair) to act as guide and adviser to those at the temple.

Because enlightenment is an innate condition it may be found not just in meditation but in any aspect of life: thus Zen places great emphasis on everyday activities as well. Dōgen, for example, wrote extensively about the correct decorum in temple life and the importance of carrying out every activity within the temple, from bowing to cooking, from washing one's face to offering incense to images of the Buddha, with a concentrated and aware mind, the mind of meditation itself.[4] Zen temple life revolves around basic physical work as much as it does around meditation, and those staying at such places will find themselves expected to scrub the floors (even if they appear to be spotless already!) just as much as they will need to be present in the meditation hall. Cleaning and scrubbing floors is a particularly prominent feature of Japanese Zen temple life, quite probably as a reflection of the importance placed on purification in Japanese culture in general. At some of the temples at which I have stayed work periods have involved, besides cleaning floors and stairs, sweeping up the falling leaves, chopping wood and, in one case, carrying buckets of water several hundred feet uphill from the river which was the only water source for that particular temple.

In each of these activities, as with meditation itself, with its focus on the form of sitting, there is an intensely physical emphasis: enlightenment, awareness, liberation and spiritual power are closely associated with, and approached through, the physical realm and the body, a theme commonly found within the Japanese religious universe that will be dealt with at length in the next chapter. This emphasis on physical discipline has been a constant theme in Zen temple life to the present and, even if modern amenities have made certain aspects of temple life simpler and more comfortable than in earlier ages, it still remains central to Zen practice. This is particularly so at the intense meditation retreats known as *sesshin* (literally 'focusing the mind') which take place periodically at major Zen temples and meditation centres. At some of these places *sesshin* occur once a year, usually in December, at others perhaps more frequently: the most common time span is eight days, during which time the temple is largely closed to the outside world and those living there do little but meditate for this period.

Lay people may take part also: I have done two such *sesshin* in Japan, one in the heart of Tokyo, the other in a mountain temple in Yamanashi prefecture, at both of which lay people as well as ordained clerics participated. In both a similar routine was maintained: about thirteen hours of meditation a day, divided into several sittings interspersed with walking meditation, some periods of work, silence, and simple food eaten sitting in the meditation posture in the meditation hall. Although such a routine naturally places a great stress on both body and mind, stretching both to the limit, it is conducive also to the process of what is known in Sōtō as 'dropping off body and mind' (*shinjin datsuraku*[5]) — letting go of all illusions and attachments, giving up internal struggles and doubts and becoming aware of one's innate Buddha nature. Such *sesshin* are the most intense points in the Zen temple calendar, but they are only part of a constant cycle of practice of the type described earlier at the Nagano temple, of early rising and periods of meditation, chanting and work, all of which are geared towards propelling the individual towards higher states of consciousness and to enlightenment.

Yet at the same time, this drive toward enlightenment that is at the heart of Zen spiritual practice is rarely far removed from a commitment to others and to the social ideals of Buddhism. Very few temples are solely, or even chiefly, meditation-centred: there are over 14,000 temples belonging to the Sōtō sect, yet only a relative handful have a meditation hall, and probably little more than 30 in all follow such strict monastic schedules. Perhaps 10 per cent of all Sōtō temples provide meditation facilities in any way at present,[6] a firm indication of the fact that meditation, while at the core of Zen Buddhism in many ways, is neither its most prominent feature nor the cause of its growth in Japan.[7]

Most Zen temples, like those of other Buddhist sects, are what are known as *ekōin* or *bodaiji*, temples whose primary function is to perform memorial services and at which households are affiliated because their ancestors are memorialised there. The priests who run such temples will have spent some time at the above-mentioned meditation centres as part of their training to become priests (in fact, the majority of those living at such meditation centres at any one time fall into this category), but generally are ready to move on and run a *bodaiji* once they have completed the requisite amount of training to get their full priest's licence. It is the meditative and spiritual training they have undergone that confers upon them the power and ritual knowledge to do this, and hence the social and funereal sides of Buddhism are intimately linked to its meditative sides.[8] There are those who continue to meditate, and there are centres whose focus is almost entirely devoted to spiritual training and the attainment of enlightenment, but these are the tip of a veritable iceberg: most people go to a Zen temple in Japan not to meditate but because someone in their household has died.

BUDDHISM, DEATH AND THE DEVELOPMENT OF THE
DANKA SYSTEM

This is not a situation that came about overnight, nor one that has
been limited to Zen: it concerns every Buddhist sect and movement
in Japan and has developed gradually over many centuries, its
origins stretching back to well before the introduction of Zen to
Japan. The association between Buddhism, death and the memorialisation of the ancestors is found from very early on in Buddhism's
history in Japan. By the seventh century it had become quite
established in this respect, as can be judged by the promulgation of
an Imperial decree of 685 AD which ordered that all households
(and it is assumed that this meant aristocratic households, as
Buddhism at the time was largely an aristocratic preserve) should
possess a *butsudan* or private family altar at which the family
antecedents could be worshipped. This is the first evidence of the
development of the family altar in Japan.[9] As Buddhism gradually
assumed responsibility for coping with the major religious role of
dealing with death it also introduced the practice of cremation as an
alternative means of disposing of the evidence of physical death, the
corpse, to accompany its role of looking after the *tama* or soul. The
first cremation in Japan was that of a Buddhist monk in 700 AD,
followed soon after by the cremation of members of the Imperial
family: this method of disposal has become more and more pre-
dominant over the centuries until by 1987 it was the means of
dealing with 95 per cent of all corpses.[10]

It was the apparent spiritual and magical powers accumulated by
those who trained in the Buddhist tradition, aligned to the powers
possessed by Buddhism in the form of its Buddha figures, statues,
prayers, incantations and rituals, that were responsible for convincing the Japanese that Buddhism had the ability to transform the
spirits of the dead and lead them to enlightenment after death,
thereby eradicating the impurities and pollutions associated with
death. Such recognition aided Buddhism's expansion, allowing it to
plant its roots more firmly in the Japanese cultural soil and hence to
expand the numbers of people to whom it could extend its teachings. It also wedded it to Japanese folk concepts of the *tama* as an
entity that continued to exist after death, a view not especially
compatible with basic Buddhist philosophical perceptions of tran-
sience, transmigration and rebirth. Such concepts still may be
discussed in philosophical terms within the Japanese Buddhist

world, yet they have never carried much weight at the popular level, where Buddhism now as in the past tends to talk of the soul as an entity that continues to exist in some form after death, a view that certainly fits more harmoniously into the Japanese religious world than do more traditional Buddhist ones.[11]

Because, also, Buddhism traditionally preached the way of celibacy and leaving one's home, it could be seen as socially antithetical to the ethos of Japan and, indeed, the rest of Asia, where the extension of the lineage and the pressure to uphold the household as an institution were vital social ideals. Thus Buddhism, in order to gain social acceptance throughout Asia and especially in China and Japan, had been obliged to counterbalance its emphasis on celibate monasticism with the promotion of familial ideals for those who did not take up ordination in the priesthood, and this stimulated the assimilation of its social role as a support mechanism for the household.

All these factors were, along with the powers of Buddhism discussed in Chapter 2 to provide *genze riyaku*, far more important in the expansion and dissemination of Buddhism than were such practices as meditation. Sōtō Zen, for instance, developed from the late thirteenth century, not so much because of its focus on meditation but because of the abilities of its priests and proselytisers to assuage the fears of the ordinary people with regard to death, to perform rites to remove the possibility of any spiritual interference from the dead soul and to mediate the powers of the Buddhas to ordinary people. It did have its meditation centres which sought to maintain strict monastic discipline of the type promulgated by Dōgen and to provide the training ground for the realisation of enlightenment, but these could only exist because of the economic support provided through the sect's expansion and development of a popular constituency. Sōtō Zen Buddhism expanded across Japan in this manner from the late thirteenth century onwards, a period in which several other major Japanese Buddhist sects, including the Pure Land sects and Nichirenism, also rose to prominence.

However, it was in the Tokugawa era (1600—1868) that Buddhism became deeply entrenched in the social system. During this era the relationship between Buddhism and the household and the position of Buddhism as *the* religion of death was formalised through a series of laws enacted by the government in the first half of the seventeenth century commanding all households to become formally affiliated to a Buddhist temple. The laws were enacted not to promote Buddhism as a religious faith but to tighten government control of the country, and were part of the move to exclude Christianity as an alien and socially disruptive force. Households, and all people in them, were obliged to register at a temple in their area, and all had to make at the temple an annual declaration of religious belief that involved a denial of Christianity. This declaration enabled them to receive a temple certificate (*tera ukejō*), non-possession of which was a serious crime. Participation in annual rituals at the temple, as well as the performance of funerals and memorial rites and various financial obligations towards the upkeep of the temple, were mandatory for all, including even Shinto priests, who had to die as Buddhists. All households were obliged to have a *butsudan* where the ancestors were enshrined and venerated.

The system enforced belonging, albeit providing an element of choice in areas where more than one temple existed. As a rule, though, belonging was through circumstance and situation rather than volition and belief: one 'became', for instance, affiliated to the Sōtō sect because the temple nearest one's residence happened to have been established and run by a priest of that sect. The temples themselves were obliged to act as a registry of births, deaths and marriages, and to enforce the oaths of allegiance. They were also very largely restricted in terms of religious teaching, being allowed to do little more than propagate the social ideals of the Tokugawa government with its emphases on obedience, loyalty and filial piety.

This system of support for the temples was known as the *danka* system: *danka* are households that are affiliated to and support a temple. The *danka* system, by making all Japanese formally become Buddhist and attend temples for ancestral rites and funerals, gave Buddhism complete domination in this area and provided it with a captive membership that, through the fees paid for funerals and other obligatory contributions, guaranteed its continued prosperity and existence. It also confirmed Buddhist rites and priests as essential factors in the transformation of the spirits of the dead into ancestors. All this did not, however, assure the continued vitality of Buddhism, for the formal, legal and bureaucratic obligations it had to shoulder under Tokugawa law made it unpopular (the Buddhist priest was frequently seen, especially in rural areas, as an outsider, something of a government agent) and reduced it virtually to being an arm of the government, while the restrictions placed on what it could teach denuded it of spiritual vitality and dynamism.[12]

The *danka* system was formally abolished after the 1868 Meiji Restoration which set about destroying the vestiges of the former regime, and for a short time a government-stimulated move took place to eradicate Buddhism completely and to make Shinto into the religion of state. Many temples were closed or destroyed and Buddhism was attacked as a foreign religion: considering that it had been in Japan for over 1300 years at this point this is a striking manifestation of the Japanocentric currents that may surface from time to time in Japan. Despite this, and although Buddhist institutions felt the anger of people who had for long been forced to support them, in the long run this did not undermine the position of Buddhism as radically as might have been expected. Many households did break away from their former obligations, yet more still continued to retain an affiliation, and support for the temples was such that the anti-Buddhist movement was a failure.[13]

The point at issue was basically that for all its faults and complicities with the previous regime, for all that it may have become, in the Tokugawa age, a ritualised and spiritually rather moribund bureaucratic institution, and for all the resentments caused by the economic demands it made, Buddhism did perform what for most people was a necessary task. Put simply, as the medium through which to cope with the bereavements of death, pacify the spirits of the dead, revere the ancestors and uphold household unity and continuity, it fulfilled a vital and meaningful social and religious role: without Buddhism and its priests, who would perform the rites for the ancestors?

The passage of time has not altered this view: indeed it has been a mainspring in Buddhism's continued influence in Japan. As was noted in Chapter 1, over 75 per cent of people describe themselves as Buddhist, almost always as a consequence of household belonging and affiliation and because of the occurrence of a death in the family, consulting priests and often finding out to which sect their families are affiliated because of this situation. Buddhism may no longer be the sole agency for this (some new religions, for instance, have instituted their own mortuary services and rites) but it remains the prime one to which the large majority of Japanese still turn in their time of need: the *danka* system might well have been abolished formally but its influences continue to colour the orientations of the majority of Japanese households and to form the backbone of contemporary Buddhism.

This has left a very deep imprint on the state and nature of Japanese Buddhism which remains, in the popular perspective, very much a ritual system to be encountered because of death. This outlook is especially prevalent among the younger generations who frequently view Buddhism as an 'old people's religion' involved with the end of life and of little immediate relevance to them. This view of affairs, which came out in my description of the rite before the *butsudan* that I attended in Nagano, where the older family members participated fully and the younger ones only ephemerally, has also been reflected in the surveys carried out on ancestral rites by researchers such as Maeda Takashi that show that participation tends to increase with age.[14]

There are few temples in Japan that do not function in some way as *bodaiji*, and the economies of most Buddhist temples and sects still rely largely on the income from fees that are paid for services connected with death and the ancestors.[15] Temples pass on a percentage of this income in sect taxes that go to the sect headquarters and are used for supporting its administration, publications on Buddhism, and social welfare and other activities including the upkeep of meditational institutions. Where the number of households affiliated to the temple is not sufficient to provide for the upkeep of the temple and a reasonable income for the priest and his family he is often obliged to take on an extra job to this end. Probably the majority of priests are in this situation, and most (80 per cent in the Sōtō sect) are also married and have inherited the temples from their fathers.[16] The priesthood, both in Buddhism and Shinto, is largely hereditary: just as in other professions, fathers are generally keen that their sons follow them, and the obligation on all temple priests to provide a successor is an added stimulus.[17]

Priests, much of whose time at the temple is spent on matters to do with mortuary rites, are generally regarded as little more than ritualists to be consulted in connection with death. The fact that many of them are non-vocational and are doing little more than following in the parental footsteps seems not to bother most people as long as the priests are qualified to perform the rites expected of them. Nor does the general perception that most priests, after they have gone through the required training to become fully fledged priests, appear to slacken off on the spiritual practices that were intrinsic to their training. As I have discussed in a previous article, Sōtō priests are, as a rule, more likely than not to cease doing *zazen* after leaving their training temples and taking charge of *bodaiji*.[18]

While none of this hinders the usefulness of priests as ritualists performing what are perceived as necessary and socially prescribed functions, it does little to improve their image, as a survey published in 1984 by the Sōtō Zen sect clearly showed. This asked over 1800 people affiliated to the sect the reasons why they would visit their temple and consult a priest. 78 per cent of respondents stated that they would visit the temple for reasons connected with mortuary rituals while only 8 per cent would do so for 'spiritual reasons': the other 14 per cent gave no response. Sixty-one per cent would visit the priest to request a ritual connected with death and the ancestors, while little more than 5 per cent would do so to learn about Buddhist teachings or to seek spiritual advice in times of distress.[19] Fewer than 50 per cent actually knew to which sect their *bodaiji* belonged.[20]

This apparent ignorance is not particularly surprising, given the pragmatic and situational nature of religion in Japan: what is important for the vast majority of people is that there is something to turn to in case of need, a means and course of action through which to deal with bereavement. The bonds that link household, ancestors and temple are far more dependent on tradition and empathy than anything else: the *de facto* continuation of the *danka* system is a result as much as anything of the importance placed by large numbers of people on the fact that a particular temple is where their ancestors once worshipped and are now buried and venerated. These are the elements of their relationship to Buddhism that are most relevant to the majority of Japanese people: in contrast the issues of what sect one belongs to, what its teachings are and who founded it pale into insignificance.

BUTSUDAN, KAIMYŌ, IHAI: THE ANCESTORS AT HOME

Although the household–temple relationship and the contact between Japanese people and Buddhist temples are primarily functional this does not mean that they lack any religious meaning or value for those involved. The rituals that occur assuage the worries of the living concerning their loved one by assuring them that he/she has attained peace and entered the benevolent world of the ancestors. This not only helps reassure the living in the face of any unease they may harbour about their own demise but also reminds them that they will not be forgotten when they die. The knowledge that one will be remembered is a strong affirmation of the meaning of one's own life in the present and is a validation of one's present existence: doubtless many taking part in rites for someone else can also read into it their own future memorialisation. Thus the ritual process is cathartic for the living, allowing them to externalise and project their personal hopes and alleviate their fears concerning death. It also helps them to redefine their own world by providing a framework through which the occurrence and grief of death may be encountered and dealt with, and through which the living group may express its renewed solidarity and structure, adjusting as it does to the upheaval created by the passing of one of its members.

Death calls into action a series of rites and actions that simultaneously remove the dead soul from this world and install it as an ancestral spirit enshrined in the home of its living kin.[21] There is a strong sense of proximity to all aspects of the living-ancestor relationship: the spirit of the dead is considered to linger around the house for 49 days after death, during which time a series of rites, including the recitation of Buddhist prayers by priests which symbolically transfer the essence of Buddhist teachings to the spirit and emancipate it, removes all the pollutions of death and prepares the soul for enshrinement in the *butsudan*. The body is cremated and the ashes and a small amount of bone are placed in an urn. After a funeral service in which priests (the number who participate depends on the amount of money the family is prepared to spend on the funeral) read Buddhist scriptures and the living make offerings of incense, the urn is interred at the grave.

On the seventh day after death the dead person is given a *kaimyō* or posthumous name. This is bestowed by the priest from the family temple (a fee is paid for this service) and consists of a number of ideograms — the number and nature of which generally reflect one's status in life, with young children usually having shorter *kaimyō* than old men who have produced children and grandchildren — which confer a new Buddhist identity on the dead person. By so becoming a Buddhist, and by 'hearing' the teachings of Buddhism through the reading of the scriptures by the priests, the dead person is popularly considered to become enlightened. At the same time this new name and change of identity is another stage in the purification process, symbolising the extinction of the physical, material presence of the person and removing the spirit of the dead from this world. The bestowal of the *kaimyō*, in conferring a new belonging and identity on the seventh day after death, in many ways parallels the custom of earlier times of naming babies on the seventh day after birth to provide them with their identity for this world, a custom that has largely died out as more and more babies are born in hospitals and given names straight afterwards. It also parallels the structure of ordinations to the Buddhist priesthood, where the initiate is given a new Buddhist name that signifies a death to mundane existence and rebirth in the world of Buddhist spirituality. The *kaimyō* is eventually inscribed on an *ihai* or memorial tablet that is placed in the *butsudan*. The *ihai* represents the spirit of the ancestor, and prayers and offerings at the *butsudan* are directed to it. At first two temporary *ihai* are made, one to be placed at the grave where it is gradually worn away by the elements, and the other in the *butsudan*.[22] The initial series of rites ends on the 49th day after death, at which time mourning ends and the soul is believed to leave the environs of its kin and enter the world of the ancestors: at this time a permanent *ihai* of black lacquer embossed in gold with the *kaimyō* engraved on it is placed in the *butsudan*. Many people consider the *ihai* to be the place of abode of the ancestors and, as Robert Smith has shown, it is often the *ihai* that are rescued first in event of fires, for 'the ancestors, after all, are members of the household and need help like anyone else'.[23] Depending on sect, regional and temple custom, a second *ihai* might be placed in a memorial hall at the family temple, where the priest will perform special memorial services for it and all the other *ihai* on a regular basis.

Buddhist memorial services continue to be held for the deceased at periodic intervals — on the hundredth day after death, on the first anniversary, the third anniversary and at fixed intervals thereafter (7th, 13th, 23rd) until the 33rd or sometimes the 50th anniversary. The Sōtō sect reports that 26 per cent of its temples cease doing memorial services after 33 years, 37 per cent after 50, and that 9 per cent continue until the 100th anniversary.[24] By later anniversaries it is unlikely that anyone who remembers the deceased as a person will still be alive, and with this consequent loss of social identity and personality memorial rites cease. Occasionally, in the case of someone whose influence transcends the bounds of lineage and extends to later ages, memorialisation may continue longer. The founders of Buddhist sects in Japan, for example, continue to have memorial services performed for them centuries after their deaths: it is over 700 years since the Zen monk Dōgen died, yet the Soto sect holds a memorial service on the day of his death each year, with a major memorial rite every 50 years. Normally, though, once individual rites are no longer performed the *ihai* is handed over to the temple where it is burnt in a ritual, and the ancestor is considered to join the general ranks of the ancestors, no longer individually identified and venerated through the *ihai*. Some households will keep a general memorial tablet made for all these unnamed ancestors in the *butsudan*.

The *butsudan* in which the *ihai* are placed is the prime focus of ancestor worship and Buddhist ritual in the home. It is basically a skilfully crafted cabinet of lacquered wood and has long been a major household expense and, to some extent, a status symbol: a large, ornate *butsudan* may cost several thousand pounds, and contemporary Japanese economic growth has enabled more and more people to acquire *butsudan* at the upper end of the market. There are also smaller ones designed to fit into small city apartments that may be acquired more cheaply, and which are within the budgets of the large majority of households.

Although one or two Buddhist sects have their own special *butsudan* which they advise members to acquire (the Nichiren Shōshū sect and its lay organisation Sōka Gakkai are especially adamant about this), *butsudan* as a rule are all very similar in style and shape. Generally they contain various Buddhist accoutrements, including candles, an incense burner, a bell and perhaps a small Buddhist statue or scroll. Each Buddhist sect encourages its members to place items specific to that sect in the *butsudan*: the Sōtō sect suggests a scroll depicting the Buddha along with Dōgen and Keizan, the two founding figures of the sect, while in the Pure Land sects a scroll or statue of Amida, the Buddha of the Pure Land, is the preferred object. Such recommendations, which are not enforceable, are seen as both affirming and encouraging a link between sect and household through the *butsudan*.

The style in which they are made has changed with the age, assimilating technological progress along the way. The development of the camera led to the installation of photographs of the deceased as well as *ihai* (in fact, it is common for people while alive to have a photograph taken of themselves wearing dark clothes, specially for this purpose) while recent technological advances have made their mark as well. The 'video *butsudan*' in which the traditional altar is augmented by a video recorder and screen which relays scenes from the life of the deceased has made its appearance recently,[25] while in late 1988 a Japanese magazine ran a report on the latest trends which show a move towards compact and even portable *butsudan* with remote controls with which to open their doors, automatically light the incense and illuminate an electric candle, and even play a recorded Buddhist prayer.[26]

These changes of style — especially the development of compact *butsudan* suited to the small city apartments in which large numbers of Japanese now live — reflect the changing social patterns of Japanese society. The *danka* system developed in an era when most Japanese lived in extended households based on patrilineal descent. The main household of the lineage would contain a *butsudan* enshrining all the ancestors of that lineage, and this would be looked after by the male head of the household and, when he died, by his eldest son who would inherit this role and pass it on to his sons. Other sons, on getting married, were likely to set up their own households as branches of the main lineage and in due course, when someone in that branch family died, establish their own *butsudan*: none the less they would continue to venerate the shared ancestors of their lineage at the main *butsudan*.[27]

The rapid urbanisation of recent decades has changed this pattern considerably. The pressures of space in the cities favour small nuclear units rather than large, extended households while economic development has stimulated the desire of couples to establish their own independent nuclear family units. As a result, in cities at least, the nuclear family has become the norm. Often a concomitant factor in this is the establishment of a *butsudan* for the new family when someone connected to it dies: the acquisition of a *butsudan* and of family ancestors is confirmation of the socially independent identity of the family unit. Death is thus an important stage in the development of the family in its urban setting, evidence that it has set down roots and established itself as an independent entity in that environment. An additional stimulus to the acquisition of nuclear *butsudan* is their increasing affordability as people in general become wealthier and as the *butsudan* become smaller.

There is no definitive rule as to whose *ihai* are placed in the *butsudan*: although it was long considered that only patrilineal members of the lineage would so be enshrined it is clear that nuclearisation has altered this somewhat. Smith reported in 1974 that *butsudan* in urban areas had a higher percentage of nonlineal *ihai* (which included relatives of the wife) than those in rural areas, concluding that this represented a changing trend towards family- rather than household-centred worship.[28] Kōmoto Mitsugu has confirmed this tendency, noting that in urban areas the direction of ancestral veneration has moved away from those concerned with the continuation of the household as an extended lineage towards those whom the living in the nuclear unit knew well and cared for.

Children and those who died in the womb may have an *ihai* and be treated as ancestors, suggesting that the idea of ancestors as those who were senior and have actively extended or continued the lineage has altered. A degree of personal choice has become apparent: the extended household system virtually required the enshrinement of certain people, while the nuclear system allows the family members the choice of whom to enshrine. Empathy and personal feelings of warmth and attachment (in other words *en*) have become primary criteria for enshrinement.[29]

Non-family members also may be incorporated, especially if they had no one else to care for them after death: this is often because of the worry that the souls of those who die an unhappy death or who are not cared for afterwards may cause spiritual interference and distress to the living. At times, too, representation in the *butsudan* may reflect a feeling of warmth and gratitude towards outsiders, as is shown by the case of the American anthropologist John Embree who conducted fieldwork in a village in Kyūshū in the 1930s and later published a monograph about it. In 1950 he and his daughter were killed in the USA in a road accident: in 1985 when Embree's widow visited the village again she found that friends of theirs had placed photographs of her husband and daughter in their *butsudan*.[30]

Offerings are made to the ancestors at the *butsudan* although the patterns vary from household to household. Some do this a number of times daily, offering foodstuffs such as rice and water from which the ancestors derive their spiritual sustenance, lighting incense and a candle, ringing the bell, joining the hands, praying and even addressing a few words, often in the form of casual conversation about family affairs, to the *ihai*. Popular manuals and pamphlets published by the Buddhist sects certainly encourage regular offerings and suggest that the ancestors be informed of events in family life such as the progress of the children at school.[31] In reality, whether this is done depends on the household for there is considerable flexibility in the nature of these observances, and while many do observe these actions carefully others may only do so sporadically or on special occasions. Besides regular (or irregular) prayers and offerings the ancestors may also be asked for their help and protection in more specific terms, for example when a family member is to go travelling or in the face of a personal or family crisis.[32] A priest from the family temple may periodically be asked to come and read Buddhist prayers before the *butsudan* for the benefit of the ancestor: this is believed to help the ancestor's progress towards full enlightenment which in turn consequently enhances the ancestor's ability to protect the living.

Traditionally it was the head of the household who was responsible for the *butsudan* and for making offerings and leading household rites at it. In contemporary urban Japan, however, where household labour patterns are quite firmly divided, with the husband working long hours and spending much of the day outside the house and wife in charge of all that goes on inside the home, it is she who is most likely to take care of the *butsudan* and the ancestors, although if a member of the older generation is living with the family he/she is likely to take on this responsibility. The younger generations are far less likely to become involved: the majority of young Japanese I have talked to whose houses have a *butsudan* have informed me that they do not make offerings at it, leaving this to a parent or grandparent, to someone generationally closer to the dead and to death itself. There remains, however, a realisation that when their time comes they will take over this role: as one male 20-year-old student remarked to me, 'when my parents die I will take over the rituals at the *butsudan*'. This sentiment, a recognition of the continuing role of filial and social obligation in Japan, is also, of course, further evidence of the situational nature of Japanese religion: when the current generation caring for the ancestors dies, their offspring will take on this task and will enshrine them as ancestors. Acceding to the responsibility of their generation they will 'become' Buddhists and play the role that is socially incumbent on them.

Besides its role within the family the *butsudan* can also provide the ideal setting for reconciliations and for expressions of intent in the process of healing social rifts, as the following incident reported in the Japanese press in February 1987 indicates. The leader of the Japanese Socialist Party (JSP), Doi Takako, while visiting the city of Okayama, called at the house of the Eda family where she lit incense and prayed before its *butsudan*. This enshrined Eda Saburō, a former JSP leader who quit as a result of factional fighting and formed a new political party in 1977. He died shortly after, unmourned at least by the JSP who viewed him as a defector: no JSP politician had previously made offerings either at the *butsudan* or at his grave. Doi had recently become head of the Socialist party and was actively seeking to create a new sense of unity among Japan's frequently feuding opposition parties: a reconciliation with Eda's party in which his son, as is common in Japanese politics, had inherited his father's mantle and had long been influential, was vital to her strategy. She had recently begun to hold talks with its leadership to this end, and the act of veneration at the *butsudan* was a way of continuing this process and expressing her wishes for the eradication of past quarrels and the restoration of harmonious relations.[33]

HAKA MAIRI AND THE RITES OF *O-BON*

Along with the *butsudan* the other great focus of unity and centre of ancestral rites is the *haka*, the family grave, where usually ashes of all the family deceased are interred. It is an important site for encountering and interacting with the ancestors: an American student of Japanese descent whom I taught in Japan reported to me that when she visited her relatives in southern Japan they immediately took her to their family grave, as they thought she would want to greet her ancestral kin before doing anything else.

The grave is simultaneously a special place of contact between the living and their ancestors, a receptacle for the spirits of the ancestors, a site for ritual offerings to the dead and a symbol of family continuity and belonging. An object of such powerful social and religious significance requires special care and consideration, and it is extremely common for diviners to be consulted before constructing a grave, just as they might before the construction of a house, to determine the orientation that is most auspicious and that will please the ancestors most. One can even buy various guide books to grave construction and maintenance to further emphasise these points.[34] The graves are usually in some sanctified ground, such as within the precincts of the family temple which thus oversees and protects the grave, with the priest conducting occasional rites to this effect. But maintaining the grave properly is the responsibility of the family and involves making offerings and periodically cleaning it, and this is a vital aspect of the relationship between the living and the dead, a means through which the living may express their feelings for the dead and uphold the vital balance and relationship through which the ancestors look after the living. Failure to do this correctly may, just as with neglect at the *butsudan*, invite problems: it is not infrequent for people who go to diviners or to the new religions for help with personal problems such as illness to be told that the cause of the problem lies in their failure to look after the grave properly or that the grave has been badly sited and requires changing.[35]

As with the *butsudan*, demographic movements have had an effect on contemporary patterns of grave ownership and of *haka mairi*, the rites of visiting the grave and paying respects to one's ancestors. There has been a general move from communal house-hold graves located in the *furusato*, the native village from which members of the family originated, to family graves in or near the cities. This is a natural result of long-term city living: as family members die and as second- and third-generation family members are born there, families find their orientations revolving more strongly around the city than the village as home. Accordingly, just as they will acquire a *butsudan*, so too will they seek to procure their own family grave in or near the city, where they can place the ashes of family members and make offerings and conduct the various rites for the dead. The ashes when interred in the earth of the family's *furusato* express a sense of belonging to that area: as the *furusato* itself is shifting focus from rural villages to urban areas, a process that can only get stronger as urbanisation continues, the wish to acquire family graves in the new family homeland is intensified. Establishing a family grave in the new *furusato* not only provides a focus of identity and marks a further stage in the development of the urban family as a new and independent unit, but also makes the practice of *haka mairi* physically more convenient, involving less of a journey, and is one reason for the growing numbers of people of all generations who have been performing the *haka mairi* in recent years.[36]

This move, ironically, is leading to its own problems of space in already overcrowded areas. Graves, unlike *butsudan* that can be easily bought and placed inside an apartment, take up space, and although some moves are being made to compartmentalise and reduce the size of family graves in a similar way to *butsudan*, this has not yet become a palatable option for most people. Temples, which in rural areas generally had a graveyard attached to them, can no longer cope in the cities: those with graveyards are full, and new temples cannot acquire, or afford, the space for graveyards. Munici-pal graveyards, an apparent solution in the 1950s, are now virtually all full as well — the last space in any Tokyo municipal graveyard was filled in 1987 — and all this has led to a growing industry in private graveyards located on the outskirts of cities, with a resultant leap in the costs of purchase.[37] Such graveyards generally have a connection with a temple which sanctifies the ground and provides a source of regular memorial services at the graveside. Often indeed the temple may eschew any formal sectarian affiliations so as to attract people of all sects (and of course those who do not know what theirs is!). Thus Myōshinji, a prominent Rinzai Buddhist temple in Kyoto well known as a meditation centre, has established a graveyard which is widely advertised by the temple in tandem with a real-estate firm controlled by the Hanshin Railway Company (which runs a complimentary bus service for those interested in checking out the facilities). In the graveyard is a memorial containing a bone believed to be a relic of the historical Buddha, and this relic acts as a symbol of power able to guard over and protect the spirits of those who acquire graves at this site. The advertising leaflets state that they have a systematised cleaning and management system which makes sure the graves never become unkempt or neglected in any way, and assure everyone that no questions will be asked about sectarian affiliations.[38] Of primary concern to most people are the facilities for maintaining the graves and the convenience of the location, all of which can be checked out in various specialist magazines and directories that have begun to appear on the market in response to this phenomenon.[39] As is generally the case, when faced with the pragmatics of the situation and the provision of an acceptable means of caring for the dead, issues of sect are of little real relevance to most people.

The grave, then, continues to be a central element in all the rites surrounding death: in fact *haka mairi* remains the single most widely performed religious activity in Japan, carried out, as was mentioned in Chapter 1, by close to 90 per cent of all Japanese people, young and old alike. It is primarily done at a number of set times in the year, especially at *higan* (literally the 'other shore'), the period around the spring and autumnal equinoxes, and the *o-bon* festival in mid-July or August (the timing varies depending on the region). Many families also visit their ancestors' graves over the New Year period as well. At these times it is customary to visit and clean the graves, making offerings of food and drink to sustain the ancestors in the other world and calling in a priest to read Buddhist prayers for the benefit of the dead and to help them in their journey to full enlightenment (the 'other shore' implied in the name *higan*). Such occasions are important for the preservation of family cohesion and unity, providing also an opportunity for relaxation, conviviality and the sharing of family news.

In March 1987 the *Japan Times*, the largest English-language newspaper in Japan, published a vivid account written by an American man who had married into a Japanese family, which described how he, along with 30 family members spanning four generations, performed *haka mairi*, gathering together at *higan*, gossiping, eating and generally relaxing together. Eventually everyone went off as a group to the family grave to clean it and make offerings. It was not a sombre occasion by any means but an outing, an expression of family togetherness: as they left the graveyard, the head of the entire family, in a reference to his own mother, the family matriarch who had been dead for 25 years but was still very much in all their minds, remarked: 'See how my mother keeps us together.'[40]

The most active and demonstrative time for family unity and festivities connected with the ancestors is the summer festive time of *o-bon*. This is the period when the souls of the dead are considered to return to earth to be with their living kin: since the ancestors are also felt to reside in the *ihai* and to be encountered at the *butsudan* throughout the year there are clearly some logical inconsistencies here, but these appear of little relevance and are hardly ever commented upon. It is a time of holidays and travel: many businesses close for a few days and those who still retain contacts with the *furusato* from which their families originated, where some of their relatives may still be living and where the main *butsudan* and grave of the *ie* may still be located, are likely to join in a mass exodus from the cities for a few days.

During *o-bon* a special altar with offerings to greet the dead souls is set up at the house, and the priest from the *bodaiji* is asked to come and read prayers before it. The demand for priestly services is great at this time, and many priests find themselves having to rush frantically from place to place in order to visit all the households affiliated to their temple. Graveyards and temples are also extremely alive and active, with lanterns and small fires set out to symbolically guide the souls of the dead back to earth (this is particularly common when the death has occurred since the previous *o-bon*), and families visiting the temple to have further memorial prayers offered for the dead and to receive a special Buddhist talisman that will be placed on the grave.

It is very much an affair of the family and household rather than of the community as a whole, as I found when I first attended an *o-bon* memorial service on a hot and sticky August evening in 1981 at a temple in the city of Nagoya. The courtyard was illuminated by paper lanterns, each of which was inscribed with the name of a household affiliated to the temple. People came to the temple as families: there appeared to be no peer groups of friends as at *hatsumōde*. The memorial service that took place involved a general offering of Buddhist chants, after which the priests chanted specific prayers for each dead soul in turn. They then handed to the family a talisman on which Buddhist inscriptions and invocations had been written for the benefit of that family's ancestor(s); they took it to the grave and placed it there as an offering. What surprised me at first was that, as this ritual was going on, just about everyone seated in the temple was chatting, greeting friends, smoking cigarettes and generally making a noise: only the family for whom the specific prayers were being said at the time appeared to be silently attentive. Family groups thus paid no attention to the memorial prayers made on behalf of those from other families, only falling silent and moving to the front of the temple when their name was called. The nature of the relationship between the living and the ancestors is highly localised, relevant to a specific lineage and family sense of identity, and consequently the prayers and talismans offered for the dead of other households were not especially relevant or worthy of much attention. As a result the service was a strange interpolation of different moods: the family noisily and irreverently talking and ignoring the religious process going on before them, and then switching in unison, when their turn came, into the seriousness of a 'religious mode'.

O-bon, although it is connected with the dead, is a brightly festive time, and community dances, *bon odori*, are held at temples and by local community associations. The basic meaning of these dances is to please and entertain the spirits of the dead but they are every bit as much for the entertainment of the living, so much so, indeed, that many *bon odori* are held after the end of *o-bon* itself as local community festivals.

Despite the joyous nature of the festival, however, it does have poignant undertones. At the end of *o-bon* the dead spirits are considered to return to the world of the dead, their way lit, as was their coming, by fires, and this departure is, for those who have died recently and their relatives and friends, a particularly striking moment of final separation. In many parts of Japan this separation is marked by the construction of small boats in which the soul of the dead symbolically rides: the boat is pushed out to sea or on to a river, thus being sent off on its journey from this world.

At Nagasaki on the island of Kyūshū this particular rite, known as *shōryō nagashi*, is celebrated in a raucous fashion on the evening of 15 August. Large model boats are constructed by the families and friends of the recent dead: the size of the boats depends to a great degree on the amount of time and money the family can put into it, with size generally being a reflection of social status and wealth in this life. Many of those I saw when I visited Nagasaki for this event in 1984 were twenty or more feet long: all were accompanied by a photograph of the dead person. They were paraded through the streets at night to the cacophonous accompaniment of firecrackers and music: the relatives, family groups and friends seemed happy as they gave their kin a good send-off while taking the boats down to the harbour, where they were pushed out to sea.

However, the physical manifestation of separation that occurred when the boats were pushed off clearly affected some people strongly. I was particularly struck by a group of young college students who had been pulling a boat with a photograph of a young girl, presumably a classmate who had died tragically young. Signs on the boat proclaimed their love for her, and while they were going through the streets throwing firecrackers and participating in the general festivities they were openly smiling along with everyone else. A short while later I saw them moments after they had pushed their boat out. They were virtually all in tears, clutching each other in the grief of the recently bereaved. It was a dramatic moment, demonstrating the intense sadness and grief that surrounds death and may still come to the fore even in the midst of all the festivities and rites that help to make it bearable for the living.

CONTINUITY, CHANGE AND THE ORIENTATIONS OF CONTEMPORARY BUDDHISM

Nuclearisation and urbanisation, even if they have changed some of the patterns of who will be enshrined, have clearly not eradicated the roles and importance of Buddhism and the ancestors in Japanese society. The high levels of participation in the rites connected with the ancestors, the continued and even growing use of Buddhist ritual processes to deal with them, and the view of the vast majority of the Japanese that they are Buddhists, albeit in a rather formal sense, testify to their enduring powers in social terms. It is indicative of this deep-rooted influence that the Buddhist symbols of the _butsudan_, the _ihai_ and the grave are as important as ever, not just in dealing with death but in affirming the social identity of the nuclear family in urban Japan.

This does not mean that the position of traditional Buddhism has remained inviolable or that it can continue to rely on a captive audience held in place by the vestigial influences of the _danka_ system. For one thing, the majority of Buddhist sects remain more strongly rooted in rural than urban society: Sōtō Zen, for example, reports that 48 per cent of all its temples are in villages, and that 64 per cent of them are in areas dependent on agriculture, forestry or fishing, all economic activities becoming increasingly marginal in contemporary Japan.[41] Consequently, as depopulation has made its impact, Buddhism has been weakened in its traditional rural constituency. People moving to cities do not always continue the relationships of the village, especially when there is no appropriate temple at hand.

For most Japanese the primary importance of rites dealing with death and commemorating the ancestors is that they should be done, not that they have to be done by a priest of a particular sect. Those affiliated with, for instance, the Sōtō Zen sect through their _ie_ in their native village are less likely to maintain that affiliation if, in their urban environment, there is no Sōtō temple conveniently at hand. They may be attracted by a particular temple because of its geographical convenience, because its priest has a good reputation or for some other personal factor such as liking its architecture or Buddhist statues. These become increasingly influential considerations when people are no longer sure what sect they ought to belong to or if they no longer feel constrained by household traditions or the obligations cast on them in earlier times. The erosion of such obligations has stimulated competition from some of the new religions, especially those of Buddhist persuasion and inclination, which also now perform their own rites of memorialisation or ask their members to change their Buddhist affiliation. Reiyūkai is one of the former, providing its own rites for the ancestors and telling its members to dispense with the services of established Buddhism, while Sōka Gakkai, which asks its followers to have their memorial services done under the auspices of its parent Buddhist body Nichiren Shōshū, has caused large numbers of Japanese to change their affiliations.

All these are, however, problems for specific Buddhist sects rather than reflections on the importance of the Buddhist framework for dealing with death and the ancestors. It is possible that contemporary change will eventually cause some realignments and weaken some Buddhist sects in terms of membership, but it is also clear, from the evidence of the last few years, that it has not greatly affected the continuing use and importance of Buddhist symbols and rituals in dealing with death and upholding social unity and family identity. The increase in *haka mairi*, the development of nuclear *butsudan* and graves, and the huge crowds that take part in *o-bon* are all evidence that, even if they profess little knowledge of the teachings and meanings of Buddhism, the Japanese still continue to die Buddhist and to regard Buddhism as having some relevance to their lives and to those of their family, both past, present and future.

At the same time, too, there has been a steady increase in the numbers of people who have shown an interest in Buddhist spiritual practices such as meditation. The Japanese media, always quick to identify and apply epithets to apparent changes of mood and behaviour in Japan, have dubbed this the 'Zen boom' (the loanword *būmu*, 'boom', being one of the most popular media words in contemporary Japan), although it is probably fair to say that whatever boom there is has been comparatively quiet and low-key. The Sōtō sect has noted a small but steady increase in attendance at *zazenkai*, meditation meetings in which lay people gather, usually at a temple under the guidance of a priest, on a regular basis to practice meditation and perhaps also to listen to a talk about Buddhism. The increase is not so much amongst the sect's *danka*, who appear largely to be content with attendance at funerals and the like, but among educated urbanites, especially those either at or recently graduated from college. As more people have become interested in meditation, more and more of the sect's temples have started their own *zazenkai*. Although only around 10 per cent of the sect's temples at present do have such meetings this none the less does represent a growing movement and an increased emphasis on the individual as a spiritual practitioner. It is a reaffirmation of the nature of Buddhism as not just a religion of the household but as a path for religious awareness not solely limited to the ordained priesthood.[42]

The sect's headquarters has greatly encouraged this, realising that Buddhism has to respond to the changing circumstances of the time and to the challenges and inroads made on its previously assured position by the new religions. It is also aware that those attracted to

Sōtō Zen through meditation may in time be liable to turn to the sect (and hence become *danka*) when they are confronted with a family death, especially if they are unaware of their own original affiliation. Thus it has, especially since the beginning of the 1980s, been producing religious literature, including magazines that juxtapose beautiful photographs of temples, Zen aesthetics, calligraphy and the tea ceremony with instructions on how to meditate and lists of temples that hold *zazenkai*, with the specific aim of attracting those whose interest in Zen Buddhism is clearly more in the area of meditation than in the rites of death and ancestorhood.[43]

Promoting the meditational aspects of Zen for lay people is something of a new departure, yet this has not been at the expense of the traditional relationship that has existed between temples and *danka* but in addition to it. Literature aimed at its *danka* still talks far more extensively if not almost exclusively of the importance of tradition and the links that this has forged between households and temple through the agency of the ancestors. For instance the Sōtō sect has, in a number of publications for its members, published a short text called *Shinkō jūkun* ('the ten articles of belief'). These ten articles are in reality mostly concerned with actions relating to the ancestors, to etiquette and to the relationship with the family temple. Article 1 is concerned with the need to clean the *butsudan* regularly and give thanks to the ancestors; Article 2 with the importance of saying grace before meals; and numbers 3 to 9 are concerned with visiting the temple in connection with the ancestors (for example, reporting events in family life to the ancestors at the temple and praying for continued family safety regularly there). Only one item, Article 10, mentions *zazen*, suggesting that on two major festival days in the year the family should go to the temple, listen to talks about Buddhism and do *zazen*. Throughout this brief list of 'articles of belief', Sōtō members are encouraged to act and to do things (for example, visit the temple and clean the *butsudan*), yet at no point are they every asked to 'believe' anything: the word *shinkō* (belief) only appears in the title, and there are no occurrences of verbs such as *shinjiru* (to believe) in the text itself.[44]

Sometimes the tone in its publications can be decidedly nostalgic, drawing pictures of idyllic traditional life in the countryside contrasted with the unease of modern, westernised, cities, and implying that the true ethos of Japanese life, and indeed the 'spiritual homeland' (*kokoro no furusato*) of the Japanese people is to be found in this traditional idyll – which of course is depicted as revolving very much around the temple, the ancestors and suchlike. This imagery is designed in particular to create an empathy and sense of belonging in its members that will help strengthen their relationship to the sect and its temples.[45]

Although the sect thus clearly recognises that the ancestors continue to remain central to the existence of Buddhism in Japan and encourages ancestor worship as an important religious activity, it also realises that to remain spiritually healthy and to encourage membership, especially in the cities, Buddhism needs to speak to people not just as members of a broader social grouping such as the household, and not just in terms of the ancestors and continuity, but also as individuals and in the context of the spiritual teachings that Buddhism offers. It is aware that these areas are not always easily linked together and may even be superficially contradictory: those least likely to want to meditate are those bound to the sect through traditional ancestral bonds, while the greatest interest in meditation is shown by the young who tend to hold the most negative views of Buddhism as an organised religion concerned with death. None the less, while contemporary Sōtō Zen Buddhist literature does tend to emphasise the ancestors or meditation, depending on the audience at which it is aimed, the sect ultimately recognises the need to synthesise the two, for ancestor worship and meditation form a dual dynamic that has been at the core of its growth and continued existence in Japan even, at times, as with the monks in the temple in Nagano mentioned at the beginning of this chapter, fused into a single whole.

Any balanced assessment of Buddhism in Japan needs to recognise that it cannot *just* be discussed as a religion of temples and meditation, nor *just* as one of ancestors and death. Certainly, for many Japanese Buddhism is associated primarily with death and the social bonding of the lineage, yet, as this chapter has shown, these cannot entirely be divorced from its orientations as a religion of individual spiritual awareness. This is an issue of relevance not only to Buddhism but to the entire spectrum of religion in Japan. Socially defined occasions, situations and actions are important components in the Japanese religious world, and it is on these that I have largely focused so far. They are not, however, its only aspects for, alongside the social constructs of religion that might require certain forms of religious behaviour from the individual in his/her capacity as a member of a wider social belonging, there exists immense scope for self-expression on a more individual basis. I have already alluded briefly to this in Chapter 1 when I spoke of the importance of individual interpretation, action and experience in the formulation of religious attitudes, but it is now time to examine this issue more thoroughly, and this will be the focus of the next chapter.

5 Individuals, Ascetics and the Expression of Power

While the religious world in Japan has provided a basis for social harmony, cohesion and belonging, it has also offered ample scope for self-expression and individuality, as the sociologists Sugimoto and Mouer have commented:

> Given the syncretic nature of Japanese religious practices and a tradition of many gods, each individual is able to choose a unique combination of gods and practices to suit his or her own individualistic needs.[1]

This individualistic dimension does not, however, go against the socially harmonising aspects of religion that have been discussed previously but rather stands in conjunction with them. As the example of the Zen priests meditating in the temple demonstrated, the path to awareness is at the same time an inextricably social affair, the meditator who lives as part of a temple community being expected to utilise what he has learned not simply for his own enlightenment but for the benefit of others.

This continuum between the social, everyday aspects of the religious world and its more austere and transcendent expressions in the activities of individual religious practitioners will be a major item of consideration in this chapter, which will examine the roles of such individual figures, the practices they undertake to attain awareness, and their continuing place in the Japanese religious world. It will also start to shed some light on the ways in which the religious world may provide the scope and opportunities for people in Japan to give expression to their feelings as individuals, moving from the social constructs of religion in which their roles and actions are clearly defined, delineated and structured, into more individual areas of expression determined by choice.

This will lead on, in subsequent chapters, to discussions of other areas in the religious sphere which offer scope for self-expression and individual action based on choice and volition. Chapters 6 and 7, for example, will examine activities connected with popular temples, shrines and pilgrimage routes, while Chapter 8, on the ever-growing legions of new religions and popular cultic practices, will demonstrate just how this scope is increasing in contemporary Japan, providing an almost untrammelled world of action and choice on an individual level to supplement, and occasionally supplant, the social framework of religion that has been dealt with in Chapters 3 and 4.

STANDING OUT FOR SELF AND OTHERS: THE SOCIAL DYNAMICS OF SPIRITUAL POWER

The religious world offers the individual various means, such as Zen meditation, pilgrimages and the religious practices of the new religions, for self-reflection, development and cultivation. Indeed, it is the realisation of such qualities, which are highly valued and emphasised in Japan not just as means of improving one's own personality but also as ways of making oneself a more valuable social being, better able to contribute to society in general and to those around one, that lies at the heart of all such religious activities and practices. Self-cultivation, as Helen Hardacre has argued, is a central facet in what she sees as the united and coherent world view of the new religions of Japan,[2] and the importance of this concept is stressed by many new religions. Tenshō Kōtai Jingūkyō, for example, a religious movement founded at the end of the war by the charismatic female Kitamura Sayo, who herself performed many austerities including the repeated recitation of Buddhist chants and long periods of cold-water austerities as part of her own process of self-cultivation, tells its members to 'polish their souls' through spiritual practice, thus developing themselves as individual and social beings.[3] It is not a concept limited to the new religions, however, but one that exists throughout virtually the entire Japanese religious spectrum, found clearly also in, for instance, Zen temple life, asceticism and activities performed at popular religious centres.

At times the notions of self-development and individual expression may come into conflict with the pressures for conformity and the principles of social cohesion that are inherent in Japanese society. To some extent it may be because of the strong group emphasis in Japanese society that the individual tradition is so alive, reacting against the constraints of the former and tempered by its pressures to greater strengths: certainly the two, group and individual, do exist in a state of some friction, the requirements of the one not always sympathetic to the disruptions at times caused by the other. Those who do step outside of group boundaries, whether as charismatic religious leaders or individuals becoming involved in a religious group that cuts across social bonds, have rarely had an easy time in Japan because they appear to go against the tide of conformity and social order. The widely used Japanese phrase *deru kugi ga utareru*, 'the nail that sticks out is beaten down', exemplifies a prevalent social attitude to nonconformity and individuality, making it clear that social forces are on hand to assert conformity and, if required, to suppress any individuality that threatens group norms. Yet this very pressure against 'the nail that sticks out' can conversely strengthen those who have the resolve to do so, intensifying their determination and feelings.

It is certainly one of the most intriguing features of Japanese social and religious history that a society so frequently portrayed as consensus- and group-oriented and with a bias towards conformity and the suppression or sublimation of individuality for the sake of the group, has such a rich and vigorous individual religious tradition of people who have stood out in some way. One of the most constant themes in Japanese religious history has been the continuing emergence of dynamic, charismatically powerful and even apparently miracle-working religious figures who have frequently, by their very natures, upset or challenged social harmony and norms. It is probably also fair to suggest that the religious sphere has been the arena for the expression of such charisma and individuality in a way that no other area of Japanese society, least of all politics, has. A cynic might even argue, at least in contemporary Japan, that a demonstrable lack of personal charisma may in fact be a positive advantage to aspiring politicians!

Such charisma and power is not so much located in and acquired through the formalities of office (even if some of these figures are at the same time priests) as through the pursuit of spiritual disciplines, generally performed outside the normal confines of society. I shall shortly describe some of the practices and settings in which power may be acquired. First, however, I shall look briefly at the social dimensions of spiritual power and of the asceticism that is closely associated with it, for the Japanese religious situation requires more than just acquiring and possessing spiritual, inspirational and charismatic powers. It demands social relevance as well: the ascetic sitting in splendid spiritual isolation on the mountaintop is of no great value to his/her fellows until s/he comes down to share, mediate and disseminate the power that has been acquired.

In a very real sense, individual religious activists and charismatic practitioners are 'standing out' on behalf of and for the benefit of all those who cannot do so for themselves, acting as a medium through which others may realise their aspirations and needs, or indeed through which they may project those needs and aspirations. The natural concomitant of the accession to spiritual transcendence and awareness through the practice of spiritual disciplines and the realisation of charisma has been the acquisition of some or a number of powers that can be used for the benefit of others. Among the abilities widely considered to be possessed in some degree by powerful religious figures in Japan are the powers of divination and of identifying sources of spiritual hindrance that are preventing individuals from attaining their wishes or that are causing them illness and misfortune, the capacity to exorcise or eradicate those sources of hindrance, and the ability to communicate with the spirits of the dead and transmit their needs to their living kin.[4] On perhaps a less dramatic level, but equally useful, is the ability to give wise counsel and spiritual advice and comfort to others, for ultimately all these powers focus on dealing with other peoples' unease and problems and the ways of counteracting them.

Thus, at core, the abilities, and the role, of religiously powerful individual figures are channelled into helping others to deal with their problems and needs. Helping others is an intrinsic part of helping oneself in the path of spiritual awareness, a notion encapsulated by the Japanese phrase *jiri rita* (literally, the process whereby benefiting oneself helps others). The essential meaning of this concept, and its relevance to the heart of the path of religious practice, has recently been explained by Gojō Junkyō, a noted ascetic practitioner and head of the temple Kinpusenji, a major centre for mountain religious asceticism at Yoshino:

> First reflect on yourself, repent your faults, and correct yourself so as to develop the great and powerful mind of *jiri rita* (this is, at the same time as cultivating yourself, to seek the happiness of other people and to strive for the betterment of others). This involves not only seeking world peace and great harmony among all people: one must also take up with determination the sufferings and wishes of every individual and must save them from their sufferings and help them in their wishes.[5]

Apart from its obvious indication of the human-centred and comprehensive nature of Japanese religion (no individual human need or wish should be neglected), this statement reflects the underlying view that human activity in the religious sphere can be effective in bringing about the realisation of those needs. Inherently, then, it accepts and affirms both the causative relationship of the spiritual and physical realms and underlines the value and importance of intercession. This drive to help others as well as oneself has always been expressed not simply on the spiritual level but also in pragmatic and civic ways as well. In earlier ages it was often religious figures who were able, through the force of their charisma, to raise funds and mobilise people into action to carry out social welfare schemes and public projects in ways that political and governmental agencies were incapable of doing. Besides mediating between the spiritual and everyday worlds, religious figures and wandering ascetics were often involved in activities of social benefit besides. Janet Goodwin, in talking of such figures of the thirteenth century, has used the phrase 'building bridges and saving souls' to describe these complementary functions of dealing with spiritual and pragmatic needs,[6] while Carmen Blacker, discussing ascetic travellers from the eighth century onwards, has written:

> With the special powers they had acquired through their austerities, they could heal sickness and prophesy future things. They seem also to have been accomplished engineers, for we read of them helping a village to dig a well or a canal, and to build roads and bridges.[7]

Contemporary society has, of course, eradicated the need for religious activists and ascetics to become involved in public building projects, but none the less this tradition lives on in new forms in the lives and actions of many of the charismatic leaders of the new religions. These, besides preaching and spreading spiritual benefits to followers, have galvanised their followers into building religious centres and networks throughout the country, often also developing social-welfare schemes, educational establishments, printing presses and the like, a theme that will be taken up in Chapter 8 when I look at the new religions and, particularly, at Agonshū, its charismatic leader Kiriyama Seiyū and the technological developments and building projects he has set in motion.

WANDERING LEGENDS, ASCETIC MEDIATORS AND PILGRIMS

Probably the most prominent and influential individual figure in popular Japanese religious history is Kōbō Daishi, whose origins are in the Buddhist tradition, but who has become a major folkloric figure in Japan, the centre of a popular cult who continues to be widely venerated as the source of numerous miracle stories and benevolences. Kōbō Daishi is the posthumous name of Kūkai, a Buddhist monk who lived from 774 until 835, during which period he travelled in Japan, at various times performing austerities in the mountains and at others studying at important Buddhist centres. He also visited China, brought back and established in Japan the esoteric Shingon Buddhist tradition, gained the patronage and support of the Imperial household and aristocracy, built the great Buddhist centre of Kōyasan (Mount Kōya) south of Osaka, wrote several important Buddhist tracts, established a number of temples and carved an indeterminate number of Buddhist statues.

Although Kūkai is still widely venerated as the founder of a major sect of Buddhism in Japan, in popular terms his reputation has gone much further. He is, for instance, credited with establishing far more temples and statues than anyone could have done in one lifetime, and with the performance of countless miracles down to the present. The roots of his mythic reputation are in the tenth century when he was given the posthumous title Kōbō Daishi ('the great teacher who spread the law of Buddhism across the country') by the Emperor, and it is under this name that he has become most widely known and venerated in popular terms in Japan. According to a legend widely propounded by the priests of the Shingon sect at the time, when Kūkai's mausoleum was opened so that a copy of the Imperial document bestowing this honour could be placed inside, his knee was found to be warm. This was taken as evidence that he had not died but had remained alive, meditating in the mausoleum: as news of this miracle spread so did the reputation of the transformed figure of Kōbō Daishi, who in popular legend descended from Mount Kōya and began to wander the byways of Japan.

The mausoleum itself developed as a centre of worship and pilgrimage, and to this day the visitor to Kōyasan will see not only streams of white-robed pilgrims coming to pay homage to Kōbō Daishi but also priests of the Shingon sect performing the daily rites of taking food to him in the mausoleum. It is also the centre of one of the best-known graveyards in Japan for it has long been considered fortuitous to be buried in a place overlooked and protected by a figure of immense holy power. Kōbō Daishi's legendary reputation did not remain ensconced in Kōyasan, however, but gradually spread throughout the country. Stories of him travelling in the guise of a priestly pilgrim, performing miracles, dispensing blessings and good luck, opening up springs and other sources of water where there were none, and developing pilgrimage routes became common.

The cult of Kōbō Daishi has continued to grow to this day, along the way absorbing elements of, and legends from, other popular and venerated individual figures.[8] In fact he is in many ways the archetypal religious figure, constantly wandering and performing austerities and miracles, and as such has formed the model for others who have set out to follow his path. The *Kōya hijiri*, ascetics from Mount Kōya, were especially active in the centuries after he was discovered to still be 'alive', travelling extensively around Japan preaching stories about his power, establishing religious sites and performing rituals to confer blessings on the populace.[9] By visiting places associated with his (historical) life on the island of Shikoku where he was born and by attempting to follow in his footsteps, performing austerities, for example, in the mountains and caves where legends said he had, these ascetics and their travels were a formative influence in the development both of his legend and of one of Japan's major pilgrimage routes, the Shikoku pilgrimage. Many of the temples along the route were, according to tradition, founded by Kōbō Daishi, and popular pilgrimage lore even attributes the establishment of the route itself to him, although with no justification outside the realms of myth.

This pilgrimage, which circles the island of Shikoku, taking in 88 temples along the way in a circuit of some 1500 kilometres, had by the mid seventeenth century begun to attract not just individual ascetic wanderers but sections of the general populace, such as peasants, farmers and artisans from the towns. These pilgrims followed in the steps of the ascetics, going outside the everyday comforts, stabilities and margins of society into the uncertain world of the pilgrim and transient asceticism.

Their clothing and accoutrements marked them out as apart from normal society while simultaneously identifying them with the prime focus of the pilgrimage, Kōbō Daishi, in a symbolism that remains relevant today. It is still common to see pilgrims in Shikoku wearing a white shirt (*hakui*) which is also a burial shroud, signifying both their symbolic death to the everyday world whilst on pilgrimage and also their readiness to meet death on the way: dressed for death, they are prepared to accept whatever fate might come to them. Pilgrims also wear a straw hat (*kasa*) that, besides keeping off the rain, snow and sun, symbolises the coffin, and is inscribed with a Buddhist poem that is frequently also engraved on coffins. They also carry a staff (*tsue*) which is useful when walking, but which also represents both the figure of Kōbō Daishi who is believed to accompany all pilgrims, and a gravestone: in earlier times when, as often happened, pilgrims died along the way, their fellow pilgrims would bury them, thrusting the staff in the ground to mark the grave and to place them under the protection of Kōbō Daishi. The pilgrim is thus set apart from the everyday world, ready to meet death at any stage. At the same time s/he is walking with Kōbō Daishi, for all the items are also inscribed with the words *dōgyō ninin*, (two people, one practice), which implies that the pilgrim is never alone but always with the miracle working figure of Kōbō Daishi.

The ascetic undertones of pilgrimage have generally been eroded by the general developments, from the seventeenth century onwards, of increasingly better facilities for pilgrims. The development of a moneyed economy along with the improved communications, routes and hostelries of the Tokugawa era made the pilgrimage more readily accessible to wider numbers of people who left their homes seeking the benefits and spiritual powers of *o-Daishi-san*, as he came to be popularly known. Twentieth-century improvements and economic prosperity coupled with the increasing pace and goal-oriented nature of contemporary society have advanced this process further, allowing the pilgrim to travel by bus and car, to stay in comfortable hotels and to complete the route in a fraction of the time it would have taken on foot.[10] None the less, the symbolism of pilgrimage in Shikoku, demarcated by the clothing the pilgrim wears, remains a potent reminder of the implicit asceticism of the route, and of the pilgrim as an outsider travelling with the wandering Kōbō Daishi, who remains very much alive in the minds of pilgrims, in the tales they relate to each other and in their journals.[11]

Even if most contemporary pilgrims are content to stand apart from society and enter the realms of asceticism only through the symbolism of their clothing while remaining very much a part of that society and its comforts in the means of their pilgrimage, there are still enduring elements of the basic asceticism of pilgrimage to be found in Shikoku. When my wife and I walked the Shikoku pilgrimage in February–March 1984 we met very few others who were walking: it was a bitter winter and most people seemed to be going by bus or car. We did, however, meet two separate pilgrims who were not just walking but were also, despite the cold and the snow, sleeping out and begging for food in traditional ascetic fashion. We walked with one of them for half a day, and discovered that he saw his pilgrimage very much in an ascetic sense, and also as a process of following in the footsteps of someone else. As we trudged through the snow he told us that his acupuncture teacher had walked the route in a similar fashion 40 years before, and that he was following his example so as to be a worthy pupil of his teacher and to prepare himself for the course he was about to commence with him. Later, as we finished our own pilgrimage just as the weather began to get warmer in mid-March, we met three more men, two in their sixties and one in his twenties, who had just set out and were also walking and sleeping out.

The vestiges of the pilgrimage's original asceticism and of the idea of the ascetic as a mediating figure also remain alive in the figure of the *sendatsu*, the pilgrimage guide or leader who often travels with parties of pilgrims, leading them in prayer at the sites and generally explaining aspects of pilgrimage to them. Many of the ascetics of earlier ages acted in such a capacity, leading groups of pilgrims around the route that they had already trodden, thus initiating them into the pilgrimage and offering them a sense of reassurance in the face of the uncertainties and difficulties of the way. To that extent the *sendatsu* could be seen as a tangible representation of Kōbō Daishi as a protector and guardian of pilgrims, their own ascetic practice enabling them to act as a channel through which the pilgrimage could be mediated to others. The tradition of the *sendatsu* still endures today, and on pilgrimages such as Shikoku and Shodōshima (an island near to Shikoku in the Inland Sea which has a Kōbō Daishi-focused pilgrimage similar in structure to Shikoku) one will often see pilgrimage parties led in this way. In 1987 we met a group of pilgrims travelling around the Shodōshima route with such a guide who told us he had been around the pilgrimage 168 times. About half of these were by foot, the rest by bus with parties of pilgrims, acting as a guide. At the sites he led them in chanting, and along the way he enlivened them with stories about the route, bringing in examples from his own deep experience as a pilgrim and from the wealth of lore concerning the pilgrimage and Kōbō Daishi's grace that he had assimilated over the years. He thus acted as guide and mediator to those who, following in his footsteps, learnt the ways and meanings of the pilgrimage. He was of course also performing the pilgrimage for himself, following in the footsteps of Kōbō Daishi and enriching his own knowledge and awareness, acting thus for self and others simultaneously.

STEPPING OUTSIDE TO COME BACK: THE DYNAMICS OF PRACTICE

The role model of Kōbō Daishi as the wandering, miracle-working and intercessionary figure linking the outside and the world of power with the inside, with the everyday life of society and the needs of ordinary people, is found widely in the Japanese religious world, for the pilgrim going outside the normal confines of society and its comforts and travelling from place to place is but one figure in Japan's rich and continuing tradition of asceticism.[12] The mountains of Japan in particular have long been a major setting for spiritual disciplines and religious cults centred on asceticism, albeit more pronouncedly so in the days before the advent of roads and cable cars made them readily accessible, thus denuding them of some of their mystery. Mountains were seen as apart from the everyday world, their very shape symbolic of the notion of reaching upwards to enlightenment, their ascent a metaphorical journey to this end. Those who climb mountains such as Fuji today can see the results of this concept: the route up the mountain is divided into ten stages, each with a rest station. These ten stages symbolise the ten realms of existence postulated in esoteric Buddhist theory, the tenth at the peak being that of enlightened Buddhas. Ascetic ascents of mountains such as Fuji would symbolically move through these realms, denoting the passage from one to the next with the performance of religious rites at sites on the mountain. The mountain thus acted not just as the setting for spiritual practice but also as a map and guide in itself to the world of enlightenment and liberation. At the sites of these ritual practices rest stations developed: Fuji, like many other mountains, is divided today into ten stages, and the rest stations on the way up are numbered from one to ten, because of the legacy of mountain religious asceticism.[13]

In earlier ages few people went to such mountains, which were seen as remote, inaccessible and dangerous, the abode of various spiritual entities including, it was widely believed, the souls of the dead: they thus formed the antithesis, the wild outside that contrasted with the safety and comforts of the towns, villages and valleys. Their very danger as symbols of the outside and abodes of the spiritual, however, made them powerful, fitting places for ascetic practice and for those who dared to step outside the normal confines of society to encounter and acquire the powers of the spiritual world. The mountain ascetic movement Shugendō, which fused together Buddhist, Taoist and folk religious themes, and its individual practitioners, the *yamabushi* (literally, 'those who sleep/ prostrate in the mountains'), were especially prominent in this tradition of entering the mountains, both in group pilgrimages and mountain ascents, especially the mountains of the Ōmine-Kumano region south of Yoshino, a practice that involves a number of rigorous austerities and that continues to this day, and in the practice of individual austerities in the mountains.[14] Through such practices and austerities they sought to emulate those who had gone before them into the mountains (notably the somewhat legendary seventh-century founder of Shugendō, En no Gyōja, who is the focus of almost as many miracle stories and legends as Kōbō Daishi), acquire the miraculous powers that they had attained and come into direct contact with the spiritual realms by visualising and encountering powerful entities such as Fudō. In returning to the everyday world below they brought back this apparent power of contact with the spiritual realm, and this further enhanced the awe with which ordinary people regarded them.

By spending periods alone isolated in the outside world of the mountains, incessantly wandering, and undergoing various physical austerities such as fasting, going without sleep or standing under icy waterfalls that are the reverse of normal activities, such ascetics and religious seekers were stepping outside the margins of society, and it is through this reversal, this standing out from the norms, that their power was enhanced and intensified. This stepping outside, however, was not an implicit rejection of the world nor an act of world denial, but a firm affirmation of its values, a means of attaining the requisite powers necessary to aid others. The *yamabushi* of earlier ages would, on coming down from the mountains, go from village to village displaying and using the powers they had acquired in the mountains through their austerities, distributing talismans and amulets representing the powers and protection of the spiritual world, performing rites to exorcise evil spirits and remove their baleful influence from the suffering and sick, diagnosing the causes of spiritual and physical problems, and seeking to effect a cure for them.

The same dynamic operates today, as we have seen, with the notion of returning to society to act as a mediator and share one's hard-won spiritual power remaining a vital element in the ascetic path as well as a motivating factor in the impulse to go to the mountains. In the present age the *yamabushi* continue to perform various rituals that seek to harness the powers of the Buddhas for the benefit of ordinary people, often incorporating into these rituals actions of a visually dramatic nature that have long been practised in Shugendō and that act as a demonstration of their acquired powers and their transcendence of normal human barriers. Fire-walking, *hiwatari*, which involves walking on the embers of a ritual bonfire, is one such demonstrative practice performed by *yamabushi* that displays their control over the beneficial yet dangerous medium of fire. It thus asserts their power and ability to subdue danger, and also emphasises their close relationship with and capability to call on the intercessionary powers of such figures as Fudō who are themselves closely associated with fire. Rituals incorporating the practice of *hiwatari* may still be seen in various parts of Japan at such places as Tanukidani, a temple on the outskirts of Kyoto associated with the *yamabushi* and Fudō, and at Mount Misen in Hiroshima prefecture, where a fire-walking rite occurs each 15 November. Often such *hiwatari* performances entail the ascetics first ritually reciting prayers and then walking across the embers, practices which are aimed at taking the dangerous heat out of the fire so that ordinary people may walk across unharmed and thus themselves receive the beneficial and purifying powers of the fire.[15] Other rites they perform are *goma* rituals in which requests and petitions to a deity or Buddha (frequently Fudō because of his association with fire) are inscribed on sticks of wood that are then ritually burnt on a pyre while invocations are chanted.

Despite the obviously dramatic and photogenic nature of their rituals which attract the attention of the media and ensure that large crowds turn up to witness them, it is probably fair to say, none the less, that the influence of the *yamabushi* as mediators and healers is not in general as prevalent as in earlier centuries. To some extent this is because of contemporary changes in society which have made

the mountains that are so important to their power far less remote
and 'other' than they were in previous ages. Now that getting to and
up them has become easier and easier, and as mountain ascents for
the purpose of tourism, skiing, hiking and climbing have become
fashionable, they have lost some of their remote otherness. Accessibility diminishes power and mystery, consequently affecting the
standing of those who formerly linked and mediated the power of
the mountains to the everyday world.[16]

Shugendō also lost some of its dynamism after its suppression and
forced merger into the Tendai and Shingon Buddhist sects after the
Meiji Restoration by a government keen to present a 'rational' face
to the West by eradicating what it saw as superstitious religions.
Merger brought increased structuralisation and a resultant loss of
vigour which has hardly been replaced since the ending of the
suppression after 1945. Perhaps more important still, though, has
been the growing influence of the new religions which have become
a primary location of the charismatic and healing powers once
prevalent in Shugendō. As Numata Kenya has recently shown,
several of the new religions have assimilated motifs and symbols
from Shugendō, including many of its dramatic and demonstrative
rituals, thus absorbing much of its former dynamism.[17] Certainly
many of the practices and rituals of the *yamabushi* have been
transported into urban settings by religions such as Agonshū, which
holds a massive *goma* ceremony every February (to be described in
Chapter 8) that is far larger than any rites the *yamabushi* do, and
hence has stolen some of their thunder. Also, many of the leaders of
new religions such as Kitamura Sayo, Kiriyama Seiyū and Itō
Shinjō, the leader of Shinnyoen, have, in developing their own
charismatic powers, assumed and assimilated the roles traditionally
played by the *yamabushi* as providers of help and of mediation
between this world and that of the spiritual realms.

They have also performed ascetic practices themselves so as to
acquire such powers, and through this, often reinforced by revela-
tory messages from various deities and Buddhas, many leaders of
new religions have come to be seen by their followers as conduits
through which the powers of the spiritual realm may be channelled
to this world. To a great extent the new religions have provided not
simply the arena for the expression of charismatic power in modern
times but also for its mediation and dissemination. The healing
powers acquired by Okada Kōtama of Mahikari have been passed
on, through short Mahikari training courses and the distribution of

holy amulets blessed by Okada and through which he is considered to have mediated and channelled the transformative, purifying and healing powers of Su-God, the central deity in the Mahikari pantheon, to Mahikari followers, thus making accessible to them the powers of spiritual healing and exorcism that once were the province of traditional religious specialists such as the *yamabushi* alone. This 'democratisation of magic' as Davis has termed it[18] will be encountered again in Chapter 8 when I examine the new religions and other contemporary religious developments. A point that is relevant here, though, is that the new religions, which are primarily urban-based, have, through their leaders and the powers and techniques they have passed on to their followers, in many ways bridged the mountain/village dichotomy that made the *yamabushi* so important by bringing the practice and acquisition of power into the cities. This has further eroded the areas within which the *yamabushi* traditionally operate and shifted their focus to the urban world of the new religions where many of the most prominent elements of charismatic religious power are expressed today.

THE DRIVE TO POWER: ASCETIC PRACTICES

It is this ability to stand out and act in a different way from other humans, forming a point of contact between them and the spiritual world and channelling its power to them that serves as the distinguishing hallmark of powerful religious activists. This ability has usually been generated by an inner drive to seek power and awareness, often stimulated in turn by misfortune and need, coupled with the performance of harsh ascetic disciplines. It is quite often the case that such figures have in some way or other been impelled to this path of action through some spiritual revelation, possession, dramatic misfortune or emotional hardship that drives them to extremes. Spiritual strength thus frequently derives from an apparent weakness or from adversity, which is used as a challenge to be overcome and transformed through spiritual disciplines. As we shall see later in this chapter, one of the most striking ascetic figures of contemporary Japan, the Tendai monk Sakai Yūsai, was impelled to the ascetic life after a failed personal life that culminated in the suicide of his wife. The life histories of many of the founders of the new religions also contain stories of misfortunes, weaknesses and sufferings that drive them to the pursuit of religious disciplines and, eventually, to transcendence and spiritual power. This again is a point that will be dealt with in Chapter 8.

A common theme basic to the path of anyone seeking to become a mediating figure or person of spiritual power in Japan, and one which fits well with the concept of going outside normal social boundaries, is a predilection for ascetic disciplines and austerities. Such austerities, generally known in Japanese as *gyō* or *shugyō*, are an intrinsic part of the development of transcendent consciousness. The physical nature of the religious path (and indeed of religion in general in Japan with its 'do it and see' culture) has already been commented on, for example in Chapter 4 which showed that physical actions and disciplines are the means through which Zen practitioners seek enhanced consciousness. Similarly they are at the core of the individual religious path, vitally important as keys to heightened spiritual awareness.

Many kinds of austerities are used to stretch the body to its limits and to break down the barriers of consciousness so as to realise awakening or the acquisition of strengths unknown to ordinary humans. All involve going outside the normal boundaries of society and everyday behaviour in some way or other. Prominent among them are standing under waterfalls, pouring buckets of ice-cold water over one's body, especially in the depths of winter, fasting, intense periods of meditation, incessant walking, isolation and the denial of sleep. Often these various austerities are combined: they are also frequently coupled with the chanting of incantations, *mantras* and other such prayers from the Buddhist tradition, prominent amongst these being the *Hannya Shingyō* discussed in Chapter 2, and invocations from the Lotus Sūtra, one of the most widely disseminated Buddhist texts in the Far East.

All of these austerities have strongly purificatory and exorcistic dimensions: the crushing or punishing of the body through, for example, the action of incessantly pouring icy water over it works to drive or wash out impurities of the mind, removing, or more straightforwardly breaking down, all the barriers, physical and mental, that might prevent the practitioner from achieving higher consciousness and powers. Here of course we are remarkably close to the techniques and practices used in Zen temple life to break down logical barriers and to achieve the 'dropping off of body and mind' discussed in the last chapter. They also serve as a way for the individual to assert his or her own willpower so as to surmount any misfortunes that may have driven them to the austerities in the first place.

The most common of all such austerities are those connected with water. Water austerities (*suigyō*) of various forms are used throughout the Japanese religious world: the *yamabushi* immerse themselves in the Doro river during their mountain pilgrimages to Kumano, the Buddhist ascetics of Hiei stand under waterfalls, and many of the founders of new religions such as Kitamura Sayo include cold water ablutions as part of their religious practices. One core reason for this emphasis on water is its purificatory symbolism and the importance this has as a means of regeneration. The image of Izanagi's bathing after his flight comes to mind yet again here: just as this purification eradicated the pollutions and hindrances surrounding him and helped give birth to new *kami* so too can the practice of water austerities be seen as exorcising the practitioner's spiritual obstructions and giving birth to a new awakening.

One can find waterfalls in numerous religious settings in Japan, in the grounds of temples and shrines and in the mountains. In the Ikoma hills east of Osaka, for instance, an area in which there are numerous religious establishments of all sorts from Buddhist temples to Korean shamanic institutions catering to the Korean ethnic minority of Osaka, to Shinto shrines and small, one-person religious centres and new religious groups, virtually every religious institution has its waterfall, either natural or man-made, which is used for the purpose of performing *suigyō*.[19]

Several of the 88 temples on the Sasaguri pilgrimage route in northern Kyushu have their own waterfalls where anyone may perform such austerities: a guidebook to the pilgrimage even provides an illustrated guide to the practice. One should, it notes, dress in white, which is both the colour of purity and death in Japan, and should purify oneself and the area of the waterfall with salt. This places oneself and the area in the correct state of ritual purity in which to carry out the austerity. Waterfalls are generally associated, in Japanese cosmology, with either (or both) the fiery Fudō or Suijin, a Shinto water deity, and the practitioner is told to invoke them during the practice, the aim of which is to become one with the deity. There is a similar motif in the fire-walking rite of the *yamabushi* mentioned earlier: by identifying and becoming one with the deity who symbolises the element (fire or water) one cannot be harmed or hurt by it. As one invokes the deity, one should become one also with the water, allowing it to permeate one's whole being, a process furthered by drinking a small draught. During the period under the waterfall one should chant Buddhist sūtras and *mantras* (it is suggested that three recitations of the *Hannya Shingyō* are normal), and perform various symbolic gestures associated with the deities. On leaving the waterfall one should clap one's hands and make an offering to the deity.[20]

The idea of becoming one with the figure of worship who forms the focus of the religious action is a common thread in much of the ascetic world and is yet another example of the closeness between humans and the *kami* and Buddhas, and of the lack of clear boundaries between them. The content of such austerities also illustrates, yet again, the overlapping nature of religious traditions in Japan: the above description shows how elements that are distinctly Buddhistic (the chanting of *mantras* and the *Hannya Shingyō*) as well as Shinto (the clapping to the deity and the use of purificatory salt) may exist together in one practice.

The continued existence of *suigyō* can be verified by anyone who is prepared to walk a little in the hills in Japan. Areas where I have come across practitioners doing *suigyō* include the Ikoma hills and the area around Yoshino that has long been associated with the mountain ascetic tradition. One can also see it performed in a slightly different form by ascetics in the Nichiren Buddhist sect who, at the height of winter, perform open-air cold-water ablutions, wearing little but a loincloth and scooping buckets of water over themselves as they and their followers chant invocations from the Lotus Sūtra, the sacred text of Nichiren Buddhism.[21] This activity usually is the culmination of an arduous ascetic retreat lasting 100 days during which the priests undergo a strict regimen of cold-water training to develop the spiritual powers which enable them to act as spiritual healers. There is a strong tradition among Nichirenist priests, particularly those associated with the Nakayama branch of Nichiren Buddhism, of exorcism, casting out spirits from those who think they are possessed, and the cold water ablutions that the priests perform are a requisite training through which to acquire the ability to perform such exorcisms.[22] There is a distinct motif of 'self and others' about this practice for, as the Nichiren ascetic Nagamura Nichihō, who has done this particular austerity five times, has written, the first 35 of the 100 days are devoted to practice for oneself after which the aim and focus turns to the benefit of others.[23]

THE *SENNICHI KAIHŌGYŌ*: THE ASCETICS OF MOUNT HIEI TODAY

Perhaps the most widely known ascetic practitioners in Japan today are the monks at the Tendai Buddhist centre at Mount Hiei near Kyoto who perform the *sennichi kaihōgyō*, or the 1000-day moun-tain-circumambulating austerity. A great deal of media attention, including books, magazine and newspaper articles, photo-essays, television programmes and full-length films, has been directed to these men in the last decade or so, and this in itself is testimony to the continuing interest in asceticism in contemporary Japan.[24]

This mountain-centred practice, which is just one of a number of ascetic practices performed by priests at Hiei, occurs either as a 100- or 1000-day practice. The 100-day practice is a necessary part of the training for all those who wish to officiate as head priests of temples in the massive Hiei complex, and is done by several priests each year. The more arduous 1000-day austerity, however, is taken on by only a few: there are no records extant of the period prior to 1571 when the whole Hiei complex was burnt to the ground by the armies of Oda Nobunaga, although it is known that the roots of the practice go back as far as the ninth-century Tendai priest Sōō.[25] Since 1571 fewer than 50 monks have done it, an average of one a decade.

The practice is a long and continuing combination of several forms of austerity traditionally practised in Japan, such as standing under waterfalls, fasting, going without sleep, and long-distance walking.[26] To undergo this 1000-day practice the monk (and it should be stressed that those who do this must be ordained and single, although some of those that have completed a 1000-day term had previously been married before turning to the monastic way of life and becoming ordained) has to remain in the Hiei region for a total of twelve years, a period which includes preliminary training and preparation, and has to get the permission of the Tendai authorities before commencing. There can be no turning back, and a symbolic dagger and piece of rope are carried by the practitioner as a reminder that he should kill himself rather than give up. There is an implicit theme of death throughout the practice: like the pilgrim, the monk wears white robes to symbolise that he is dead to the mundane world, standing apart from it and ready and prepared to meet death at any step. Besides the white robes the practitioner's outfit includes a long, narrow hat woven from strips of *hinoki* wood:

it is not worn, except during rain, for the first 300 days of practice. He wears straw sandals, many pairs of which wear out in the course of walking, and may only wear *tabi*, traditional Japanese socks, after 300 days have been completed.

The 1000-day practice is basically an extension of the 100-day one, but lasts over a period of seven years. The major focus is on traversing a route through the forests and hills of Hiei every day for 100 days in a row, usually beginning in early spring, a time when there is still snow on the ground at the higher reaches of Hiei. There are two routes that may be followed: that which starts from the temple Mudō-ji is just under 35 kilometres long, and the other, far less frequently done, goes through the Imuro valley area of Hiei and is around 40 kilometres in length. The practitioner commences early in the morning, usually rising around midnight, performing a Buddhist service at the temple and then standing under a waterfall before setting out on the route. Along the way he stops to pray and chant *mantras* at 260 sites which cover the entire gamut of objects worshipped in Japan, from Buddhist temples and Shinto shrines to wayside stone Buddhas, trees, rocks and waterfalls, a graphic reflection both of the inclusiveness of the Japanese religious world and of its perceptions that all aspects of the physical world are settings for the existence of the spiritual. Usually the priest will return to his temple at some time in the morning (it takes six or seven hours to go around the route once the body has become hardened to it) and then has to take part in the normal cycle of temple activities, from performing rites at the temple to seeing and counselling visitors. Normally he will get to sleep around 9 p.m., and will live on sparse and simple food and a minimum of sleep. On one of the 100 days the practitioner will visit various religious sites in Kyoto on a 48-kilometre circuit known as the *kirimawari*, during which he will give blessings to people along the way, a first step in the process of transferring the powers and merits he attains to others.

This basic 100-day practice is, in the 1000-day setting, performed every spring for three years: in the fourth and fifth years it is extended to 200 days, starting in spring and ending in autumn. At the end of the second 200-day term, when he has completed 700 days, the ascetic enters the most stringent phase of all, the *dōiri* (literally, 'entering the hall'), a nine-day total fast in which he must abstain from food, water and sleep: he may not lie down either. This is the crux of the whole practice, a turning point when he will come close to death and after which the focus of the ascetic's practice is turned from himself to the benefit of others.

In the *dōiri* the monk is secluded in a Buddhist temple, and sits in the lotus posture in front of a statue of Fudō, reciting prayers and invocations as well as conducting Buddhist services. Two attendants stay with him to make sure he does not fall asleep. Each day, at 2 a.m., he leaves the hall to make a 200-metre journey to a well, where he draws water and carries it back to the temple to offer to Fudō. On this journey he is accompanied by several attendants who chant prayers such as the *Hannya Shingyō* and the *mantra* of Fudō. The journey may take only a few minutes on the first day, but by the last days, when the effects of fasting and sleeplessness have become intense, it may take 40 minutes or more.

It is common for people to gather at the temple during the night to offer support to the ascetic as he makes the increasingly arduous journey to the well: when, in October 1984, Sakai Yūsai did the *dōiri* for the second time (having completed one 1000-day period he had decided to do it again), I went to Hiei on three nights to witness the walk to the well, and noted that the numbers of people in attendance grew until perhaps 500 or so were present on the last night when he left the hall at 2 a.m. to draw water for the last time before the retreat ended (with a symbolic bowl of herb tea) a short while later. As the ascetic, by now emaciated and drawn, made his slow and painful progress between the temple and well, the crowd chanted along with his attendants. The whole area resonated with the sound of the prayers, and I was left with the feeling that everyone was willing him forward, seeking to give their strength to him in his austerity. Later, when he emerged, having completed the *dōiri*, people bowed to him and to the power he had acquired which would henceforth be directed back to them.

The ascetic confronts death, and in doing so throws off his former self and is reborn as an enlightened being, becoming one with Fudō. From this symbolic rebirth his practice should be devoted to the help of others. The *dōiri* takes place in the autumn of the fifth year, and in the following spring the ascetic embarks on a new round of 100 days, this time extending the walk to a route of 60 kilometres that takes up to fifteen hours to complete. In the seventh and final year he performs the *ōmawari*, a 84-kilometre route through Kyoto, during which he worships at various shrines and temples in the city and dispenses blessings to and prays for people along the way. This route may take eighteen or more hours to complete, and during this

100-day period the ascetic has to make do on virtually no sleep at all. The last 100 days revert to the original short course, after which the austerity is complete.

Most of those who have done the austerity do not undergo it again, although they have invariably continued to perform various ascetic disciplines and to use their spiritual prominence to further the cause of Buddhism. Hagami Shōchō, who completed the austerity in 1953 (and who had become a monk after the tragically young death of his wife), was a major religious activist who wrote books on Buddhism and travelled widely promoting religious understanding and peace, while Utsumi Shunshō, who completed it in 1979, runs a temple on Hiei and from time to time takes groups of interested lay people along the route and gives talks about the practice.

Sakai Yūsai, however, decided to perform the practice again and, even after his second completion, shows no inclination to give up the harsh disciplines of the ascetic life. He did not become a priest until he was almost 40 years old, after a rather drifting and unhappy life full of business failures, lost jobs and a tragic personal life in which his wife committed suicide. Eventually he turned, in his distress, to Hiei, becoming a novice monk and gradually undergoing various ascetic practices until determining to do the 1000-day practice. During it he was apparently, during the first four 100-day periods, beset by visions of his dead wife and of friends who died in the war, before these troubles fell away.[27]

The life of ascetic practice has suited him well, and he has stated on occasions that he does not ever wish to cease, for the religious path has no end. He has also remarked that this was the only thing he had been able to do properly in his life, and hence was something he ought not to cease. He remains perhaps the most widely known of all contemporary ascetics in Japan, cheerfully receiving the large numbers of people who come to him for advice or simply to talk, and telling everyone of his immense gratitude for the natural world around him. The austerities themselves are something to be grateful for, for they offer the path to true understanding: even the rain that hinders his progress at times is a cause for gratitude, for it means that the crops will grow and that people will have food to eat.[28]

Hiei is not the only place in Japan where such extreme austerities are found, although it is perhaps the most active and well known. The practice of long and absolute fasts may be found at Kinpusenji in Yoshino, where Gojō Junkyō completed a nine-day sleepless fast in 1974.[29] Versions of the 1000-day mountain practice are extant at several mountain centres including Yoshino and Kubote in Kyūshū, where in 1986 a *yamabushi* named Yamada Ryushin became the first person for 116 years to complete the austerity which involved ascending to the summit of Mount Kubote (a round trip of almost 30 kilometres) to perform offerings, as well as various stringent fasts.[30]

Many of these ascetics have written books on their experiences, and have used them, and their recent fame in Japan, to encourage others to heighten their own religiosity. This need not be in the severe manner of the trained ascetic, but may be of a type more readily accessible to the ordinary lay person. Yamada, for example, talks not only about the ascetic practices of religious specialists such as himself but also relates the concept of spiritual practice or training, *shugyō* to the world of the ordinary lay person. Yamada asserts that *shugyō* or spiritual practice is not something reserved for specialists, writing of it as accessible to lay people in the following terms:

> greeting the ancestors every morning and evening would be good [*shugyō*]. This means greeting the ancestors with words such as 'good morning' and 'good evening', just as you would greet family members with the same greetings. Spiritual practice [*shugyō*] is everywhere in life. . . . there are all sorts of *shugyō* that you can do without having to do such unreasonable things as emulate ascetics who pour water over themselves and fast. For instance, just carrying on quietly with your work is also a great spiritual practice.[31]

By placing spiritual practice and training directly in everyday life Yamada is clearly reiterating, in different terms, the basic Zen concept of enlightenment as an ordinary, everyday experience to be encountered in cleaning the floors as well as in meditation. Implicit in this statement is the idea that religiosity is not in any way divorced or separate from ordinary life but is an intrinsic part of it, accessible to all. This, again, is a strong reaffirmation of the fluid continuities of the Japanese religious world, providing a related means of action for everyone, whether it is the ascetic Yamada standing under waterfalls and ascending mountains, or the ordinary person carrying out his or her job with sincerity or greeting the ancestors correctly. It is also a further affirmation of the mediating role of the ascetic himself, acting as a means of directing the lay person into a religious awareness of his or her own life.

DIVINERS, MEDIUMS AND OTHERS

Besides such powerfully dynamic ascetic figures there are also countless other religious practitioners ranging from diviners to spirit mediums and shamanic healers, all of whom incorporate several of the themes of ascetic practice, often as a result of some affliction or calling, leading to the ability to mediate in some way between human beings and the spiritual world. This often involves the manifestation of a facility to predict the future, communicate with the spirits of the dead, or perhaps identify the spiritual cause of a problem or illness and eradicate it in some way.

It is unclear quite how many diviners, mediums and the like currently operate in Japan, nor how many people regularly seek their counsel, although it is clear that there is, at the very least, a sizeable minority who do so on a casual or regular basis. In its survey on the attitudes of its *danka* cited in Chapter 4, the Sōtō Zen sect asked how many of them visited *ogamiya-san*, faith-healers and practitioners of magical cures. Of the respondents 26 per cent had done so, and when all the interviewees were asked whether they believed what such figures said, 14 per cent responded 'yes', 11 per cent 'no', 19 per cent 'sometimes' and 54 per cent did not answer.[32] This at the very least represents a small but significant minority of people who do go to and take note of such figures outside the formal religious structure.

Often one can find in the areas around major religious centres numerous diviners and *ogamiya-san*. The streets leading to Ishikiri shrine in eastern Osaka are a good case in point, with many independent religious specialists with their own stalls or premises, offering to divine fortunes, predict the future, give counselling about siting the family grave or provide spiritual and occasionally herbal cures for maladies. Whenever I have been to this area, especially at weekends and public holidays, such practitioners appear to attract a good number of clients.

Some of these figures do little more than seek to divine the future, while others lay claim to greater powers, often of the level of those that have established new religions. Indeed, besides the larger new religions of Japan there are countless other small-scale religious groups, usually gathered around one figure of power who caters to the needs of a small following. A recent popular book entitled *Nihon no reinōryokusha* ('People with Spiritual Power in Japan'), which outlines the biographies of nineteen religious figures who are active in Japan today, is but one of a number of recent books drawing attention to such figures, and it indicates clearly how they are as likely to be found in the hearts of the major cities as in the mountains, for many of those profiled operate in urban centres such as Tokyo and Osaka. While they all have small groups of regular followers they are also actively concerned with dealing with people on a more casual and need-orientated basis.[33]

This is the case also with the *itako* of Osorezan, a group of blind female mediums who are widely known for contacting and relaying words and messages from the spirits of the dead in seance-like rites. The *itako* deserve mention here not just because they incorporate many of the elements that have been discussed so far but also because they have become extremely well known in Japan, as much as anything because they represent the last and dying vestiges of a shamanic tradition that once was very strong in northern Japan. Their first qualification for undergoing the training that is needed to become a medium is their blindness, which marks them out (or selects them) for this role, but they also need to have a long period of arduous ascetic training involving a long apprenticeship to another medium, during which they learn the techniques of summoning the spirits of the dead and undergo long periods of intense asceticism, especially of cold-water ablutions, which hone their abilities to do this.

Osorezan, which is located at the very northern tip of the main island of Honshū, is a wild and desolate mountainous and volcanic area of hot springs and barren rocks with sulphur fumes seeping out of the ground. In Japanese folklore it has long been regarded as a place where the souls of the dead may return to earth to be contacted by the living, a view clearly endorsed by its eery atmosphere which readily conveys an other-worldly impression. Especially during the two festivals for the dead held there each summer, at which the *itako* gather, it is a place of great activity. Besides the *itako* there is a Buddhist temple run by priests of the Sōtō sect, at which memorial services may be said for the souls of the dead. Every summer busloads of visitors make the journey there for such a purpose, consulting the *itako* to find out what the dead require in terms of offerings, memorials and the like, and what they have to say to the living, and going to the Buddhist temple to carry out the requisite memorials and to acquire talismans dedicated to the dead from the Buddhist priests who here, as elsewhere, are the agency for dealing with and memorialising the dead. This is an interesting example of how the established and popular folkloric traditions may interact and exist in tandem: people visit the *itako* and the temple as two interlocking parts of the process of contacting, finding out the needs of and memorialising the dead.

The established tradition, on the surface at least, appears to distance itself from this interaction and from the *itako*, who are seen through official eyes as representing something akin to superstition: one might also suggest that their supposed abilities to communicate directly with the dead pose an implicit threat to the role of the Buddhist priests, who may find themselves carrying out formalised rites on behalf of the dead as a result of what the *itako* have said. A notice at the temple informs people that the *itako* have been allowed to use the temple grounds during the festival because of tradition and historical circumstances, and that they really have nothing to do with the temple and its practices. However, the notice, at least in 1981 when I saw it, was small and placed in a dark corner where few would notice it. Official disapproval fades into the background when confronted with popular reality and with the ways that people utilise both the formal and informal religious traditions as a coherent whole. In reality, the two, temple and *itako*, are linked together in the practices of those who visit Osorezan.

It is clear that the *itako* depend less on personal power than on the processes of theatrical drama. When approached to contact a dead person's spirit the *itako* go through a standardised ritual of chanting, rattling their long rosaries and relaying messages from the dead in a rather formalised response. Although it is generally considered that they are generally following a rather formatted procedure (as Blacker has pointed out, the questions and answers they give are somewhat standardised[34]), when the theatrical nature of their performance is set against the background of the rather exotic atmosphere of Osorezan and placed in conjunction with the emotional states of some of those who call on them, they clearly make some form of impact. When I was at Osorezan in 1981 I was struck by the numbers of people who managed to find meaning in what the *itako* were 'relaying' to them from their dead relatives, and recall more than one person in tears at what was said, although it should also be mentioned that I also met people there who affirmed that they had seen little more than a ritualised drama. Performance in itself is, of course, a form of therapy, and the drama of the rite, with its rattling of rosaries, its chants and its rather exotic performers, was enough to satisfy most, if not all, of those who called on their services. The *itako*, at least symbolically and in the minds of those who visit them, act as bridges and mediators between this and other worlds, thus acting in much the same way as other religious figures already encountered in this chapter.

NOSTALGIA, REVIVAL AND THE IMAGES OF ASCETICISM

The *itako* represent a rather faded and almost extinct form of spirit mediumship in Japan. Indeed, it is probably as much as anything because these are the last vestiges of what was once a far stronger tradition that they continue to attract a large amount of attention. The busloads of people who go to Osorezan are evidence of this: a recent estimate suggested as many as 100,000 people now visit Osorezan during the two festivals each year.[35] There is, in general, a great amount of interest in all forms of asceticism and figures of power in Japan today. Books such as *Nihon no reinōryokusha*, mentioned above, can be found in large numbers in Japanese bookshops, while the numbers of people visiting Osorezan, turning to the charismatic leaders of new religions or showing an interest in the performances of the ascetics of Mount Hiei, are indications that the highly motivated and driven individual religious figure remains, even in the midst of modernisation and the changing patterns of Japanese society, a figure of significance and interest. The ascetic and individual religious traditions of Japan with their deep roots in Japanese religious history and their emphasis on harsh physical austerities as a means of attaining awakening and spiritual powers to be used for the benefit of others have not been displaced by modernity and contemporary change. In fact they have probably been stimulated and encouraged by them: certainly the development of the modern media has helped make their practices and messages more widely known than ever.

   The interest that is displayed in asceticism is often tinged with nostalgic nuances, chiefly because such asceticism and the underlying concepts it involves represent a vital part of Japanese cultural history and because they thus represent the idea of a strongly rooted and continuing sense of tradition, of cultural roots and hence of identity in a society and age that continues to undergo rapid changes. Thus one full length film shown widely in Japan in the mid-1980s, which was entitled *Yomigaeru: Tōtō* (with the English sub-title 'The Eastern Pagoda-Phoenix of Mount Hiei'), focused on two events: the rebuilding of one of the pagodas of the temple in traditional style using no modern materials, and the performance of the 1000-day practice by Utsumi Shunshō. The juxtaposition of these traditional images, especially of the ascetic clothed in traditional white against the modernised background of contemporary Japan, was used to great effect to suggest that somehow the former, representing the traditional, held more depth than the latter with its inherent modernity, and to impart the message of implicit revival inherent in the film's title. Two commentators on the film reflected these nuances with similar remarks in a booklet published to accompany the film: the Buddhist academic Nakamura Hajime wrote that the film should be sub-titled 'the revival of the Japanese spirit', and Matsumoto Kenichi stated that the ethos of Japan was to be found in the traditional form of the ascetic and his white robes rather than in the westernised background against which he stood.[36]

The nostalgic feelings expressed here are elements in a wider and more general revival of interest in traditionalism in contemporary Japan, a revival that of necessity must be seen in relation to the rapid tides of modernisation and the intrusion of Western influences in Japan. These again are issues that will be commented on more fully later in this book. What is of interest in relationship to the present chapter is the ways in which both Nakamura and Matsumoto projected their views and feelings on to and through the figure of the ascetic who thus, in his practice, becomes more than a medium through whom power may be disseminated. In performing his *gyō* he comes to represent, and even be a substitute for, the wishes, feelings and needs of others. In acting out his own struggle for awareness he becomes a vessel and a means through which others may reflect and project their own feelings and emotions. This is further affirmation of the ways in which the individual religious practitioner, in the very act of standing apart from and following a way of life that is antithetical to the normal, remains at heart an intensely social being, pointing the way to self-expression and individuality while mediating the qualities thereby attained to others. This not only reiterates many of the basic themes of individual practice discussed at the beginning of this chapter, but shows the extent to which these themes, so basic to Japanese religious history, continue to be alive and relevant in Japanese society today.

6 Sites and Sights: Temples and Shrines as Centres of Power and Entertainment

There are enormous numbers of shrines and temples in Japan: some are primarily local community shrines or temples for memorialising the ancestors, yet others extend their influence beyond the environs of their local community. Many of the religious centres that permeate Japan's landscape have widespread reputations as locations and centres of religious power, and as arenas at and through which the spiritual world and power of the *kami*, Buddhas and other entities may be contacted, encountered and assimilated for human benefit. Often there is a link here to the powerful individuals and ascetic figures discussed in the previous chapter, for the reputations of many of these religious centres are founded in oracles, omens, stories of miraculous events and transcendent deeds that centre on or are attributed to ascetic wanderers and sages of the distant past. When, as is common, these are aligned to such additional factors as a beautiful physical setting, fine architecture and good transport access they become magnets drawing in large crowds.

Many religious centres, besides providing a setting in which Japanese people can express their individual volition in religious terms, are also well-known tourist attractions. Indeed, it is more likely than not that visitors to Japan will find themselves being encouraged to go to various famous shrines and temples, especially in the great tourist centres of Kyoto, Kamakura and Nara, by their guidebooks, by Japanese tourist organisations and by their Japanese friends. Travelling further afield the picture is no different, with every region and local tourist office drawing attention to the famous, scenic and culturally rich shrines and temples of the area. It is much the same for the Japanese as well: throughout Japan shrines and temples form an intrinsic part of the tourist route. Famed religious institutions such as Tokyo's Sensōji temple (better known as Asakusa Kannon) with its crowded street-markets and frenetic activity, the great Shinto shrines at Ise with their simple yet refined architecture, Kyoto's Kiyomizu temple propped on massive supports over a ravine, Risshakuji, better known simply as Yama-dera ('mountain temple'), which hovers along the sides of a mountain in Yamagata prefecture in northern Japan, the huge Buddhist temple Shinshōji, a mecca of popular religious activities at Narita near Tokyo's international airport, and the resplendent shrines and temples of Nachi in the Kii peninsula, surrounded by deep mountains, still forests, rushing streams and the roaring power of Japan's highest waterfall, are but a few of the myriad religious centres that have for centuries drawn vast crowds of Japanese visitors seeking out their own country's famous sights and praying to the *kami* and Buddhas.

Visiting such places today one is liable to be swept up in a swirl of activity amidst crowds of people jostling alongside bus parties of Japanese led by whistle-blowing guides, groups of pilgrims dressed in white and chanting the *Hannya Shingyō* in unison, and swarms of black-uniformed schoolboys and girls, especially in Kyoto, on their statutory school trips designed to instil in them some awareness of Japanese culture and history. Thrust into a confusing array of sounds, sights, smells and other stimuli, the visitor passes by ferocious and glaring statues at temple gates or through brightly coloured shrine gateways and by purificatory water fountains to be enveloped in swirling clouds of incense smoke and the cacophonous noise of ringing bells, clapping hands, coins rattling as they are tossed loudly into offertory boxes, and discordant sounds of intermingled laughter and chanting.

No doubt the visitor will quickly become aware of the immense array of tangible objects to worship and enter into a relationship with: most shrines and temples are not single places of worship but complexes encompassing numerous halls enshrining a variety of *kami* or Buddhas as well as trees, rocks and other natural phenomena demarcated with Shinto regalia to denote the presence of a *kami* or with various offerings placed at them to imply the presence of some spiritual entity or other. Buddhist temples may also have rows of stone statues depicting various figures from the Buddhist pantheon as well as little shrines for the local guardian *kami*. There will normally also be a large array of talismans, amulets and trinkets of all shapes and sizes on sale, all apparently promising good luck or protection from misfortune and sold by a shrine maiden, robed Buddhist or Shinto prelate or lay helper. The ways that people relate to all these objects, and to the whole arena in general, may appear bewilderingly complex if not downright chaotic. Certainly there will be an immense amount of variation, from those who dutifully wash their hands and mouths in purification and offer coins and possibly items of food while bowing and praying reverently at all the sub-shrines or statues, to those who appear to select a few objects for reverence, to those who rush past the purificatory water and the objects of worship to bring out their picnic lunches while chattering noisily, laughing and giving the air of having a good day out.

Some visitors might also be struck by the seemingly undifferentiated admixture of religious and commercial motifs. Often the temples and shrines themselves are surrounded by a web of commercial enterprises from souvenir shops to restaurants catering to every need and providing visitors with food, trinkets and various items of religious paraphernalia from incense holders to books of Buddhist texts and even cartoon books about various *kami* and Buddhas. This religious/commercial mixture might appear even more intense if one were to go to one of the famous shrine or temple fairs, such as those held at Osaka's Shitennōji temple, Nagoya's Nittaiji or Kyoto's Tōji, all on the 21st of each month, or at Kyoto's Kitano Tenmangū shrine on the 25th. At these times the streets around and the precincts of these religious centres become a mass of stalls selling everything from antiques to old clothes and bowls of noodles. One may note, too, that the crowds there appear to combine with ease praying, shopping for bargains and having a good day out, a fair indication of the close and overlapping bonds between ludic, economic and religious modes of behaviour.

Although the above outline is certainly impressionistic, based on a pastiche of experiences and images that I have gleaned from several years of avid temple and shrine visiting, it has been given in order to convey some of the atmosphere of religious centres in Japan and to serve as a preliminary introduction to some of the things that may occur there. This chapter and the next will attempt to provide some meaning to these impressions in such a way as to both provide further understandings of the Japanese religious world and to give some insights into the meanings behind the things and actions seen at such centres. In this chapter I shall be concerned with why certain places have come to be regarded as powerful and famous, how they are so demarcated as holy, what motivates people to visit them, and some of the things they may do at them: in the next I shall look at how the merits and powers of the temples are accessed by visitors and will discuss the underlying meanings of the requests they make and the talismans and trinkets they acquire there. Taken together it is hoped that these chapters, besides providing another angle on the Japanese religious world in general, may help those who visit shrines and temples in Japan to acquire some understanding of what they might see there.

POWER, PLACE AND DEMARCATIONS OF THE HOLY

As was noted in Chapter 2, the entire geography of Japan is laden with markers indicating the presence of the spiritual world, with temples and shrines on mountains and in the heart of red-light districts, and statues on mountain passes and department-store roofs. This omnipresence reflects both the notions implicit in early Japanese folk religion and expressed in Shinto and its myths that the whole of Japan is the abode of innumerable *kami*, and Buddhist ideas that since the Buddhas are all-pervasive they may manifest themselves at any time or place, and that since enlightenment itself is rooted in life, each and every place is inherently a potential setting for its realisation and manifestation. Potentially, then, everywhere is, or may be, the grounding of and a place of contact with the spiritual world that exists in direct and close relationship with the present world.

This is an important consideration in viewing the nature of temples and shrines as centres of religious power for it implicitly means that it is not the building and consecration of a religious institution that sacralises a place and marks it out as a holy arena. Rather, the religious institution has been built because some sign or incident has occurred to convince people that the place in question has manifested its potential as a setting for the spiritual and hence is able to stand out as somewhere special and beyond the ordinary. The institution is thus an acknowledgement and a recognition of the special nature of the location. Because one place is so designated it does not preclude others in the near vicinity from also being recognised in a similar way and often, in fact, one finds such places in clusters, for one overt expression of the spiritual in the physical world is an indication that others may occur close at hand. Such is the case with the proliferation of major shrines and temples in Kyoto and the complex of religious centres at Nachi, where the Nachi falls, demarcated as a Shinto shrine yet traditionally identified in Buddhist and Shugendō eyes with Kannon, stands close by a major Buddhist temple and another important Shinto shrine, all of which have their own legendary founding stories replete with miraculous happenings.

Temples and shrines thus may be seen as locations at which spiritual power, usually manifested by the *kami* and Buddhas, may emerge into this world in such ways as to be accessible, either mediated through statues, prayers, priests and rituals, or by direct supplication, to all and sundry. In this respect as centres and gateways to power there is little if no differentiation between shrines and temples, and similar, overlapping motifs and activities are found at both.[1] Both are demarcated as special gateways to power by a sign, or series of signs, that mark out the religious centre from the surrounding area and signify to all who enter that they are moving from the ordinary world into something special, into the powerful presence of the spiritual realms.

Especially outside urban areas, the approaches to shrines and temples may be signified by rows of small shrines and statues as well as by avenues of high trees, all of which help to confer a special presence on the place. Even in the midst of cities this sense of transition may be transmitted, with the streets before shrines and temples crowded with not just small shrines, statues and other religious symbols, but with souvenir shops, restaurants and throngs of people, all testifying to the interwoven nature of religious and commercial themes to be found around all major centres.

One of the most familiar sights in Japan is the *torii* or traditional Shinto gateway consisting of two pillars with two crossbeams at the top, sometimes built in grey concrete but more commonly of wood painted a resplendent vermilion, a colour manifesting the sense of brightness and life always associated with Shinto. *Torii* stand before shrines, often straddling the roads leading up to them, to inform all visitors that they are entering the realms of the holy and the presence of the *kami*. Often there may be more than one *torii* before the shrine, as is the case with the Heian shrine in Kyoto whose huge *torii* on the roads before it denote a gradually increasing proximity to the *kami* prior to entering the main gateway that takes one into the precincts of the shrine itself. *Torii* may also be found inside shrine and temple complexes in front of subsidiary shrines within the precincts: they may sometimes be arrayed close together, especially before shrines dedicated to Inari, for the donation of *torii* as votive gifts accompanying a request or as gratitude for help provided by the *kami* is a common practice, often done by companies and organisations as much as by private individuals. The most prominent example of this practice can be seen at Fushimi Inari in Kyoto where, behind the main hall of worship, a series of paths go up the hillside, linking together a series of subsidiary shrines: the path is lined with thousands of *torii* (shrine estimates suggest there are at least 10,000 of them) placed so close together that they form what is virtually a covered walkway. Similar, if shorter, avenues of *torii* may be seen inside Buddhist temples as well: at Chōgosonshiji, a popular temple at the southern crest of the Ikoma hills near Osaka, the temple complex contains two such avenues, one containing over 100 and the other over 700 *torii*, each leading to shrines (neither connected to Inari) within the temple grounds.

The Buddhist counterpart of the *torii* is the *sanmon* or *niōmon*, a gateway usually two storeys high with a tiled roof and enclosures on either side in which stand two *niō*, celestial guardians whose ferocious faces symbolically ward off evil and warn all who enter to do so with a pure mind. Usually the *niōmon* is slightly elevated, making one go up a few steps to pass through it in a symbolic ascent to the realms of the holy. One can see examples of this type within the confines of cities such as Kyoto as well as in the mountains beyond: the great gate of Chionin, a Pure Land temple in eastern Kyoto much visited by worshippers and tourists, stands atop a steep flight of steps and appears to hover over the visitor and convey a sense of imposing grandeur.

In architectural terms it is a general rule of thumb that a *torii* signifies a shrine and a *niōmon* a temple, but as in all matters concerning the relationship of Shinto and Buddhism, the centuries of constant interpenetration have led to some fusions in styles that mean it is not always possible to differentiate, especially from outside, between the two. The gateway of Yasaka shrine in Kyoto, for example, standing atop a short flight of steps, looks like a *niōmon* from a distance, and it is not until one comes closer that one realises that its guardians are Shinto warriors rather than ferocious Buddhist *niō*. Buddhist temples can be even more confusing for they invariably contain one or more *torii* in their precincts to signify the guardian *kami* of the site, and sometimes may even have a *torii* at their entrance. Chōgosonshiji has both a *niōmon* and several *torii* along its approaches, although most of those who arrive by car, bus and funicular railway now do not pass through the *niōmon*: the car parks and the path from the railway station give access directly to the temple through the *torii*.

The motif of purification so conspicuous throughout the Japanese religious world is strongly in evidence in this transition from the everyday to the holy. Water, so prevalent in Shinto rites as a potent symbol of purity and life, is a constant factor, used to wash away the pollutions and evils accruing to visitors so that they may greet the *kami* (and the Buddhas) in a state of ritual and mental purity. Often, especially with shrines, one may cross a small bridge over a stream whose water thus symbolically washes away the impurities and evils from those who traverse it. Examples of this motif may be seen at both the Outer and Inner shrines of Ise and, in a Buddhist context, at the entrance that leads up, through a kilometre-long avenue of high trees and graves, to Kōbō Daishi's mausoleum at Kōyasan. Virtually all shrines, and large numbers of temples besides, have a *temizuya*, a place for ablutions, usually a fountain of running water, perhaps issuing from the mouth of a bronze dragon or from a bamboo water spout, so that those who wish to do so may rinse out their mouths, clean their hands and further purify themselves. At temples the purificatory motif is often reinforced both by the ferocious stares of the *niō* and by incense burners at which one may light sticks of incense as offerings, waving the smoke over oneself in a ritual gesture of purification.

Within the precincts also are numerous objects that illustrate the presence of the spiritual world: thus a large Buddhist temple may have several sub-temples, each enshrining Buddhas offering specific forms of benefit to those who pray to them and make offerings there, as well as many, perhaps hundreds, of statues of all sorts scattered throughout the temple compound. Equally a major shrine will contain all manner of holy symbols, from ropes tied around trees to denote their holiness, to numerous sub-shrines and images of animals who act either as guardians or messengers of the *kami*: the presence of an Inari shrine may be indicated by statues of the fox who is this deity's messenger, while it is common to see a pair of stone animals, one a lion, the other a dog, sitting guard in the precincts to protect the *kami*.

All these symbols and objects are indicators of the special nature of the place, a setting in which unusual concentrations of power have shown through and been manifested in the physical world. The processes whereby such places have become so recognised and hence marked out from the rest of the (potentially holy) world around them are generally complex, involving a mixture of factors from popular legends that often incorporate various extraordinary

events and happenings, oracles, miracles, and the deeds of holy
wanderers and ascetics, to the support of powerful patrons such as
emperors and great historical figures, and the confluence of economic and touristic factors. All of these will come under scrutiny in
this chapter, but first I shall look at the founding stories on which
the recognition of the presence of the holy, and hence its resultant
development as a site, is based.

LEGENDS, MIRACLES AND THE DEVELOPMENT OF POPULAR LORE

Most temples and shrines have their own *engi* or foundation stories
that generally involve stirring accounts of miracles, messages and
oracles transmitted from the *kami* and interpreted by empowered
individuals, along with dramatic events involving the deeds of
powerful individuals, manifestations of Buddha figures, apparitions
and messages transmitted in dreams, and other such phenomena.[2]
These frequently involve some of the most famous figures in
Japanese religious history such as Kōbō Daishi and Shōtoku Taishi,
the sixth-century prince widely revered for his Buddhist learning:
countless temples throughout Japan attribute their founding in some
form to one of these figures who thus, because of their great fame as
religious leaders, serve to legitimate the site and provide it with
religious validity. Accordingly, there is clearly a degree of fiction
involved in *engi*: indeed, since the possession of a good, rousing *engi*
acted as a vital factor in transmitting to others the impression that a
particular site was special, thus promoting its development as a holy
centre while simultaneously serving as a mode of teaching that
informed worshippers of the powers of the *kami* and Buddhas that
could be encountered there, it is not surprising that the creation and
narration of *engi*, usually by those concerned with developing the
shrines and temples themselves, came to be something of an art
form in itself. It would, however, be wrong to regard them as just
fiction for, as manifestations and explanations of a world view that
accepts the potential presence of the spiritual directly in this world
and recognises the immanence of religious experience and of the
intercessionary powers of the gifted individual figures that related
them, they are projections of implicit religious views and meanings.
They are often also expansions of a core of events surrounding the
founding of the site, perhaps projected on to a major figure such as

Kōbō Daishi for the sake of legitimation, and embellished and related with artistic licence so as to transform such events on to a miraculous plane and intensify the importance of the site, thus drawing more people to it and into a relationship with the *kami* and Buddhas.

In order to give a perspective on the themes involved in *engi* and to show how these can contribute to the importance of a site, I shall briefly outline four *engi* here. The first is the story of the origin of the famous Kiyomizudera in Kyoto, founded by the priest Enchin whose dream in 780 of a spring of pure water (Kiyomizudera means 'temple of pure water') led him to set out from Nara to seek its source. Reaching the valley where the temple now is he recognised it as the site of his dream and, establishing a hermitage by the spring, carved a figure of Kannon from a piece of wood received from another hermit in the area and enshrined it there. His meditations were interrupted when Sakanoue Tamuramaro, a powerful military figure, came hunting a deer for his pregnant wife: the blood of a freshly killed deer was then widely believed to be a magical potion that facilitated easy childbirth. Enchin, admonishing him for taking life, preached the mercies of Kannon, and instilled such remorse in the warrior that he became devoted to Kannon and built a temple there, which became Kiyomizudera.[3]

The establishment of the city of Kyoto in 794 not only drew more and more people to this site but led to the development of other religious institutions in the region, such as the shrine Iwashimizu Hachimangū atop Otokoyama at Yawata a few miles south-west of the city. Here again there was a spring of pure water from the rocks (the name Iwashimizu means 'pure water from the rock') which was marked by a shrine, and this appeared especially propitious as the south-west was, in the Taoist geomancy then highly regarded by the court, an unlucky direction from which misfortunes were likely to come. Consequently the shrine came to be seen as a protector of the capital, warding off the evil spirits and bad fortunes that might otherwise come. In 859 the Buddhist priest Gyōkyō of Nara visited the main shrine of the powerful *kami* Hachiman, who was closely associated, as the spirit of the former Emperor Ōjin, with the Imperial family, at Usa in Kyushu, and the *kami* expressed to him, and hence to the Imperial family, through an oracle the wish that a shrine be built for him at Otokoyama, from whence Hachiman could more readily pacify the land, guard the capital and be venerated by the Emperor and court. This message from the *kami* (incidentally transmitted by a Buddhist priest, a sure indication of the degree to which the two traditions were intertwined) led the Emperor Seiwa to build a new and magnificent shrine to Hachiman on the peak of Otokoyama, to which the Imperial family could easily go to venerate their ancestor Hachiman and which was a suitably powerful protector for the city. The shrine remains prominent to this day, and a representative from the Imperial Household visits the shrine at its main annual festival every 15 September to pay homage to the *kami*.[4] From the ninth century onwards the Buddhist temple Enryakuji, established by the monk Saichō at the peak of Mount Hiei, where he had spent several years performing austerities, also became a protector of the capital, for Hiei stands to the north-east of Kyoto, the other major unlucky direction, and hence the two institutions, one a Buddhist temple, the other a Shinto shrine, came to function in tandem to guard the city.

My third example concerns the temple Enkyōji on Mount Shosha outside the town of Himeji in western Japan. This famous pilgrimage site is, like Kiyomizudera, one of the 33 temples on the Saikoku pilgrimage route and draws visitors and pilgrims from far and wide. Its founder was a tenth-century ascetic named Shōkū who, in the temple *engi*, saw during his ascetic wanderings a purple cloud which seemed to float in front of him. He followed it and it led him to Mount Shosha, where it stopped: Shōkū took this as an omen that he should build a hermitage on the mountain and so began to practise austerities there. During these he had a vision that convinced him that one of the trees on the mountain was a dwelling place of Kannon and this inspired him to carve a statue of Kannon from the tree and to worship it. Gradually word of Shōkū's powers as an ascetic began to spread far and wide, and this led to a growing tide of visitors who came to pay homage to him and to the statue. The end result was the establishment of the temple Enkyōji as a centre of popular worship and as a site on the Saikoku route which is focused on the veneration of Kannon.[5]

The last and most complex example is from the temple Shinshōji at Narita, popularly known as Narita-san (the suffix *san* means 'mountain' and is frequently used in the names of religious centres, especially temples, even when, as with Narita-san, they may be located not on a mountain but in the plains). This *engi* starts with an attempted insurrection by the ex-Emperor Heizei in 810. As part of the campaign against this rebellion the monk Kūkai (referred to in the *engi* as Kōbō Daishi) was asked to carve a statue of the Buddha figure Fudō and perform a *goma* (fire) ritual before it to seek Fudō's help in subduing the uprising, thus bringing the spiritual realms into play to help solve a political and military issue. He did so, and performed the *kaigen* (eye-opening rite to empower the statue) as well as *goma* rites to help the Imperial forces, at Takaosanji near Kyoto: after the defeat of the rebellion, the statue and the temple were regarded as special protectors of the state.

Over a century later, in 940, in the reign of Emperor Tengyō, a subsequent uprising led by Taira Masakado took place in the Kantō region east of present-day Tokyo, and a force was sent from the then capital Kyoto to quell it. Along with the troops went the priest Kanjō, who carried the image of Fudō carved by Kōbō Daishi as a talisman of support. On arriving in the region he erected an altar and performed a *goma* rite praying for Fudō's aid and for the defeat of the rebels. When the rebellion had been quelled and the region pacified, Kanjō, along with the victorious troops, prepared to return to Kyoto, but the statue, although small and light, could not be lifted. Instead, an image of Fudō appeared and spoke to Kanjō, expressing Fudō's wish to remain there to protect the people of the region and to ensure continuing peace. Kanjō returned to Kyoto to report this news to the Emperor who commanded that a temple be built in the Kantō region to house the image.[6]

This temple, Shinshōji (the name means 'temple of the newly won victory'), has ever since been a major centre of religious power, drawing large numbers of worshippers who seek Fudō's power, grace and protection. The power of the Narita Fudō has subsequently been spread throughout Japan via a whole series of Narita-san branch temples, one of which is the Kōrien Narita-san temple near Osaka from whence come the protective amulets carried on trains and buses of the Keihan Railway Company. The temple was sacralised in 1934, using a replica of the original Fudō carved by Kōbō Daishi as its main image so as to make the power of this Fudō accessible to the people of this region: in fact, there are now Narita-san branch temples throughout Japan. The replica was empowered through rituals performed by priests of the temple following forms of practice originally established by Kūkai when he established Shingon Buddhism, to which the Narita-san temples belong, in Japan in the ninth century. Through these rituals the innate powers of the original statue (which is regarded as Fudō incarnate) are symbolically extended to the replica, which in turn is sacralised and transformed, becoming Fudō just as had the original. The statue itself is considered to be a *bunshin* (literally, offshoot) or *bunrei* (spiritual offshoot) of the original, and this process whereby an original statue gives birth, as it were, to an offshoot while continuing to retain its own power is very much the same as that through which the various amulets and talismans distributed by shrines and temples are sacralised, an issue to which I shall return in the next chapter.

The statue was then brought to the Osaka region and installed in a temple there, with the Keihan Railway Company providing the means of transport and the major financial backing for it. The area where the temple was sited was to the north-east, the primary unlucky direction or *kimon* ('devil's gate'), of Osaka: consequently the temple has come to be seen as the protector of the city. In addition, because of this unlucky geomantic position the area where the temple is now sited was at the time sparsely populated. According to sources at the temple, the Keihan Company (which had substantial property as well as transport interests) hoped that the siting of the temple there would help eradicate the general reticence of people to live in what was seen as an unlucky area. It is probably because of the increased urbanisation and pressure on the land that the region has turned into a densely populated commuter area since the war, but none the less the Keihan Company has benefited from this, both from its real-estate interests in the area and from the increasing numbers of commuters who use its trains and buses. The continuing links between the temple and company are shown not just by the talismans in the trains and buses or by the company memorial services held at the temple (see p. 74) but by the announcements made on every train as it enters Kōrien station, informing prospective visitors to alight there for the temple.[7]

In all the *engi* cited here one can see the importance of individual figures of power: Gyōkyō through the oracle, Enchin, Shōkū and Kōbō Daishi play major roles in creating the holy site. Enchin recognises, in his dream, the special nature of the place through its natural qualities (the fountain of water), as did those unnamed people who first saw, in its spring of water, the essence of holiness at Otokoyama that was later ratified by Hachiman through Gyōkyō. Enchin's powerful vision and asceticism in selecting the site of Kiyomizudera is reinforced by Kannon's compassion that leads Tamuramaro to repent of his ways and build a temple, while Shōkū's oracular vision of the cloud leads him to see the holiness inherent in Shosha and to realise Kannon's immanence there, from which derives Enkyōji's continuing popularity as a centre of Kannon worship and pilgrimage.

The root source of the power of the Narita temples is also located in the world of individual practitioners. While the statue of Fudō 'chose' the site of the present temple and subsequently sacralised further sites through its offshoots, it was through the spiritual power of Kōbō Daishi and the rituals he performed that the power was generated in the first place, transforming the statue from what was originally just a piece of perhaps artistically carved wood into something else entirely, the actual embodiment and manifestation of Fudō.

Engi provide shrines and temples with foundation stories or myths rooted in the miraculous that legitimate their foundation and show that the site they stand on is especially marked out as a centre of power. They also simultaneously help to attract the patronage needed to make a place into a major institution: it was Emperor Tengyō, grateful for the suppression of the 940 revolt, who established Shinshōji, and the patronage of Emperor Seiwa that turned the shrine at Otokoyama into a major centre. It may be a reflection of the underlying continuities of religion in Japan that the institution patronised in the tenth century by Emperor Tengyō has spawned a twentieth-century branch temple under the patronage of a modern business enterprise that has in its way sought and received the help of that temple and its figure of worship just as the Emperor did a millenium before. In both cases this patronage has served to draw people to the temples, the earlier one through the prestige of association with the Imperial court and the later, perhaps more mundanely, through the publicity of the company itself.

In each case such associations have helped spread the oral lore that is a vital aspect in the development of a temple or shrine's reputation. The continuing and vibrant nature of popular lore, originating in the tales and promises of intercessionary power and miracle contained in the *engi*, creates reputations and assigns powers, often for specific forms of *riyaku*, and hence is a constant dynamic creating and reinforcing the reputations and statuses of shrines and temples. Shrine and temple visitors continue to pass on to each other stories of the powers and benefits of different places: thus, one will be told that a certain shrine, temple, Buddha or *kami* is particularly efficacious for prayers and requests for, say, helping one pass examinations or avoid road accidents.

In such respects it is clear that the *engi* and oral lore point not just to the special nature of the place and to the holy power enshrined there, but to a special conjunction of the two. Kannon and Fudō are, in Buddhist terms, universal figures who can manifest anywhere and spread their *riyaku* anywhere, and Hachiman is a powerful *kami* with shrines all over Japan, yet what is often especially relevant in terms of their popular fame is their special relationship to the site at which they occur. One talks of the *Narita-san* Fudō, the *Enkyōji* Kannon and the *Iwashimizu* Hachiman. These are not terms of limitation, for their power remains ubiquitous, but of nature, implying an unique configuration of potency between the spiritual entity and the special place of manifestation. Where this configuration and conjunction occurs one is liable to see the development of major popular power centres.

Temples and shrines have an obvious and vested interest in the promotion of such oral lore, for this helps bring people through their gates. Thus visitors to religious centres may well be confronted by signs and pamphlets published by the institutions that highlight the various forms of *riyaku* of the spiritual beings enshrined therein. Some may go further still, placing advertisements in newspapers, especially before festivals and special prayer days, and on trains, buses and in other public places.[8] The media in general have actively reinforced these processes: newspapers often carry articles about popular religious centres, while guidebooks to temples, shrines and the *riyaku* they offer are published with some regularity. Thus we find the *Fuku o yobu jisha jiten* ('Dictionary of Shrines and Temples that Summon Good Fortune'), published by one of Japan's major publishers, Kōdansha, which is divided into sections covering everything from educational success and promotion inside one's company to the preservation of good health, traffic safety and the conception of babies, with relevant shrines and temples for each of these on a regional basis.[9]

The categorisation of *riyaku* into types, coupled with the acquired reputations of certain places for specific forms of *riyaku*, serves to create a bond and a link between certain religious sites and special-interest groups and trades. Sumiyoshi shrine in Osaka is a popular place for prayers for *riyaku* of all sorts, but its reputation as a protector of the city's business prosperity has forged a bond between it and the city's merchants, shopkeepers and traders who go there to pray for continued business success. Hōzanji, a temple in the Ikoma hills which enshrines Kankiten, a deity noted for production, fertility and prosperity, is another place closely associated with the businessmen, traders and merchants of Osaka, many of whom make a *hatsumōde* visit there to seek Kankiten's help in the coming year. There are many shrines and temples, notably the Narita-san temples, associated with travel safety that receive the prayers and attention of those in the transport industry and of car drivers in particular, while those involved in education may particularly visit Tenjin shrines, or temples dedicated to Monju, a Buddha of wisdom and learning.

Young lovers and those seeking marital partners may be drawn to one or more of the many shrines and temples associated with *ryōen* (making good marriages) and *enmusubi* (linking two people together as a couple). In the former, a person of marriageable age (or more likely still, the parents) will beseech the *kami* or Buddhas to help them find a suitable partner, while in the latter, those who already have their eyes on someone will pray for help in cementing the union or bringing it about. Couples may also visit such places together to make pledges of *enmusubi* as a signal of their determination to make their relationship last. Izumo shrine in Shimane prefecture, one of the most ancient and important Shinto centres in Japan, is one of the most popular shrines in Japan for such prayers, attracting especially young women and worried parents seeking to find them a husband, for prominent among the powers of its *kami* is the *riyaku* of *ryōen*. Another shrine well known both for *ryōen* and *enmusubi* is Jishu shrine, in the precincts of Kiyomizudera in Kyoto: set behind the main hall of the temple this shrine performs various ritual services and does a brisk trade in various talismans for both these requests. The shrine itself makes great play of the powers of its *kami* to help people find good partners and make relationships last, placing advertisements for the shrine on trains in the Kyoto region and in other prominent places. The shrine also hands out a leaflet which states that the roots of happiness are in making a good marriage, from whence comes family happiness and other fortunes, but then goes on to note that there are many people who are unable to find a partner, for:

> there are still many things in this world that are unattainable through human power alone. At such times how grateful we are that we can depend on the power of the *kami* to eliminate all the hindrances [that prevent us finding a partner].[10]

The leaflet naturally goes on to extol the merits of the shrine and its *kami* in doing this and in aiding people to achieve happiness. This is naturally a clear statement of the causative themes behind such prayers, and it is an issue to which I shall return in the next chapter when I examine the meanings behind such prayers and behind the talismans that people may acquire from places such as Jishu shrine.

SEEKING CONCEPTION AND SAFE BIRTH

Most large temples and shrines are in reality complex configurations of numerous subsidiary centres of worship arranged around a main hall of worship enshrining the prime spiritual entity of the site. As such they are often settings in which all manner of *riyaku* may be — at least according to temple and popular lore — available. To illustrate this point, and to show how the workings of popular lore crystallise into action, I shall examine in some detail the temple Nakayamadera in Takarazuka near Osaka. This temple is on the Saikoku pilgrimage route and is dedicated to Kannon who, in her manifestation at Nakayamadera, is most closely associated with easy childbirth, an issue that, as the *engi* of Kiyomizudera shows, has long been of great concern in Japan.[11]

The temple itself is said to have been founded by Shōtoku Taishi in the sixth century as a centre for the veneration of Kannon. Like Shōkū at Enkyōji, Shōtoku was guided there, according to the Nakayama *engi*, by a purple cloud, a popular good omen in Buddhism. Since then the temple has become the centre of numerous legends, stories and embellishments of stories concerning both the site and the Nakayamadera Kannon. These relate in particular to its role in conception, safe childbirth and the raising of children, which at Nakayamadera can be traced back at least to the sixteenth century when the wife of the political and military leader Toyotomi Hideyoshi is said to have prayed there because she seemed unable to conceive. Shortly after she did, and this naturally helped develop oral traditions that were further enhanced when the mother of Emperor Meiji, after praying for safe delivery there in the nineteenth century, had an easy birth. Such stories, linked to important figures in Japanese history, have served to ensure that Nakayamadera has grown into probably the major centre in the Kyoto–Osaka region, if not in Japan in general, for anything to do with pregnancy, childbirth and babies.

Women visit the temple to pray and acquire amulets for safe birth and also to ask for Kannon's grace to help them become pregnant. For pregnant women the most common course of action is to acquire a *hara obi*, a long strip of cloth that is commonly worn around the stomach by pregnant women in Japan from the fifth month of pregnancy onwards. This is considered to keep the baby warm and also, at least in popular belief, small so as to allow an easy birth. Although the *hara obi* can be bought elsewhere besides shrines and temples it is most common for women to acquire it at a religious site with a reputation for *anzan* (safe birth) such as Nakayamadera, and to have it inscribed at the same time with a prayer for safe birth. At Nakayamadera the custom is for women to purchase the inscribed *hara obi* at the temple (along with it they receive also a lucky talisman for safe birth); when the child has been born safely the grateful mother returns to the temple bearing a new *hara obi* she has bought at a shop. This is given to the temple to be inscribed, after which it will be passed on, via the temple, to someone who comes, pregnant, to make a prayer for safe delivery. This process in which the good luck one woman receives from the temple is passed on through the donation and transmission of the *obi* to someone else, follows a traditional custom in which women who had had successful births would present their pregnant friends with an *obi*. The custom of wearing the *obi* remains extremely strong: the anthropologist Emiko Ohnuki-Tierney, in surveying 149 pregnant women at a hospital in the Osaka region, found that 139 wore the *hara obi*. Of these, 106 had obtained them from temples or shrines, and 81 of these were from Nakayamadera.[12] I once asked a Japanese friend if she had worn such an *obi* when pregnant, and if so had she got it at Nakayamadera: she replied 'of course', adding that she thought most women in the region would do this, at least during their first pregnancy, very often, as in her case, due to the encouragement of the mother or mother-in-law.

Certainly, visitors to Nakayamadera will not fail to notice the importance of this tradition, for the temple, especially on Sundays, swarms with pregnant women as well as women with young babies returning to thank Kannon for their safe delivery and to ask for further protection. Because of its close association with birth the Nakayamadera Kannon is regarded as a protector of children in general, and many parents take their babies to the temple for *miyamairi* and, when the children are a little older, for the *shichigosan* (7–5–3) festival. To the side of the Kannon hall is a subsidiary shrine for *miyamairi* where babies are blessed by a Buddhist priest: the attendants are dressed in the clothing of shrine maidens with a white blouse and a red split skirt. That

Nakayamadera is a temple and not a shrine (the normal setting for *miyamairi* and *shichigosan*) appears of little consequence: certainly the priest when asked appeared to see no incongruity in this admixture of apparently different themes. In reality such centres of power transcend any theoretical differentiations between, say, the roles of Shinto and Buddhism. This also indicates the pragmatic attitudes that Japanese people are liable to take in such terms, choosing to visit places that seem relevant for the purpose required, regardless of any technical religious differentiation.

Like all large temples and shrines, however, Nakayamadera does not consist of just one focus of worship but of a whole range: within its precincts are dozens of buildings, some devoted to temple administration and living quarters for the priests and officiants, others used as teaching halls for lectures and for major functions, and still others as focuses of worship. Besides these there are also numerous Buddhist statues throughout the precincts, behind the main hall and lining the path behind the main temple up into the hills. The power of the site illustrated through the legends surround-ing Kannon, coupled with the throngs of people who visit the place, has led to the development of various other subsidiary temples within the complex, each enshrining numerous figures of worship and offering different forms of *riyaku*. The nature of the *riyaku* accessible to the visitor is not limited to the special benefits of the main image but involves many others besides, although many of these, reflecting the primary orientations of the temple, are con-nected in some way with caring for children.

There are several temples on the path leading up from the main gate to the Kannon hall. One, just inside the temple gate, is dedicated to the Buddhas Jizō, Fudō and Monju, the last of whom is widely petitioned for help in education. Next to that is a temple enshrining Dainichi (the sun Buddha of the Shingon sect to which the temple belongs) and Benten (one of the seven gods of good fortune, a syncretic group of deities who will be discussed separately later in this chapter). According to signs at the temple the chief attribute of Dainichi here is *yaku yoke*, prevention of danger, while Benten's is *gōkaku*, educational success. A general examination of the *ema*, the votive tablets on which people write petitions and requests to the *kami* and Buddhas, left at this site suggested that most of those who worshipped here were seeking Dainichi's grace, although there were also petitions to Benten for educational success.[13]

The next temple enshrines the Bodhisattva Fugen, here particularly well known for preventing diseases that afflict children. Priests at the temple perform *kitō* (special prayer services that direct entreaties to and seek the help of the Buddhas) whose aim is the prevention of various afflictions such as general weakness, crying at night and sleeplessness. Here again people had hung *ema* asking Fugen to help their children avoid such problems. Opposite this is a temple enshrining Amida, the Buddha of the Pure Land, Daikokuten, another of the seven gods of good fortune, and Jizō. One *riyaku* of the Buddhas here, according to the signs posted outside, is traffic safety (*kōtsū anzen*), but most of the activity in this particular temple revolves around Jizō in his capacity as *mizuko Jizō*: the guardian of the souls of those who die in the womb (*mizuko*). It is an active place at which people — predominantly female, but often in couples — seek Jizō's help and protection for the soul of the dead foetus, often expressing their own remorse (for the vast proportion of *mizuko* are the result of abortion) by giving form, through their actions, to the baby who never saw the light of day. As is common at many temples that provide the setting for the expression of such wishes small effigies of Jizō can be purchased: these represent and give form to the child and are left at the temple before a large statue of Jizō who is thus entreated to look after its soul. Often other offerings are made of flowers and various objects that would give special pleasure to children, such as dolls, toys and the like. Through such processes those who feel responsible for the state of an aborted child or who feel grieved at the loss of a wanted child who died in the womb may give vent to and externalise their feelings, for giving form helps direct and bring emotions out into the open where they may be properly confronted and dealt with. These rites of offering accompanied by prayers for the sake of the spirit may also be seen as similar to the actions performed for the ancestors, aimed at transforming the spirit after death and making it into a benevolent guardian of the living. The *ema* that many people write at this temple (as at many places that deal with *mizuko*) reflect these themes well, and also show the ways in which people may speak directly, through the votive tablets, to the spirit of the child. Most offer simple apologies (*gomen ne*: 'I'm sorry') but others relate further messages, even explaining why the parents felt it necessary to have an abortion: both at Nakayamadera and elsewhere I have seen messages suggesting that the time was not right, that the parents could not have coped, or that their economic situation made it difficult for them. Some may announce the birth of another child, often asking the spirit of the *mizuko* to guard over it and give it spiritual support. Although it may at first appear incongruous, in a complex devoted to safe childbirth, to have a temple focusing on the souls of dead — especially aborted — foetuses, it is not really so: the overall focus of the temple is in caring for children and, by extension, giving a sense of reassurance and peace of mind to their parents. Thus, the action of performing memorials for the unhappy souls of babies whose lives were abruptly terminated is itself a projection of caring, and its role in helping the parents come to terms with the situation, perhaps by making a gesture of atonement and thereby attaining some form of peace, is very much in line with the overarching sense of compassion manifested through the realms of temples and Buddhas.

There are many more focuses of worship and action besides. As is common in Buddhist institutions there is a memorial hall dedicated to the temple's founder, in this case Shōtoku Taishi, various other statues of Kannon and Jizō, and, behind the main hall, a temple dedicated to Kōbō Daishi. This contains a miniature pilgrimage route, in which scrolls depicting the main images of worship of 33 temples on the Saikoku pilgrimage (including Nakayamadera) as well as of eight major Buddhist sites of India and China are arranged around the walls. Before each scroll is a small box of soil from the courtyards of each of these temples and sites. Anyone who wishes may thus enter this hall and, walking around the room treading in turn on each piece of soil and praying before the replicated images, thus perform the pilgrimage and imbibe its merits and powers in microcosm.[14] Beyond this hall there are steps and paths leading up to an inner temple some kilometres away, and all along this path there are various statues and other religious insignia.

In sum, then, Nakayamadera is a composite centre in which all manner of *riyaku* and different entities may be encountered. Its core is in the compassionate Kannon it enshrines and in the power she, according to legend, may bestow. The acquired reputation that draws people to the temple of course helps develop and stimulate other aspects of activity that go on there: clearly, the temple's close association with birth and children has made it a logical focus also for the growing practice of performing memorial services for *mizuko*.

CONCEPTION, FERTILITY, BIRTH AND THE DYNAMICS
OF ORAL LORE: A SHORT POSTSCRIPT

As a postscript to this general discussion of reputations and the
transmission of oral lore, and of relevance particularly in connection
with the importance placed on fertility and safe birth in Japan, I
should like to introduce briefly the following short story relating
how my wife and I encountered the workings of popular lore in a
rather amusing way when we were walking around the island of
Shodōshima visiting some of its pilgrimage sites in May 1987. At
one small temple set right at the end of a valley of steeply terraced
and abundantly green rice fields we fell into conversation with four
female pilgrims who were, I judged, in their sixties. After telling us
about various sites on the island where one ought to pray for
particular *riyaku* they asked if we had any children. At the time we
did not and I said so, adding (or at least intending to add) that it
was because we did not have children that we were able to do the
pilgrimage (that is, with children it would not be possible to go off
walking for a week as we were doing). A mixture of poorly phrased
Japanese and their interpretation (and perhaps expectation) of what
I said made them decide that we were doing the pilgrimage because
we did not have children (that is, could not conceive and hence were
performing a pilgrimage to seek the help of the *kami* and Buddhas
to this end).

From their outlook this was not an unreasonable thing to do:
praying for the ability to conceive is a fairly common request and
there are a number of religious centres in Japan famed for fertility,
including Nakayamadera. It also fits, if one is allowed a pun, with
the conceptual orientations of the Japanese religious world in which
the spiritual realms may intercede to remove a hindrance that has
been preventing something happening. As a consequence, they
began to tell us of all the religious sites on the island whose deities
helped facilitate conception, and to which we should go and pray.
Two days later we were walking along a small road when a car drew
to a halt and one of the ladies leapt out: they were so glad to have
found us again as they had just remembered another good place for
fertility and procreation, this time near to our own home in the
Osaka region, to which we could go on our return to the mainland.
In such ways we became privy to items of popular lore passed on to
us by other temple and shrine visitors who clearly assumed that we
shared similar views about the nature of causation and the power of

spiritual entities to aid one even in such aspects of life as procreation. It is, of course, not inconceivable that these same ladies might not pass on the story of the two Westerners who came to Shodōshima seeking the help of the Buddhas in conceiving a child, thus further enriching and reinforcing popular traditions.

SCENIC SETTINGS, TOURISM AND CABLE CARS

Popular lore fired by miraculous tales of the past and by the pronouncements of the shrines and temples themselves, and the apparent benefits and *riyaku* that may be acquired, are not the only factors in the development of religious centres or in motivating people to visit them. Accessibility, transportation, cultural and touristic motivations and scenic location are also important. When various of these elements intersect with the constructions of popular lore certain locations are transformed into magnets drawing large crowds.

Situation itself may be especially important in enhancing the appeal of a shrine or temple as a centre of power: shrines centred on natural phenomena such as the waterfall at Nachi, whose very height and force clearly marks it out as something removed from the everyday, and temples perched on mountainsides or overhanging ravines appear to be metaphorically set apart from the ordinary world and are hence suggestive of the immanent proximity of spiritual realms. Many of Japan's religious sites are stunning in their settings deep in the mountains amidst trees that come ablaze with the blossoms of spring, the colours of autumn or the deep silence of winter snow. Many of the temples on the Saikoku pilgrimage, which circles most of the Kansai district of Japan from the Kii peninsula up to the Japan Sea coast, passing through Osaka, Nara and Kyoto and taking in 33 famous temples all dedicated to Kannon, are set in dramatic places: Kiyomizudera and Enkyōji, straddling ravines, Hōgonji, which dominates the island of Chikubushima in Lake Biwa, and Sefukuji high in the Katsuragi hills south of Osaka are just some examples of temples whose very location is designed to stimulate a sense of something special, apart from the routines of everyday life.

Often religious institutions have been constructed to utilise their natural surroundings in ways that convey religious teachings. Iwayaji in Ehime prefecture, one of the temples on the Shikoku pilgrimage, is not so much set in the mountains as built into the wall of rock that towers above the pilgrim as s/he climbs up to it. The temple hovers over a sheer drop, seemingly suspended between worlds, an image that was almost certainly in the mind of its builders and which fits well with the position of the pilgrim as a transient being for the duration of the journey, having left home and stepped outside the normal parameters of society. Similar imagery is seen at some of the temples on the Shodōshima pilgrimage, several of which have been fashioned from caves that were once, it is generally believed, inhabited by mountain ascetics. Such sites are dramatic in the extreme, for one walks up steep inclines, past rushing streams, sharp rocky outcrops and rows of statues and stones erected by pilgrims to commemorate their journey, to small temples that have been sited within caves, or which have been built on to the front of recesses in the mountain walls, and from which the views are often breathtakingly dramatic.

Cultural and historical factors also are important, for shrines and temples in a very real way represent some of the richest outpourings of Japanese cultural history. The architecturally simple grandeur of the shrines of Ise, for example, or the buildings, sculptures and art works of Hasedera, itself one of the Saikoku temples in Nara prefecture, are but two of the many examples of sites whose cultural heritages have made great tourist centres as well. In a very real sense, shrine and temple visiting is a way of learning about Japan's cultural history, much of which is written, as it were, in the structures, sculptures, paintings, scrolls and other art works of the religious world. This, in many respects, is why Japanese school-children are to be seen being herded in great throngs around the shrines and temples of Nara and Kyoto on their school trips: in visiting these religious centres they are being taken on a tour of their country's cultural roots and history.

A visit to any major religious centre will underline these points graphically. Mimurotoji is a well-known pilgrimage temple on the Saikoku route just outside the town of Uji near Kyoto. Set against a hillside and surrounded by trees, its location is beautiful at any time of the year and attracts a constant stream of visitors besides pilgrims. In November 1987 I spent two days in the grounds of the temple, doing research on pilgrimage. It was during the brief period when the autumn colours were at their best, ringing the temple complex in a fiery circle of reds, yellows, russets and browns, and this drew more visitors than would be there on an average weekend.

White-coated pilgrims lighting candles and chanting in groups mingled with photographers seeking to capture the colours of the leaves, while family groups ate packed lunches and made offerings of incense and prayers while reading about the temple's history and art treasures in guide books. The pilgrims did not just pray nor the photographers just take pictures. While many of the former pulled out cameras to memorialise their visits, some of the latter clearly did likewise by acquiring talismans or praying at the temple. In all, there was a general diversity of actions covering cultural, religious and touristic themes simultaneously, reflecting the nature of the holy place as site and sight together.

PILGRIMAGES, CULTURAL TOURS AND HOLY PLACES

Like other Japanese pilgrimages such as Shikoku, the Saikoku route involves the pilgrim in visiting a number of linked centres of power. While the Shikoku pilgrimage mentioned in Chapter 5 involves 88 sites connected with Kōbō Daishi, the 33 Saikoku temples all enshrine Kannon. Their *engi* and oral traditions abound with tales of her great compassion, mercy and intercession, while their images of Kannon are widely venerated as sources and embodiments of her infinitely compassionate power. The combination of a series of places of power in such a route serves, at least in the perceptions of the pilgrims themselves, to heighten the sense of relationship between the pilgrim and the figure of worship, and also to increase the potential *riyaku* and spiritual benefits that accrue from visiting centres of power in general. Most Japanese pilgrimages have evolved on these lines, incorporating a number of centres of power in a linked route, and this remains a prominent factor in the continued development of pilgrimages in Japan today, with temples often co-operating to establish pilgrimage routes as a way of encouraging more people to visit them and enter into a relationship with the Buddhas.

There are also important touristic and cultural themes to pilgrimage as well, just as there are to general shrine and temple visiting. As has already been noted, the Saikoku route includes many beautiful temples, such as Enkyōji, in striking locations which have built up a store of popular legend testifying to their power. Many of these temples are repositories of some of the greatest artistic works in Japan, and many of the temple buildings themselves, as well as the statues and images housed in them, are designated as important cultural properties.[15] The route itself takes the pilgrim on what is virtually a cultural and historical tour around western Japan, incorporating also many of its most famous touristic sites as well, from the natural beauties of the Kii peninsula and its hot spring resorts, through Nara and Kyoto, to Nariaiji in northern Kyoto prefecture, which overlooks the famous natural sight of the sand bar and bay of Amanohashidate and then across Japan's largest lake, Lake Biwa, to the hills of Gifu beyond. The route also goes through several of Japan's most famous castle towns, such as Himeji and Hikone.

There is some evidence to suggest that the feudal authorities in Tokugawa Japan encouraged people from Edo (present day Tokyo) and its environs to go on pilgrimages to Saikoku because this helped develop a sense of national identity, opening their eyes to the cultural and historical splendours of Japan.[16] These cultural perceptions of pilgrimage continue to be a very major element in the pilgrimage today: many of the pilgrims whom I interviewed at a survey I carried out with a fellow researcher over two days in 1987 at Mimurotoji and others I have interviewed elsewhere on the Saikoku route, have stated that learning about Japan and its cultural history was a major reason for undertaking the pilgrimage. The ways in which the Saikoku pilgrimage is done in the present age tend to reinforce this, for most pilgrims dress in casual clothes, rather than the traditional white garb still worn on the Shikoku route, and large numbers of them do not complete the route at one time, preferring to incorporate it into their daily lives by going occasionally, usually on a Sunday or day off, to one or two sites, until eventually they have visited all the temples.[17]

Pilgrims usually carry a scroll or book which can be stamped by each temple on the route. Originally used as proof that the pilgrim had been where s/he had received permission to go (in the Tokugawa era, people had to obtain permits if they wished to travel), these have become important mementoes of the experience of pilgrimage. Nowadays most pilgrims on Saikoku carry an elaborate scroll with a depiction of Kannon in the centre, around which the temple seals, beautifully illustrated also with brush calligraphy, are affixed. When completed this constitutes a representation of the powers of the images of worship of all the temples, a symbol of Kannon's mercy and, perhaps most importantly for many people, a beautiful, and often costly, work of art to be hung in the home as a decoration and as a memorialisation and reminder of their journey. Many of the pilgrims I have interviewed stated that one of their primary motives for doing the pilgrimage was that they saw such a completed scroll at someone else's house and felt they would also like one.

The survey we carried out at Mimurotoji showed also the extent to which the ways in which pilgrims travel mirror contemporary developments in society. In the pre-motorised era everyone, save the few who could afford horses, walked: today there are still a very few who go by foot. As mass transport became available more and more people made use of it, until by the 1950s organised bus tours had become a standard way of going on pilgrimages.[18] Increased wealth and car ownership have further affected this picture: our survey showed that, out of a total of 449 pilgrims surveyed, 51 per cent were travelling by private car (compared with 40 per cent who used buses and trains), and 55 per cent were with their spouse; 18 per cent more were with other family members and only 8 per cent were alone.[19] This is very much in line with the increasing sense of nuclearisation: going out with a spouse and perhaps other family members in the family car on a series of Sundays to complete the scroll that would be hung in the home as a family treasure is both a further strengthening of the identity of the family as a unit and an expression of the importance of sharing such activities, both religious and cultural, with the family. Many Saikoku pilgrims are thus taking part in a cultural tour of their country while having a nice day out with the family, and these interlocking themes, incorporating national pride, family solidarity and enjoyment, are intrinsic to contemporary Japanese pilgrimage and are found in shrine and temple visiting in general.

Yet this does not mean that pilgrimage, or shrine and temple visiting, should be seen solely as cultural and touristic: just as with the actions performed at *hatsumōde* and other such times in the social religious calendar, pilgrimage does involve people in some form of religious interaction. Of our respondents in the survey, 32 per cent stated that they did little else at the temple besides getting their scroll stamped, which implies that for them this was primarily a touristic, cultural, souvenir-gathering exercise. Yet the rest did take part in all manner of activities, from lighting candles and incense (49 per cent), chanting prayers (18 per cent), chanting prayers as well as the special pilgrimage song of each temple (11 per cent), buying various religious amulets and talismans (20 per cent), offering special prayers for the benefit of their ancestors (9 per cent) and leaving a *fuda*, or slip of paper marked with religious inscriptions and with the pilgrim's name, at the temple (6 per cent). This at the very least represents a broad diversity and multiplicity of actions from a group of people who could all be placed under the single rubric of pilgrims. Some pilgrims had an explicit concern with issues of faith and religious action that left little room for any cultural motivations. This was the case with one man we interviewed who, dressed wholly in the traditional white garments of the pilgrim, was performing the pilgrimage as a memorial service on the seventh anniversary of the death of his wife. He spent a long time at Mimurotoji praying and lighting candles to her memory, but evinced little interest in the autumnal colours or the general mood of enjoyment that permeated the temple. Others, especially those in large groups led by *sendatsu*, not only chanted prayers and pilgrimage songs but devoted a long time to it. An example of this was a group of pilgrims from Kyushu who, led by their female guide and all dressed in white, arrived early in the morning and chanted in unison for close to 30 minutes at the temple before setting off for the next site on the route.

In reality, of course, there are multiple reasons — and ways — in which people visit shrines and temples, and perform pilgrimages, just as there are immense diversities in the ways they behave there. There are those who will walk a pilgrimage route even in winter, sleeping out and seeking spiritual awareness through their physical austerities, and there are others who will cheerfully drive around in a car, doing the pilgrimage as a series of days out, with the aims of learning something of Japan's cultural history while completing a lovely scroll to display in their home. All these are manifestations of the fluidity of Japanese religion in general and the extent to which personal choice and interpretation are important, for each person determines the manner in which s/he will approach the site or perform a pilgrimage. This does not make one less or more valid than any other: all are in some way moving into a sphere in which they may interact with the religious world in the light of their own perceptions, requirements and wishes.

One can see in all this the multidimensional nature of temples and shrines, which operate simultaneously as tourist, religious and cultural institutions. The ways that people actually behave at shrines and temples may incorporate all these themes at once, as with our pilgrims visiting Saikoku temples to imbibe the cultural heritage, see some memorable places and pray for Kannon's grace. I shall return to these themes in the next chapter when I examine the content of such shrines and temples and the meanings of the actions that people perform at them, but before I do this I shall briefly examine one final element in the process whereby people are drawn to certain centres of religious power, and this brings us on to the question of economic factors and the development of modern transport facilities.

ECONOMICS, MODERN TRANSPORT AND THE PROMOTION OF CENTRES OF POWER

Economic factors and the development of transport and communications have played a large part in transforming religious sites into centres of mass activity. Temples and shrines, by acting as magnets for large numbers of people, have for centuries been the natural focus of economic activities such as markets, stalls and entertainment catering to the every need of visitors. They have provided major crossroads for trade routes or, because of the numbers of people they attracted, have stimulated the development of trade routes and markets around them. Special festival days at such religious institutions were often the occasion for market days, and the regular monthly *ennichi* ('days with good *en*'; that is, when the *kami* or Buddhas are especially receptive to prayers) at places such as Tōji and Kitano Tenmangū mentioned at the beginning of this chapter are products of this coalition of religious and economic factors. Temples and shrines have often served as the nuclei around which urban areas have grown, as is the case with Narita which developed as a *monzenmachi*, or 'town before the temple gate', of Shinshōji, as its increasing numbers of visitors led to the growth of a network of shops, stalls and other establishments seeking to cater to their needs — and of course to relieve them of some of their money.[20]

The development of centres of power has been greatly encouraged and stimulated by the continuing improvements in communication routes and means which encourage and facilitate travel, thus making the visiting of temples and shrines and the performance of pilgrimages progressively more comfortable and easier. The ease with which one can now do, for example, the Shikoku pilgrimage has allowed more and more Japanese people to take part in this religious activity without having to undergo the trials and tribulations that pilgrims of earlier ages had to face. No longer does the pilgrim have to experience the discomforts of his/her predecessors: while the choice remains for those who wish to walk as an austerity, there are organised bus tours and warm hotels for the vast majority who prefer to go in this manner.

Since modern comforts facilitate the widening accessibility of pilgrimages and holy sites, stimulate further crowds of visitors and increase the custom for those involved in the business of transporting them and catering to their needs, it is not surprising to find not just the shrines and temples themselves but the transport and tourist networks avidly publicising religious sites and pilgrimages. The Iyotetsu Bus Company of Matsuyama in Shikoku, for instance, which has long run organised pilgrimage tours around the island, tells its potential customers that the route has become 'completely comfortable' and can be done without worry and with complete peace of mind on buses run by the company.[21] The activities of transport consortia that have helped to promote the contemporary world of pilgrimage in places such as Shikoku have been complemented by the work of regional tourist authorities in areas such as Shikoku and Shodōshima. Both these areas, which have suffered from rural depopulation, are dependent on tourism as a major local industry that can help regenerate the local economy, and consequently few items of tourist literature about either island fail to make use of the photogenic nature of white-coated pilgrims photographed against the backdrop of the more visually dramatic parts of the pilgrimage route, usually accompanied by a few words on the cultural traditions of the pilgrimage.[22]

The image of tradition thus created, of the pilgrim walking in the wilds dressed in traditional clothing and escaping the confines of the present, acts as a powerful message encouraging people to visit the islands and to participate in the pilgrimage. It does not matter that most who do so will travel, albeit dressed in white, on luxury buses rather than in the style depicted in the image, for it is the implicit theme of the encounter with tradition and cultural roots that is at the core of the imagery, rather than the manner of its performance. These images of nostalgia and emphases on tradition have been encountered elsewhere in this book and will come up again later. What is of relevance in connection with the issues of shrine and temple visiting, and of pilgrimages, is that the stories and reputations that are passed on about the sites themselves are often reinforced and strengthened by the activities and co-operation of transport firms and tourist organisations and the publicity that they generate.

It is not publicity alone that does this, of course, but the provision of new and better ɪneans of communication. The construction of new railways, roads and cable cars has brought many religious sites closer and more readily accessible to increasingly large numbers of people. The modern visitor, for example, can have ready access to Kōyasan, the Shingon centre where Kōbō Daishi's mausoleum is, from the centre of Osaka via a railway line and funicular railway built by the Nankai Railway Company, while the Keihan Railway, besides giving access via a regular bus service to the Kōrien Narita-san temple, also provides ready access to Iwashimizu Hachimangū shrine via a funicular railway running up the slopes of Otokoyama from the local Yawata station. Enkyōji on Mount Shosha, where Shōkū once performed austerities, now may be reached by cable car. A similar pattern is found throughout Japan, with funicular railways, cable cars and, now, skyline drives making the ascent to once-remote mountain temples and shrines swift and comfortably cushioned.

Two examples from the Ikoma area near Osaka should suffice to show the ways in which transport developments may increase the number of visitors to religious sites and the resultant changes in the environment at and around them. Ishikiri shrine is one of the major religious centres of this area, receiving, according to estimates, around 3.5 million visitors a year. Although locally popular for prayers connected with healing, especially the healing of tumours, it was, by all accounts, not especially widely known or visited by people from outside the locality. The opening up in 1914 of a railway line from Osaka to Nara, which passed through the Ishikiri area, made the shrine readily accessible to the citizens of Osaka, causing a rapid growth in the numbers of visitors and a consequent boost to its reputation as a healing centre. At the time the railway was opened there were no shops on the road leading up to the shrine: by the mid-1920s there were fifteen, and the numbers of visitors enabled the shrine to support ten priests and other offi-ciants. By the mid-1980s the numbers of officiants at the shrine had risen to over 50, and the number of shops and stalls in the street leading to the shrine had risen to 140, of which six dealt in herbal medicines and fifteen specialised in divination or spiritual healing.[23]

Similar developments have occured at Chōgosonshiji, popularly known as Shigisan, at the southern end of the Ikoma hills: although it had long attracted visitors it was the building of two rail routes up the hillside by the Kintetsu Railway Company in 1915 and 1930 that caused their numbers to grow enormously. This in turn led to the development of a *monzenmachi* of restaurants, souvenir shops and inns catering to the flow of visitors. The subsequent opening of a scenic toll road along the crest of the hills, which also links Shigisan with a major amusement park, has since placed the temple firmly in the network of bus tours and has further swelled the tide of visitors.[24]

Transport companies do not, of course, build cable cars or railway lines to religious centres purely for altruistic reasons. Transporting pilgrims around Shikoku is a major source of income for the Iyotetsu Bus Company, giving it a vested interest in supporting and publicising the merits of the pilgrimage, while the Nankai Railway has an economic interest in displaying posters of Kōyasan and encouraging people to visit it, in much the same way that, as was mentioned in Chapter 3, many railway companies publicise the temples and shrines on their routes at major festive times such as New Year. Shrine and temple visiting in general is big business, a major outdoor, weekend and holiday activity of millions of Japanese that generates a series of interrelated economic concerns from souvenir shops, restaurants, hotels and the other trappings of the tourist industry to the interests of the transport industry. Running trains and buses to religious centres guarantees a good supply of customers and is an important commercial concern, which of course encourages the further development of communications and the possibility of even more visitors. Thus, as we have seen with the case of the Kōrien Narita-san temple and the Keihan Railway, there is frequently a close and mutually beneficial relationship between religious centres and commercial organisations that serves to maintain the continuing tradition of shrine and temple visiting.

THE SEVEN GODS OF GOOD FORTUNE AND RAILWAY PILGRIMAGES

In order to illustrate further the involvement of business, tourist and religious themes and to shed light on an area of great popularity in contemporary Japanese religion, I shall end this chapter with a brief look at a syncretic group of deities known as the *shichi fukujin*, or seven gods of good fortune, that have become increasingly popular in contemporary Japan. These seven deities have individually been venerated in Japan for many centuries, but have been associated together also as a group since at least the seventeenth century, although they have especially enjoyed a contemporary wave of popularity since the mid-1970s. Before that time various pilgrimage routes incorporating the seven existed, but since then there has been throughout Japan a general increase in the numbers of regional pilgrimage routes incorporating temples and shrines dedicated to different members of the group.[25]

The seven gods come from a variety of different traditions: three — the deities of contentment and magnanimity, Hotei; of longevity, Jurōjin; and of popularity, Fukurokuju — are of Taoist origins; two — Bishamonten, a symbol of authority, and Daikokuten, who personifies abundance — are Buddhist; one — Benten, a deity of music and the arts — is originally Hindu but came to Japan along with Buddhism; and one — Ebisu — is an ethnic Japanese deity personifying honesty and prosperity. Despite their diverse origins they have, reflecting the syncretic and Japanising tendencies of the religious culture, become as a group a distinctly Japanese entity, generally portrayed sailing in a treasure boat bringing wealth and happiness with them and promising the types of this-worldly wishes that are at the heart of Japanese religion. They are especially prominent at New Year, for in their boat sailing across the seas they epitomise the sense of coming good fortune that is associated with this time of year, and thus New Year is the prime time for pilgrimages to the *shichi fukujin*. It is a mark of the fusions between the various traditions in Japan that this is possible, for some (for example, Ebisu) may be enshrined in Shinto institutions, and others, such as Bishamonten, in Buddhist ones. Still others, such as Benten, may be found at either: most *shichi fukujin* pilgrimage routes incorporate both temples and shrines.

.On 4 January 1989 my wife and I followed one such route that ran through one Tokyo ward along the banks of the Sumida River. We did this with a group of Japanese friends, at the start buying, like everyone else, a small model of the boat on which the gods travel and then at each of the shrines and temples in turn a small figurine of the particular deity enshrined there, until at the end we had assembled the complete set of the seven aboard the treasure boat. The whole tour was about five miles long and took about two and a half hours to do. Our party of six adults and four children all had an enjoyable time. The children delighted in acquiring the various figurines, looked around the souvenir and food stalls at each of the sites and prayed with their parents at each place visited. The adults kept the children happy while showing their friends (us) around and imbibing their own religious culture, and we were pleased to be seeing another side of Tokyo, having a good time with our friends and doing a little research besides.

They provide not just the means of performing a relatively short and accessible pilgrimage (almost all the *shichi fukujin* pilgrimages in Japan can be done in a day or less) but one through which people may legitimately express their desires for the happy and joyous benefits the gods appear to offer. The benevolent and happy nature of the seven also seems to fit with the relaxed, touristic approach possessed by many of those who perform these pilgrimages. It has also helped make the *shichi fukujin* popular with tourist and commercial agencies: probably the most flourishing of all these routes was established in 1973 around the island of Awaji as a result of co-operation between some of the island's temples, bus companies and the tourist board which was eager to stimulate the island's rather weak tourist industry. This now attracts many thousands of visitors each year and its example has provided a stimulus for others to follow suit.[26]

The promotion and development of *shichi fukujin* routes has also been actively encouraged by many railway companies. The Hankyū Railway of Osaka, for example, widely publicises over the New Year period a *shichi fukujin* route that it helped to develop and that can be done entirely on its trains, visiting two shrines and five temples all within a few moments' walk of stations on its line from Osaka to Takarazuka. The company even sells special concessionary train tickets for the pilgrimage and gives pilgrims a special sheet of paper on which the seals of all these institutions may be affixed. One of the temples of this route is Nakayamadera, for it enshrines in its precincts the figure of Jurōjin. Other companies have 'their' routes as well: the Ōmi Railway Company that services the eastern shores of Lake Biwa and the Meitetsu Railway of Nagoya also patronise and promote routes comprising shrines and temples dedicated to the gods and accessible via their railways. Besides the obvious commercial aspects that may be involved, such activities also help the companies concerned to promote their own corporate images and depict themselves in a caring light, supportive of tradition and religious customs.[27]

An article in the religious newspaper *Chūgai Nippō* in July 1987 illustrates the mechanisms behind the formation of many such routes. This reported the formation of a *Kōbe shichi fukujin kai* (Kōbe Seven Gods of Good Fortune Society) consisting of the heads of seven prominent shrines and temples in the city plus various representatives of local government, tourist and business concerns. The aim was to start and promote a *shichi fukujin* pilgrimage incorporating all seven sites, with the additional aim of contributing to Kōbe's drive to increase tourism to the city (itself a motivating factor behind the Kōbe Festival discussed in Chapter 3). Through various promotional activities the route has been nurtured as one of the city's tourist attractions, and at a reception to mark the beginnings of this effort Yoshida Akira, the head priest of Minatogawa shrine, one of the pilgrimage sites, expressed his hopes that the cheerful nature of the *shichi fukujin* would help develop Kōbe's tourist prosperity.[28] Elsewhere the relationship between business and religion has been expressed through the *shichi fukujin* in even more vivid ways, perhaps the most engaging of which, in my view, has been the production by the Asahi Beer Company of a can of beer bearing the smiling faces of the seven gods and publicising the Izumo region's *shichi fukujin* pilgrimage.[29] No doubt the jollity of the deities helps to sell the beer just as the can sells the pilgrimage!

Besides being examples of the syncretic and co-operative aspects of the various traditions that have appeared in Japan, then, the seven gods of good fortune illustrate in a light-hearted manner many of the dynamics of contemporary shrine- and temple-going and of the ways in which these along with commercial enterprises may play their part in developing and encouraging activities connected with the religious world. Their association with various benefits further makes them good representative examples of some of the contemporary dynamics of Japanese religion, while their current popularity provides the Japanese with one further medium through which to engage in religious actions and express their needs and desires.

7 Actions, Amulets and the Expression of Meaning: Reflections of Need and Statements of Desire

Japanese people are rarely passive within the framework of temples and shrines, but generally interact actively with the religious environment around them and with all the diverse objects signifying the presence and nature of the spiritual within that environment. Religious sites are basically settings in and through which religious power may be accessed and diffused, and the various signs and symbols present within them are vehicles of that power, conduits through which its beneficial aspects may be disseminated and shared out. All these signs and symbols, from the rows of statues and the myriad signs of the presence of *kami* indicated by the ropes tied round trees and rocks to the numerous talismans and amulets signifying good fortune and protection, provide enormous scope and choice of action, each providing an opportunity and setting for interactions through which relationships may be created, whether temporary and conditioned by needs and circumstances or regular and underpinned by personal affinity and devotion.

A significant element in all this is that the benefits, compassion and spiritual help that are, as it were, on tap are untrammelled by any sense of sectarian or religious affiliation but are open and accessible to everyone without question. In this there is a forceful sense of fairness, an implicit recognition and assertion that no one should be turned away or prevented from sharing in the benefits and grace of the spiritual world.

This implicit recognition of fairness, that everyone should equally be able to imbibe and assimilate these powers and that no one should be left out, is well illustrated by the widespread prevalence at many temples of miniature pilgrimage routes such as the one at Nakayamadera which I described in the previous chapter. This practice of condensing pilgrimages into concentrated and readily accessible copies of the original has its roots in the seventeenth century, when the Saikoku and Shikoku pilgrimages first widely developed as popular practices. At that time, however, it was not always possible for people, especially from outlying regions, to find the time and wherewithal to embark on a long journey, and consequently smaller, localised versions of these pilgrimages, many copying the names and images of the Saikoku or Shikoku temples themselves, were created throughout the country, often by dynamic individuals who, having gone on a pilgrimage, determined to enable others from their region who were less able to travel to do the same. By bringing back soil from the pilgrimage sites of Saikoku or Shikoku they helped bring the pilgrimage to those who were unable to go to it. Most of these earlier small-scale pilgrimages still took a number of days to perform and so gradually even smaller versions, usually ranged around a temple courtyard and perhaps only a few yards long, began to appear so that those who wished to encounter the merits of the pilgrimage and of Kannon and Kōbō Daishi, but who were too poor or infirm even to travel for a few days could symbolically walk with Kōbō Daishi around Shikoku or go on pilgrimage to Saikoku.[1]

Large numbers of them remain in use today and many more are being created. Advances in transport, communications and economic wealth have brought the major routes within virtually everyone's potential, thereby increasing the numbers who do perform the major pilgrimages. This has stimulated a general interest in pilgrimage and, rather than making the miniature versions redundant, has encouraged their further development. Examples of these microcosmic pilgrimages may be seen at large numbers of temples throughout Japan: the Kōrien Narita-san temple has a Shikoku route perhaps 80 metres long, each 'temple' a small wooden structure with a miniature altar inside. Within the huge temple complex at Shigisan in Ikoma there are actually *two* miniature Shikoku pilgrimage routes. At Kiyomizudera at Yonago in Tottori prefecture (a temple bearing the same name as its more famous counterpart in Kyoto, but well-known in its own region as a prayer centre) there are stones under each of which is soil not from one but from three different sites from the 33-stage Saikoku, Chūgoku and Izumo Kannon pilgrimages, the last two of which are themselves copies of the first.

A recently built courtyard in the grounds of Sumadera, a popular prayer temple in eastern Kōbe, houses a new pagoda around which have been erected statues representing each of the 88 Shikoku temples: before each is a clear panel of plastic containing a small amount of soil from the relevant temple. There is also a sign informing visitors that in walking around this pilgrimage one may receive the same merits as if one performed the Shikoku pilgrimage itself.

Whether performing the pilgrimage in microcosm is the same as doing the actual route and whether the same merit may accrue is, as an officiant at Sumadera remarked in response to my question, to be determined in the minds of those who do it.[2] What it does suggest, and what underlies all activities that occur at popular centres of power where the emphasis is on the transmission and acquisition of *riyaku*, is that the interpretation of what is done rests very much with the participants themselves.

Every person interacts with the site and its entities in the manner and on the levels s/he thinks fit and receives from that interaction and encounter what s/he wishes to take. As we shall see in this chapter, the range and levels of activity that do take place at popular religious centres are extremely diverse and cover just about everything from forms of asceticism performed with immense seriousness and determination to acts of an extremely folkloric nature tinged with humour and a sense of frivolity. The efficacy of each of these actions is for the doer to decide, as is to be expected in a religious culture which emphasises the importance of the experiential dimension, of 'doing it and seeing'. This populist nature is further underlined by the ways in which the forms of benefits and support offered by the *kami* and Buddhas are responsive to the contemporary needs and insecurities of those who visit religious sites, a point that will be discussed later. The sites that have been discussed in this and the previous chapter can, to this extent, be seen as popular centres of power that transcend narrower distinctions such as 'temples' (Buddhist) or 'shrines' (Shinto). They are, rather, centres of a genuinely popular religiosity whose actions and themes cut across any boundaries of differentiation: such boundaries are, anyway, as we have seen in earlier chapters, more artificial than anything else in the overall Japanese religious perspective.

THE DIVERSITY OF ACTIONS: A BRIEF OVERVIEW

The diversity of actions and customs found at religious sites in Japan is immense, ranging from local practices specific perhaps only to one site to others found almost universally. To describe here more than a few would be impossible and consequently I shall present a brief overview of some of the more commonly seen ones, as well as of the more common forms of talismans, amulets and other lucky charms and this in turn will lead on to a general discussion of the meanings behind these things and of their relevance in contemporary Japan.

While some of the activity is formal and channelled through priests and ritual officiants, much is informal, personal and individual. As with the rites before the *butsudan*, one may engage the services of a priest to act as a mediator in invoking the powers of the *kami* and Buddhas. People who feel the need for the additional emotional comfort that a formal religious service may produce could ask the priest(s) of a particular site to perform a special ritual there invoking the powers of the enshrined Buddha or *kami* and sacralising a special talisman. For this they would also pay a suitable, usually predetermined, fee. Such fees, and those for talismans and amulets, often form an important part of the economy of a temple or shrine, and this certainly encourages priests to promote the putative powers of their centre and its enshrined entities, much as they have encouraged the development of *engi* and miracle stories to draw people to them. In addition, priests as guardians of the site and of the *kami* and Buddhas enshrined therein are naturally likely to have some faith in the efficacy of these figures and to encourage others to do likewise, for this in turn is a means of drawing them into a further relationship with the religious world, through which deeper faith and belonging might result.

The regular priesthood is the official channel to and mediating agency of this religious power, and thus to a great degree retains an element of control over access to and usage of such places. This does not, however, mean that the priesthood is solely in control of the types of activities and, especially, of the nature of the prayers and requests that are made. While temples, shrines and priests can to some extent create or stimulate certain areas of religious activity and prayer (the role of temples and some new religious groups in persuading people of the necessity to hold memorial services for aborted foetuses is certainly a factor in the growing *mizuko kuyō* phenomenon) this does not mean either that they alone can manipulate or guide popular religious sentiment and action. As we saw in the earlier discussion of the relationship between Buddhist temples, the priesthood and the issue of death and the ancestors, the priesthood acts in many respects as a service agency for the needs and requirements of people in general. Just as priests are expected and required to perform memorial services for the ancestors so are the guardians and controllers of sites enshrining powerful *kami* and Buddhas expected to facilitate the transmission of requests of all sorts to the spiritual world. In numerous conversations with both Buddhist and Shinto priests I have been repeatedly told that should a person make a petition they would transmit it to the *kami* or Buddhas. It is, in short, their duty to do so and to thus react to popular needs and requests. Thus popular prayer activities develop both from the impetus provided by the priesthood and through the demands exerted by the populace.

People do not, in any event, have to go through the priests in their relationship with the objects of reverence but may also make their own informal and direct approaches. Many people, indeed, are content just to place a small coin before a statue, or a can of drink before a shrine, clap their hands, bow and mutter a few words of prayerful request; or to purchase for a small sum a talisman or amulet. There is a very strong focus throughout all these actions on giving form to the religious interaction that takes place with the spiritual world. As we saw in the previous chapter, people do not pray just for the benefit of a baby that died in the womb, but will give a shape and form to their feelings, and to the child, by purchasing a small figure of Jizō and by presenting offerings suitable for a child. The talismans and amulets that may be acquired are another means through which a tangible dimension and form may be given to a wish, feeling or prayer.

Statues of Buddhas, as we saw in Chapter 2, are not simply to be worshipped but are presented with offerings and perhaps decorated. Further extensions of this interactive process involve the symbolic transferral either of merit or pain: by rubbing part of a statue and then the same area of their own bodies people are symbolically extending its merit to themselves. When the action is performed in reverse and they rub themselves first they are calling on the compassion of the spiritual entity (usually a Buddha) to absorb and take from them a pain or illness, as can be seen, for example, at the Saikoku pilgrimage temple Kegonji at Tanigumi in Gifu prefecture. Behind its main hall there is an enclosure housing a statue of the healing Buddha Yakushi. The statue is frequently swathed in clouds of incense lit by the many people who pray for his assistance in overcoming pains and sickness. To the side of the statue is a small kiosk where one can purchase strips of paper with Buddhist spells written on them: the purchaser then places the paper on Yakushi's body and, while reciting a prayer, pours over it water from a ladle, thus symbolically washing the pain from the afflicted area.

This focus on physical action as a means of eradicating worries and problems may be followed by those facing the uncertainties of their *yakudoshi* or unlucky age, which, as was mentioned in Chapter 2 is 33 for a woman and 42 for a man. Many religious centres provide amulets to protect people of this age and may also provide special purification rites to symbolically sweep away the potential misfortunes and dangers believed to surround people during this year. Another way of counteracting and clearing away the pollutions of this unlucky age is through the ascent of special flights of steps that may be found at many religious centres. At Yakuōji, a pilgrimage temple at Hiwasa in Shikoku famed for its protection of those in their *yakudoshi*, there is a flight of 42 steps on the way up to the main hall. Signs tell those in their *yakudoshi* that they should walk up them, depositing a coin on each step in turn, men for the whole 42 and women for 33 steps. At the top there is a board that should be struck the appropriate number of times with a wooden mallet. Those who are not in their *yakudoshi* are also encouraged to do this to ward off potential misfortunes, by placing coins on the number of steps and striking the number of blows relevant to their age.[3]

Sometimes the means by which one enters into a relationship with a Buddha or *kami*, or creates the merit by which one is worthy of the *kami* or Buddha's compassion and help, may involve a greater degree of commitment and perhaps even some limited expression of asceticism. One such practice is *hyakudo mairi* ('100 times around'), in which people circumambulate (usually 100 times) two stone markers set several metres apart in the grounds of shrines and temples for this purpose. It is performed for many reasons: as a penance for a fault or wrongdoing, as a form of asceticism designed to polish the soul, or, more commonly still, to demonstrate one's sincerity when seeking the deity's benevolence and help for oneself or someone else. Hōzanji and Ishikiri shrine in Ikoma both have active *hyakudo mairi* places: at the former I have seen people doing this barefoot, while at the latter the courtyard before the main shrine is very often thronged with people walking purposefully around the stones. The shrine is associated with healing (particularly of cancers and tumours), and many of those performing this practice are doing so to invoke the *kami*'s help in curing such a problem or for the benefit of someone else, such as a friend or family member who is sick or undergoing surgery.

Behind the main hall of worship at Shigisan is a shrine dedicated to one of the temple's guardian deities: to reach it involves a 30-minute climb up a steep path lined by over 700 *torii*. At the top of the hill there is no water, and the common practice of those who ascend the hill to seek the support of this powerful *kami*, who is said to help in the successful completion of all wishes, is to carry a pot of water up the hill as an offering. Empty pots are provided at the foot of the hill for this purpose. Many of those who ascend the hill also perform further acts of service, collecting brooms from the shrine attendant and sweeping part of the courtyard or path, or do *hyakudo mairi* there.

Yet side by side with these clearly serious practices are others that appear to be little more than folkloric customs to be indulged in with a sense of amusement and fun. This admixture is evident at most religious centres, and Shigisan with its *hyakudo mairi* and hill ascents is no exception. Before Senjuin, one of its many sub-temples, is a row of Buddha statues, and a supply of holy water, *reisui*, that, according to the notice, can prevent cancers. The incidence of water imbued with some sort of special power is widely found at religious centres in Japan, especially for wisdom (as at, for example, Kyoto's Kiyomizudera) but also for various cures and preventions of disease. As at Shigisan, it is generally quaffed with a degree of relaxed humour.

After drinking this miraculous water one can walk the Shikoku pilgrimage by crossing stones representing each of the 88 temples and enter a 'money' *kami* shrine. Here one can purchase for 300 yen (a little over £1) imitation and oversized 10,000 yen notes with pictures of Shōtoku Taishi on one side (until a few years ago his picture was on the genuine 10,000 yen notes) and a prayer on the other. These are then placed, along with one's purse or wallet, on a rock inhabited by the *kami* and turned clockwise three times while chanting a short prayer. This would, the old lady officiant was informing everyone with a chuckle the day I visited this site, make one's own money grow: 'Just go to the bank on Monday and see!' Several people participated, all of them laughing and clearly enjoying the fun.

The spectrum of activity within one place may thus be extensive, from earnest devotion to amused irreverence, from ascetic practices to folkloric customs: the same person may relate in all these ways within the same religious centre. It is clear that this is not a religious system that involves fear and trembling but one that evokes a sense of healthy interaction and allows participants to return home feeling good, happy and positive. In these interactions a series of transfers – of merit and help from the spiritual, of pains, problems, entreaties and gratitude from the human – is activated. I shall shortly turn to a discussion of the inner meanings contained in these interactions, but first, to conclude this outline of the activities at popular religious centres, I shall describe the most common types of amulet and talisman that are found there.

REQUESTS, TALISMANS AND AMULETS: *FUDA*, *O-MAMORI* AND *EMA*

Most religious centres provide an immense array of talismans, amulets and other religious paraphernalia that can be acquired as symbols and representations of the religious power and protection of the Buddhas and *kami*. These are usually bought for a small fee (for example an amulet for educational success might cost 300 yen, the same price as a cup of coffee), although the religious centres themselves prefer to see this as a form of merit-making and receiving, in which a donation is made and a talisman given in return. The basic underlying aims of such talismans and amulets are to provide good luck, protect people from bad luck and ward off misfortunes and any hindrances that might block the successful pursuit of a goal. As with the reputed powers of the *kami* and Buddhas themselves, some talismans and amulets may be specifically for a particular desire, goal or benefit, while others may be more general and all-embracing.

They fall into two broad categories: those that are to be taken away from the religious place as representations of its power, and those that are left there as a means of sending messages and transmitting requests to the *kami* and Buddhas. While the first variety operates more clearly as a protective agency and the latter as a means of expressing a desire or wish for *riyaku*, both in the final analysis seek the same ends, concerned with the well-being of the person who receives the object concerned.

The most common of the first category are *fuda* and *o-mamori*, both of which may act as talismans (that is, bringing good luck) or as amulets (warding off misfortunes and protecting against dangers), depending on the particular prayer or category of *riyaku* they represent: a talisman for *gōkaku*, educational success, seeks to bring good luck, while an amulet for *kōtsū anzen*, safe travel, aims to protect against potential misfortunes and bad luck. In reality these two functions are barely differentiated and form interlocking aspects of the same overall process.

Fuda are generally made of a flat piece of wood often both slightly pointed and broader at the top than at the bottom, on which an inscription of some sort, often the name of the shrine/temple and its *kami*/Buddha, has been written in cursive brush strokes. They are generally also wrapped in white paper so that the inscription is visible and are tied with a bow of coloured string. They are of various sizes: while most, such as those in Keihan trains, are usually about fifteen centimetres high, one can acquire larger ones which are considered to have proportionally more power. The Kōrien Narita-san temple, for example, has a whole array of *fuda* for traffic safety (the primary *riyaku* associated with the temple), up to approximately a metre in height: the prices vary accordingly. Another common type of *fuda* is a piece of paper on which an image (usually of a Buddha), often accompanied by a sacred inscription, has been imprinted.

O-mamori are smaller, usually consisting of a small brocade bag or sachet with draw strings. On the bag are written the shrine or temple name and the particular *riyaku* it is for. Inside the bag there is usually a piece of paper or wood with a further inscription such as the text of the *Hannya Shingyō*.[4] Like much else in the world of Japanese religion, styles may change to reflect the contemporary mood: in the 1980s plastic *o-mamori* shaped like credit cards (and indicative of Japan's growing development of plastic money) have come into prominence. Many shrines and temples now provide, besides the more traditional *o-mamori*, some in the form of a credit card. Kiyomizudera in Yashiro, Hyogo prefecture (yet another popular temple with this name), provides such an *o-mamori* with, on one side, a Buddhist inscription and the words *kanai anzen* (family safety), *kōtsū anzen* (traffic safety) and *shogan jōjū* (completion of all wishes), plus the temple's name, address and telephone number. On the reverse is the *engi* and further information about the temple. *O-mamori* that double as telephone cards, which themselves have become increasingly popular since the mid-1980s in Japan both for use in telephones and as collectors' items, have also become increasingly prevalent. Inscribed with inscriptions, prayers for luck and protection and often pictures of the religious centre, these can be used to make telephone calls but also act as an amulet or talisman.

Basically *fuda* sacralise an area: once acquired they are placed in, for example, the *butsudan* or *kamidana* or elsewhere in the house from whence they protect the environment and surroundings. The *fuda* in the Keihan train and the amulets in the *kamidana* on the bridge of the ferry from Kyūshū mentioned in Chapter 2 protect those environments and those within them. Similarly I have a paper *fuda* depicting Fudō, given to me by a priest in Shodōshima: I was, he told me, to place it in the hallway of my house facing the door, and this would keep the house safe from burglars and other miscreants.

O-mamori are more personalised in that they protect (the word itself comes from the verb *mamoru*, to protect or guard) a particular person: they are worn on or about the person. The credit and telephone card types may easily be carried in a wallet, while the sachet type may be tied, for example, on to a bag. It is quite common to see schoolchildren with *o-mamori* for educational success tied to their satchels, and *o-mamori* for traffic safety hung inside cars to protect those within them.

The reasons why these are religious objects, and the manner in which they are supposed to work, are interrelated. Although when made they are, even if carefully crafted and pleasing to the eye, merely pieces of paper, brocade or wood, they are then empowered in religious rituals that transform them into manifestations of the *kami* and Buddhas in just the same way as a statue is changed from being merely an object into a Buddha through the 'eye opening' rites (see Chapter 2). At Narita-san, for example, *fuda* and *o-mamori* are placed before the image of Fudō (which *is* Fudō, the spirit having been put into it by Kōbō Daishi, as we saw in Chapter 6) and, through rituals performed by the priests, Fudō's power and spirit passes into the talismans and amulets. They are sacralised, no longer wood and paper but actually Fudō himself. They are, like the temple image at Kōrien, *bunshin*, spiritual offshoots, of the main image, fields of power in their own right. Of course, at the same time this means, at least in the case of Narita-san amulets, that the source of their power emanates from the power of Kōbō Daishi himself. Thus the talismans and amulets at Narita-san, as at other centres whose origins stem from the actions of such powerful religious practitioners, stand at the end of a long chain of religious transmission extending from Kōbō Daishi via Fudō to the present day.[5]

The person who acquires them, then, does not receive a piece of wood or paper but a charged concretisation of power, the essence not simply of the *kami* or Buddha's power and compassion but of the entity itself. Thus they, the *kami* and Buddhas, may be carried with one or kept in the home or elsewhere to bring in good fortune, ward off spiritual impediments and absorb bad luck that otherwise would afflict the person concerned. Unlike statues, however, their power and efficacy are transient: having absorbed bad luck or having opened the way to good, they may need to be changed. The general custom (encouraged by shrines and temples, for whom the sale of amulets and the like can be an important element in their economies) is to change them yearly, with the major period of exchange being at New Year, as we saw in Chapter 3. They may also be purchased for a specific purpose or situation; for example, because of an examination, and may thus be disposed of once that need has been dealt with.

Besides *fuda* and *o-mamori* there are many other items of religious paraphernalia that may be taken away from the centre. Some religious centres distribute sachets of earth from their precincts to act (as with the soil from Shikoku temples in miniature pilgrimages) as extensions of the power of the centre itself. Kiyotakisan, a cave temple and pilgrimage site in Shodōshima, distributes soil empowered through rituals that can, according to the words on its sachet, be scattered on the fields to help provide a good harvest, or around the house to lead to household prosperity. At Imakumano, a Saikoku pilgrimage temple in south-east Kyoto, one can buy specially empowered pillowcases which can, according to the temple, prevent headaches and senility, make one wise and improve health and longevity. Kiyoshi Kōjin shrine in Takarazuka, like many other places, vends lucky frog figurines: the symbolic efficacy of this frog derives from a linguistic pun, for the word for frog, *kaeru*, is pronounced the same as the verb *kaeru*, to return. Hence the frog symbolises both the idea of returning safely (that is, it has a function connected to travel) and returning to health. Through all these means people are able to take away with them the power of the holy centre, extending its influence to their homes, cars, persons and wherever else they wish in an unending process of accessibility.

Besides this array of means for bringing away power and protection, visitors to religious centres can also choose a variety of objects through which to express their feelings and requests to the *kami* and Buddhas. The most common of these is the *ema*, the small wooden votive tablet mentioned in earlier chapters. Usually a few centimetres across, these flat board-like objects carry various colourful pictures as well as the name of the religious site, and often a specified wish as well. Many are hand-painted and are genuine representations of folk art, avidly collected as such. The name *ema* means 'horse picture', and derives from the traditional Shintoesque concept that horses were messengers and mounts of the *kami* and could readily transmit entreaties to them. Presenting a horse to the *kami* as part of a ritual, or to accompany an important request, was the most prestigious and efficacious offering one could make, yet in early Japanese society this was an extremely expensive matter, beyond the reach of all but the very rich. Consequently the practice of substituting a horse figurine or, later, a picture of a horse (*ema*) developed: excavations have shown that this custom was extant by the eighth century. The practice of submitting petitions to the *kami* on wooden boards depicting a horse became standard, spreading also to Buddhist temples, and gradually the symbols inscribed or painted on the *ema* themselves became diversified, with the shrines and temples producing their own for the benefit of visitors.[6]

The contemporary small *ema* is the legacy of this development, found at virtually all religious centres in Japan and in diverse and varied designs, from year animals and figures of worship to depictions of scenes from *engi*. Frequently the design may involve a motif symbolising the intent of the *ema*, as is the case with the temple Kokawadera in Wakayama prefecture, whose *ema* shows an arrow with the words *shogan jōjū* (successful completion of all wishes) striking the centre of a target. Usually *ema* have a space for people to write in their own messages, wishes and, if they wish, their name, age and address. They are then hung up at the shrine or temple as a petition or message to the *kami* and Buddhas. At most religious centres they will eventually be ritually burned to make way for more and symbolically to liberate the request. In general terms the requests are directed to *kami* or Buddha, the exception being *ema* or *mizuko* which, as was noted in the previous chapter, are directly addressed to the spirit of the child and are usually concerned with relating expressions of remorse and informing the spirit about family developments.

As with all that has been discussed in this chapter, the requests written on *ema* cover a wide range of issues. Where a shrine or temple is noted for a specific form of *riyaku*, most or all of the *ema* left there may reflect that theme: thus at Tenjin shrines, with their focus on education, the requests on *ema* are largely connected with passing examinations, improving the ability to study and being able to enter a good university or high school. One of the powers of Kankiten at Hōzanji in Ikoma is to give support to those who make vows to give up something. The *ema* here depicts a padlock superimposed on the ideogram *kokoro* (heart, mind) to symbolise the binding nature of the commitment to the resolution being made. In 1938 Holtom published a detailed list of the resolutions written on *ema* at Hōzanji over 50 years ago: most showed men and women asking for help in giving up, usually for a fixed period, alcohol, tobacco, betting or sexual relations, either entirely or, more commonly, with partners other than a spouse.[7]

Similar investigations into the Hōzanji *ema* by Japanese researchers in the mid-1980s have shown that some of these vows are still made: of 998 *ema* investigated at the temple in August 1982, 196 centred on abstention from something such as tobacco, alcohol, gambling and, a sign of contemporary social problems, drugs, including glue sniffing. Interestingly, possibly also a sign of changing social mores, very few (less than 2 per cent) were concerned with sexual abstention and infidelities. Besides these vows there were many other, more direct requests for various forms of *riyaku*, the most common being for *gōkaku*, educational success (205 of the *ema*), followed by business prosperity, family safety, and good health.[8]

Over several years of reading *ema* I have noted a general preponderance of requests connected with education, signifying a high level of *ema* writing among young people, especially those under the age of 22 (the normal age of university graduation, when people leave examinations behind). These may be general, as with pleas for help in studying well or passing examinations, or direct and specific: it is common to see *ema* requesting help in getting into a specific high school or university, or even a particular department in a university. Besides education they can express various other ambitions, as with the *ema* I saw at Chionin in Amanohashidate, northern Kyoto prefecture, where a 19-year-old girl had written that she wanted to make a lot of money, go to London and meet a 'really great person'. One can make multiple requests on the same *ema*, my favourite being one I read at Ichijōji, a pilgrimage temple near Himeji, presumably written by a young boy, making five requests:

'more pocket money, may the Tigers [a baseball team] win the championship, may I have good health, may I be able to study well, and may we soon find someone to look after the kittens'.

At many places, including Jishu shrine, the popular lovers' shrine in Kyoto, people (more commonly girls) write *ema* expressing their feelings for someone else, in a form of graffiti that sends a message not just to the *kami* but to the desired person, should they also frequent that religious centre. Couples may write a joint *ema* pledging their eternal affection, as with the following from Chionin in Amanohashidate:

> May we always live together harmoniously and in good health.
> May we have a healthy baby.

While many of the requests may thus be happy and often amusing, they can also strike poignant chords of genuine need and despair: at Yoshiminedera near Kyoto a couple aged 30 and 32 asked that they might be able to have a baby soon, while a man of 36 requested that he find a wife, again soon. Perhaps more desperate still was the following, written by a female person, who gave her name but not her age, at Kokawadera:

> May I soon be able to pay back the money I owe and get some peace of mind, and also may I overcome my illness.

Relief from illness and pain is another common entreaty, as with the plaintive 'my hip hurts: please do something about it' that I saw at Ishikiri shrine. They may be written for the benefit of others, for example a member of a peer group or for a friend or family member, as with these two examples, the first from Zōjōji in Tokyo and the second from Shigisan:

> May Jun-chan somehow get into university (signed: Mami).
> May father's diabetes get better, and may mother's hip and heart problems clear up.

I have outlined here just a few of the enormous variety of requests that I have observed written on *ema* over the past few years so as to provide some idea of what people might seek through them and also to illustrate what an interesting pastime reading *ema* can be, not just because of their variety but also because they provide a very direct window into the fears, worries, needs, desires and contemporary orientations and values of Japanese people. This is a point to which I shall return later.

Besides *ema* there exist a number of other means for transcribing and conveying one's feelings and wishes to the spiritual world. The small sticks of wood incinerated in the *goma* ritual mentioned in Chapter 5 may be purchased at many temples and shrines: one writes a request on the stick and then leaves it at the religious centre, where it will be ritually burned along with others in a ceremony that 'liberates' the messages on them and brings them to the attention of the *kami* and Buddhas. Stones are another popular medium of transmission, and at many religious centres one may see piles of small round stones inscribed with requests which have been left for the *kami* or Buddha to 'read' and act upon.

USES AND MEANINGS

The acquisition of such charms and talismans is carried out by a broad section of Japanese society: the five-yearly NHK surveys from 1973 onwards show a steady growth in the numbers of those who state that they carry *o-mamori* or keep *fuda*, rising from 30 per cent in 1973 to 36 per cent in 1983.[9] A more detailed 1981 NHK survey on religious attitudes shows a broader picture, with those using them 'often' ranging from 29 per cent for teenagers to 56 per cent for those over 70, and 'sometimes', from 48 per cent of teenagers to 24 per cent of those over 70. Combining those who do so often and those who do so sometimes the total for all age groups is over 70 per cent, ranging from 72 per cent of those over 70 to 80 per cent of those in their thirties.[10]

I carried out a brief survey on four classes of students aged between 18 and 20 at two universities at which I taught in the Osaka—Kōbe region, and although I cannot claim the results as comprehensive (the sample itself being rather small) the figures produced do show high levels of acquisition of *o-mamori* as well as of *ema*. I asked the following questions: Do you buy *o-mamori*? Do you write requests on *ema*? Do (1) *o-mamori* and (2) praying to the *kami* and Buddhas help in passing examinations? The following totals and percentages, out of a response of 151, were the result:

1. Buying *o-mamori*. Yes: 112 (75 per cent) (of these 16 did so often and 96 sometimes); no: 37; no response: 2.
2. Writing on *ema*. yes: 51 (33 per cent); No: 89; no response: 11.
3. *O-mamori* as helpful in examinations. Yes: 86 (57 per cent); no: 64; no response: 1.

4. Praying as helpful for examinations. Yes: 93 (61 per cent); no: 56; no response: 2.[11]

There are two preliminary points that should be made concerning these figures. One is that the overall high levels of acquisition should be taken in conjunction with the generally prevalent customs, often interfused with ludic themes, of shrine and temple visiting in Japan, and of taking part in mass activities such as *hatsumōde* and festivals. As my descriptions in Chapter 3 illustrated, part of the ambience of such occasions involves buying talismans, often on a casual basis inspired by the festive atmosphere. The second is that the comparatively high levels of occasional use by young people, shown both in the 1981 survey and my own, are clearly influenced by the heavy involvement of this generation in educational matters, and especially in the periodic and important examinations that control their progress up the education ladder.

These points are also valid in searching for explanations of the general nature and efficacy of the actions performed at religious sites. Much of this activity is spontaneous and casual, influenced by the convivial atmosphere, innate humour and the warmth that permeates the world of shrine and temple visiting. This certainly, far more than any firmly held belief that such actions will necessarily work, is what conditions participation in such amusing folkloric customs as Shigisan's miraculous means of 'increasing' one's bank balance. Besides being carried along by the ambience, of course, many people feel that no harm can come of the situation: one has more to lose if the proposition (that certain water contained holy powers, for instance) were true and one did not do it than if it were false and one did. A student at examination time seeing his/her peers writing *ema* for success or buying *gōkaku* talismans is liable to follow suit if only because of this 'insurance factor' dimension. In such terms the 'do it and see' dimensions of Japanese religion clearly have a 'nothing ventured, nothing gained' angle as well.

None the less, this does not mean that the actions performed or the amulets obtained are merely magical and coercive: nor does it mean that people expect a direct material reward for their actions or from the talismans. In questioning those who acquire amulets and talismans and the priests at whose temples and shrines they are sold, I have yet to find anyone who has positively asserted that such objects work as a matter of course. As my survey of students demonstrates, many people do consider that praying and acquiring *o-mamori* help them in the face of difficulties, but this is far from saying that they have an automatic effect that mechanically manipulates or coerces the spiritual world.

When I was questioning some students on their attitudes to *ema* and *o-mamori* one girl who regularly used them expressed her attitude by using the phrase *shinjireba kanau* ('if you believe, it will happen'). This did not mean, she added, that she would not need to work before an examination: naturally, she would have to study at least as hard as everyone else. However she could also feel reassured in her own mind that she had, by praying and expressing her inner wishes through an *ema* or amulet, 'got the gods on her side', and the emotional sense of ease that would come through this would enable her actually to work better. Believing that something will happen was thus the first step to its actual occurrence. The importance of this sense of emotional ease was further emphasised by another student who, commenting on his purchase of *ema* and *o-mamori* prior to university examinations, informed me: 'It won't mean I can pass, but it means I will relax: it gives me peace of mind [*anshin*] when I take the examination.'

We have already encountered this idea of a prayer or religious talisman providing a sense of calm that can help in achieving ends or overcoming obstacles in the example of the young woman, cited in Chapter 2, who steadied herself before her driving test by reciting the *Hannya Shingyō* and by carrying a copy of the text with her. The importance of feeling at ease and in command of events, and the role that prayers and amulets may play in this, are perhaps felt more overtly in the world of education than anywhere else in contemporary Japan. The pressurised and competitive Japanese education system with its famed 'examination hell' (*shiken jigoku*) places immense stress on its students, especially in the university entrance examinations, where success or failure can have drastic career consequences, and by thus creating such a sense of uncertainty and unease virtually drives those within it to the *kami* and Buddhas. It can do the same for the students' parents who frequently become avid procurers of talismans and amulets as their children progress through the educational system and who often become so committed to their offsprings' success that they work themselves into states of insecurity. Such feelings were expressed to me by a woman who used to come and meditate at the temple at which I lived in the winter of 1981–2 at Sendai in northern Japan. During the *hatsumōde* period she came to the temple and had a special prayer request said by the priest and acquired a *fuda* for educational success for the benefit of her son who was going to take his university examinations that spring. She explained to me that she felt he would pass because he was bright and worked hard, but nevertheless she could not help worrying about the matter. As a result she felt she was transmitting her nervousness to him and consequently unsettling his studies and perhaps implanting seeds of doubt in his own mind. By coming to the temple and seeking the Buddhas' support and getting a *fuda* she felt she had set things in harmony on the spiritual side: this would make sure no unforeseen problems would arise and would thus reassure her. Indeed, immediately afterwards she said she felt calmer and more confident that things would be alright. The result of this new sense of calm confidence would be that she would not disturb his studies and this would enable him to get on with the business of studying through which he would succeed in his task.

Underpinning these remarks and attitudes is the feeling that all enterprises need psychic support and that human beings need to recognise the importance of working with the *kami* and Buddhas and in harmony with their environment. As the pamphlet from Jishu shrine quoted in the previous chapter made clear, inherent in this is an understanding that there may be times when human power alone cannot attain things and a recognition of inherent human frailties, and that at such times one needs the support and reassurance of the *kami* and Buddhas. The *ema* at Hōzanji show this well, with supplicants asking Kankiten to give them the strength and support to carry out their vows to avoid temptations to which they are clearly prone. The person rubbing a statue may be expressing a similar message: the need for help and support in the face of pain and ill-health. There is here an implicit recognition that there are times when events are outside one's control: the student, no matter how good, is still faced with the uncertainties of what will actually appear on the examination paper and in consequence may find that the therapies provided through shrines, temples and talismans provide a way of assuming some sense of reassurance and control.

The same may be true for the driver who has his/her car ritually purified (this can be done at the Narita-san temples and at many others, as well as many shrines besides) or who places a traffic safety amulet in it. Such actions do not guarantee that s/he will have no accidents but they can serve to provide a sense of well-being, a feeling that one has done what one possibly can in psychological terms to guard against unforeseen circumstances. One female student I taught briefly during my first stay in Japan in 1981 was given a new car by her parents: her first act, she told me, was to take it to the Nagoya branch temple of Narita-san, get it blessed and purchase an amulet for it. This, she stated, helped give her a sense of peace of mind and confidence when she drove it, and this was in itself conducive to being a better, safer driver.

Talismans, amulets and prayers for welfare — and consequently the inner ethos of *genze riyaku* — are concerned to a great extent with liminal points in life where the individual or group cannot otherwise be sure of the outcome of an event. Villagers in pre-modern Japan dependent on a good harvest for their continued well-being, women nervously awaiting the birth of a child, students preparing for university entrance examinations that could affect the rest of their lives, and people embarking on voyages or acquiring a new car are all, in their different ways, stepping into the unknown, into areas of potential danger. The reassurance provided through religious action thus symbolically and psychologically serves to hem in that danger, making it safe and reassuring those who pray that they have done everything possible to bring it within the sphere of human control. It thus also provides a sense of solace and peace to those who, like the woman whose *ema* showed her turmoil because of debts and illness, find themselves otherwise in a state of despair over the condition of their lives.

Many prayers and amulets express a concern for safety and protection: common requests centre on *kōtsu anzen* (traffic/travel safety), *kanai anzen* (safety in the family), *anzan* (safe birth) and *yaku yoke* (prevention of danger). This is indicative of a deeply entrenched preoccupation with security and safety within Japanese society in general: one does not have to live long in Japan before becoming aware of this, largely through the numbers of signs admonishing one to keep safety in mind. Station announcements warn one about the dangers of standing near the edge of the platform when a train is coming in, warning lights flash in buses when the bus is about to stop so that passengers are not taken unaware and thrown off balance, and ubiquitous *anzen daiichi* ('safety first') signs may be found on buildings and anywhere that construction is taking place. This overriding concern for safety and security also contributes to the pressures of the education system, for success here is a virtual passport to the warm security of a lifelong company job.

This preoccupation with messages and reminders of safety is manifested also in the use of *fuda* and *o-mamori*. A traffic safety

o-mamori hanging in the car is, as a Buddhist priest at Narita-san
informed me, a reminder that one should drive carefully and remain
ever-vigilant and aware. It is by maintaining this state of mind that
accidents can be prevented. Thus the practical prevention of accidents does not come about because of any magical propensities in
the amulet so much as through the messages they transmit to make
people feel at ease and to remind them to be vigilant and constantly
do their best to drive safely. Signs at the Narita-san temples and
inscriptions on their amulets read: 'With the mind of Buddha at the
driving wheel there will be no accidents' (*Busshin nigiru handoru
jiko nashi*).

In a similar vein, the traffic safety amulet from Kasuga shrine in
Nara carries a message beseeching people to drive safely and 'maake
this a world without traffic accidents'. Through such messages
o-mamori and *fuda* may be used to promote social ideals and
responsibility and thus play their part in the propagation of a
harmonious society. Around November 1986 when the law to make
the wearing of seatbelts compulsory in the front seat of cars came
into effect, seatbelt *o-mamori* began to appear at some temples and
shrines. I bought one at Daisenji in Tottori prefecture, asking the
priest as I did so why it was being sold. His response was that
Japanese people, few of whom had previously worn seatbelts,
needed to be encouraged to wear them as it was now clear that they
did save lives: thus the *o-mamori*, which could be clipped to the
seatbelt, was a reminder of the need to use the belt whenever one
got in the car.[12]

Prayers, amulets and talismans are also, as the student cited
earlier expressed, externalisations of inner volition and thus may be
seen as means through which internalised feelings and intents move
towards transformation and realisation. By defining and bringing
into the open an inner feeling, that wish or need is structuralised
and given form, and as such its realisation as an actuality is set in
motion: will is turned into actuality by being stated outwardly
through the form of a prayer, a talisman or a ritual. They provide a
cathartic function as well, providing valuable emotional release
mechanisms, especially for those, like the students in the 'examination hell', under some stress. By acting out feelings and emotions
and externalising those inner desires, fears and worries Japanese
people have a channel through which they can therapeutically
liberate those feelings and get them out in the open rather than
bottling them up.

The importance of this public performance, of making a vow before the *kami* and Buddhas to demonstrate one's true intent and to express inner feelings and desires, plays an important part in the process of seeking *riyaku*. On the one hand it demonstrates one's sincerity and, hence, the worthiness of the benefit that is sought, and on the other, it helps to channel what may be personally beneficial and aggrandising wishes into a legitimate framework. Prayers for success manifest the element of competitive concern in Japanese society, in which success and 'getting on' are desired goals. At the same time, of course, it is a society that likes to stress the ideals of harmony, conformity to group norms and not standing out. The religious milieu through which such ambitious desires for success are externalised via supplications to the gods and fortune-beckoning talismans thus provides an ideal setting through which the apparent contradictions between the ethics of competition and conformity may be harmonised. Students can ask the *kami* to bestow success in a university entrance examination — a situation where some have to stand out to the disadvantage and distress of those who fail — within a context that removes from them the naked gloss of ambition by apparently placing their fate in the hands of the gods. In such ways the socially desirable pursuit of success may be legitimated so as not to clash with the prevailing images of harmony that are widely promoted as social ideals in Japan.

During his campaign to succeed Nakasone Yasuhiro as Prime Minister of Japan in 1986, Takeshita Noboru, one of the leading contenders for the office, was pictured on the front page of Japanese newspapers receiving a talisman for *daigan jōjū* (successful attainment of a great desire) at Zenkōji, a famous prayer temple in Nagano.[13] Takeshita was not simply rationalising his ambition within a legitimate framework of expression, however, for this public performance also provided an ideal photo-opportunity through which to send out to all those who were involved in selecting Nakasone's successor a clear message of his sincere determination to win.

Thus prayers and the messages conveyed by *fuda*, *o-mamori* and *ema* act also as a medium through which one can transmit messages to others. Students who buy *o-mamori* and affix them to their satchels in the period before examinations can send reassuring messages to their teachers and parents of the sincerity of their intent. Equally, as we have already seen, amulets displayed in railway carriages serve to assure the public of the concerned intent of the company, just as those displayed in shop *kamidana* are symbolically informing the public of the shopkeeper's good faith and best intentions.

Beyond such personal and psychological dimensions there are also social factors involved in all these activities, for the religious world provides a means of expressing one's concerns and cares for others, as with those who write *ema* seeking some benefit for their parents or friends, or perform the *hyakudo mairi* for a sick friend or relative. A certain amount of the acquisition of *o-mamori* is not for oneself but for others: mothers visiting temples and shrines may puchase talismans for their children, both to remind them of the importance of studying and doing well in their examinations and as gestures of their concern for them in their studies. Older children may do the same for younger siblings, as was the case with a friend of ours, a university graduate, who bought an *o-mamori* from the major education shrine Kitano Tenmangū in Kyoto at New Year, to give to her younger brother prior to his university entrance examinations.

My wife and I have been given *o-mamori* by Japanese friends in similar gestures of friendship: shortly before one university holiday when we were about to embark on a journey a Japanese colleague gave me an *o-mamori* and said she had said a prayer at her local shrine for us. Later, shortly before we returned to the United Kingdom for good, the local beer shop owner gave my wife, by then several months pregnant, an *o-mamori* for safe birth that he had purchased at a nearby shrine.

A final element that may be relevant in the acquisition of *fuda* and *o-mamori* is the extent to which they may be bought as souvenirs by those for whom shrine and temple visiting is also a touristic exercise. They may also be taken back as souvenirs for others, for Japanese social customs and etiquette decree that those who travel should bring back *o-miyage*, souvenirs, for their close family and friends.

The acquisition of an *o-mamori* or *fuda*, then, and the performance of any action at a religious centre may express a complex web of themes, motives and meanings. Not all of them are necessarily present on each occasion: some people may simply buy an *o-mamori* as a souvenir or present, or rub a statue just because everyone is doing the same, while others will be more concerned with the sense of mental peace they might attain from carrying an amulet or performing an action. As with the actions performed at religious centres in general the nature of the motivations and the interpretations that may be placed on them are for the individual to determine. What is clear, however, is that the orientations of all these actions and objects are concerned with the creation of a sense of ease and with helping people to feel happy and bright in some way, whether through the reassuring peace of mind that can come from having an amulet in one's car and the *kami* on one's side, or from bringing into the open an inner wish or worry, or even from the enjoyment that may flow from buying a talisman as an expression of love or even simply as a souvenir for a sibling, parent or friend.

REFLECTING CONTEMPORARY INSECURITIES: PRAYERS AND *O-MAMORI* AS MIRRORS OF CONTEMPORARY SOCIETY

Prayers, *ema*, *fuda* and *o-mamori* in many respects act as mirrors and barometers of contemporary social moods, worries, insecurities and preoccupations, for one of the most striking things about their content and the themes they express is the degree to which they remain in step with the changes and advances of contemporary society. The *ema* at Hōzanji are a good example, showing both how certain problems endure over the generations (the enduring human struggle with the problems of gambling, alcohol and tobacco) and how changing social circumstances and attitudes have their effect, with the appearance of the drug problem and the comparatively diminished interest in the upholding of sexual mores.

In general the requests that are made and the desires, needs and worries that are expressed at popular religious centres are very much issues of contemporary concern. The extent to which the messages written on *ema* show the immense importance of educational success and the pressures inherent in that system has already been commented upon. Here I shall briefly outline two further examples of this contemporary reflection of worries and insecurities.

The first concerns the rapid rise over the past two decades of the numbers of people who ask temples and shrines to conduct purification rituals for their cars to prevent traffic accidents. This has come about as the number of cars on the roads has grown, as public concern about and awareness of traffic accidents and deaths has developed and as the Japanese have become increasingly mobile both at home and abroad. In 1963 the temple Kawasaki Daishi near Tokyo performed about 100 such purifications per year: by 1970 the figure had gone up to 25,000 and by 1982 it was 67,000.[14] Shinshōji at Narita, which is probably the best known religious centre for traffic safety in Japan, estimates that it performs some 100,000 purifications a year now.

According to temple informants the association of the Narita-san temples with traffic safety really began in the 1950s and 1960s because of popular demand and was a natural extension of the traditional role of the Narita-san Fudō as a guardian of travellers. The gradual increase in car ownership in those decades led to a growing number of requests for special protective amulets for automobiles. The temple further realised that both a need and a source of insecurity existed because of the growing number of memorial services it was asked to perform for those who had died in traffic accidents, and consequently it developed a special amulet and car purification service as a response.[15] The temple was, in fact, quick to understand that such a need existed and to promote and establish itself as the primary centre for the *riyaku* of traffic safety in Japan. In subsequent years both its reputation and the desire of people for this protection have become widespread, enabling it to acquire new levels of prosperity and to build further branch temples throughout Japan: equally, many other shrines and temples throughout Japan now provide similar services. In a further extension of this capacity to protect travellers Narita-san has begun to produce amulets specifically for overseas and air travel, an area of need and request that can only grow in the next few years as increasing numbers of Japanese start to travel abroad.[16]

The second example of the responsive nature of the religious world to the contemporary needs of worshippers and to problems of present concern in society concerns the growing number of places (in this instance, mainly temples, and especially those enshrining Kannon) offering prayers and amulets of various forms for *boke fūji* (literally, the suppression of senility). In this activity elderly people pray to Kannon, asking that they will not go senile and lose their dignity before they die. This in itself is an indication of the growing problems of ageing in an increasingly urban and nuclearised society that has developed better medical techniques for keeping people alive longer. The Japanese have very high life expectancies, but the downside of this has been an increasing incidence of senility: in 1984 there were 500,000 people suffering from this problem and estimates suggest this may rise to one million by the next century.[17]

Medical science has so far not found an answer to the problem, while the attention paid to it in the media has both heightened public awareness and simultaneously increased the worries of many old people. While there is perhaps little that people can do to avoid the reality of such things happening, what may cause them even more distress is the *fear* that it might occur to them. Many old people dread either becoming a burden on their families or, as is more likely these days, ending up alone in an old people's home: perhaps they are even more terrified of the loss of human dignity that senility and Alzheimer's Disease may bring.

Consequently many have turned to the religious world to seek psychological support and assurance in the face of their unease. The *boke fūji* phenomenon, with Kannon, because of her compassionate and caring image, its primary focus, is a product of this. Imakumano temple in Kyoto, for example, now has a *boke fūji* Kannon statue depicting Kannon blessing two old people who clutch at her robes. At the temple one can purchase small statues of an old person, which are inscribed with one's name and presented as offerings to Kannon: these beseech her to intercede and save the donor from the fate of senility. To the side of the Kannon is a rack where *ema* requesting Kannon's help in preventing senility are hung. A pilgrimage linking 33 temples with *boke fūji* Kannon statues, including Imakumano, has also developed in recent years. This is an area of religious activity that will probably continue to grow because the increasing incidence and awareness of the problem coupled with the apparent lack of any material progress towards its prevention in effect leave many people with little but the insecurity of worrying whether they will be affected, and with few means through which to express and assuage that anxiety apart from the religious world.

THE CONTINUITY OF CHANGE

The Japanese religious world is, especially at popular levels, constantly changing, developing and responding as the surrounding society and its needs change. In the Kisogawa region in the mountains of Nagano prefecture, as Josef Kyburz has recently shown, the major local religious cult used to be the worship of Batō (horse-headed) Kannon, a manifestation of Kannon especially popular among farmers and horse-breeders. Horse rearing was traditionally the major economic activity of the region, and this naturally emphasised Batō Kannon's prominence. After the war, however, this trade was gradually marginalised, eventually becoming extinct as motorisation made the horse redundant as a means of transport and in agriculture. With this demise the Batō Kannon cult has fallen by the wayside, its centres of worship falling into disrepair and its statues overgrown.[18]

This says much about the dynamics of popular religious orientations: when a form of *riyaku* or a figure of worship is no longer in tune with the changing circumstances of the age or becomes obsolete it ceases to have any real significance and value for those around it. This does not, of course, signify any form of religious decline but of change, of regeneration, for shifting social patterns create new circumstances and needs that elucidate fresh responses and manifestations in the religious sphere. Spiritual entities may assimilate new functions as circumstances arise, or may be adapted to changing conditions. Inari's growing role in the securities business, mentioned in Chapter 3, is an indication of this, as is the role Kannon has assumed in connection with the increasing problems of senility and the fears that accompany it.

The spiritual world remains malleable and ever-changing in line with the patterns of the environment around it, able to adapt and be adapted to any problem or change that occurs. This flexible responsiveness is central to the nature of popular religious centres. Thus they are not simply enjoyable places to visit because of their inherent vitality, dynamism and vibrant colour: they also provide a direct window on the nature of Japanese religion and on the contemporary insecurities, needs and orientations of Japanese people that are reflected in the activities, amulets and talismans found there.

8 Spirits, Satellites and a User-Friendly Religion: Agonshū and the New Religions

Probably the single most discussed and dynamic phenomenon in the Japanese religious world in the past few decades has been the rise and proliferation of new religions (known in Japanese as *shin shūkyō*).[1] Since the early nineteenth century many hundreds of religious movements have developed in Japan in a constant process of flux, growth, decline and renewal. Some have flourished and grown into massive organisations.

Tenrikyō, for example, claims over one and a half million members and maintains a multidimensional organisation centred at the city of Tenri (named after the religion), near the old Imperial capital of Nara. Tenri is a veritable relgious capital that has grown around the sites where Nakayama Miki, Tenrikyō's foundress, lived and received the revelations and spiritual powers that led to the formation of the religion in the nineteenth century. Spreading out from the main religious centre at Tenri are a complex of hostels for pilgrims and visitors from all over Japan and the rest of the world, administrative buildings, teaching centres, shops selling Tenrikyō publications, and various other institutions, including a major university with one of the best libraries in Japan and a modern hospital. It also has overseas branches, especially in areas with a large number of Japanese immigrants such as Brazil and Hawaii.

Sōka Gakkai is larger still, claiming millions of followers, and with huge headquarters in Tokyo and centres all over Japan, its own university, Sōka University, and newspaper, the *Seikyō shinbun*, which is one of the largest-selling daily papers in Japan. It has also given birth to, and retains close links with, one of Japan's major political parties, the Kōmeitō.

At the other end of the scale are countless small groups with a handful of members centred around one individual teacher who provides them with guidance for living and solutions for spiritual problems. For example, the Taiyō Shinjiru Piramiddo no Kai ('Sun Worshipping Pyramid Society') which venerates the sun as a mani-

194

festation of the *kami* Amaterasu and believes that performing special memorial rites for one's ancestors will purify and eradicate all one's bad deeds, has fewer than 500 members and meets at the bar run by its foundress and leader Kamei Miyoko in Sapporo, Hokkaidō. Many new religions, especially such small and person-alised ones, flourish briefly then fall into decline, often on the demise of a charismatic founder, or are rent with secessions, as was the case with Mahikari cited in Chapter 1.

Their rise has often been stimulated by social factors: some of the greatest developments and expansions of new religions have occurred during periods of social crisis and unrest. The transition period from the Tokugawa to Meiji regimes, with its resultant social upheavals in the mid-nineteenth century, the years of economic depression and urban poverty in the late 1920s, and, especially, the catastrophic period after the end of the war in 1945 when Japan was defeated and occupied with her cities in ruins and her government and religious establishment disgraced, have all been times when new religions have developed and grown rapidly.[2] In the 1980s a wave of active and brash new religious movements (usually called the 'new' new religions (*shin shinshūkyō*) to distinguish them from earlier movements[3]) has come into prominence in Japan, expanding their membership rapidly and attracting the attention of the media and academics alike because they appear, in the midst of a rapidly technologising, modernising and internationalising society, to express anti-modern and Japanocentric sentiments, focusing on miracles, spirit possession and a view of causation that is rooted very firmly in the Japanese folk tradition. As we shall see in this chapter, these 'new' new religions, amongst the better known of which are Mahikari, Agonshū, Shinnyoen, Byakkō Shinkōkai, Ōyama Nezunomikoto Shinshikyōkai and Shinreikyō, are in many respects also a response to the social uneases of the age, providing a forum through which Japanese people may express their concerns about various worries and fears on wider social levels as well as on personal ones.

Many of them have grown rapidly: while membership statistics are notoriously unreliable (see above, Chapter 2) several of this newest wave of religious groups claim huge growths in their numbers during the 1980s. Ōyama Nezunomikoto Shinshikyōkai, a Shintoesque spiritual healing new religion based in Yokohama, claims a tenfold growth during a ten year period up to the late 1980s, and puts its membership now at over half a million.[4]

Shinnyoen also claims a tenfold increase in the same decade and states that it now has two million followers[5] while Agonshū, which will be the main focus of this chapter, also asserts a tenfold increase during the 1980s. These increases mirror the rapid increases of other new religions in earlier eras: Oomoto, for instance, experienced similar rapid growth in the 1920s, while Sōka Gakkai expanded its membership from a few thousand in 1950 to (according to its own rather optimistic estimate) 16 million in 1960.[6] In general, even when accepting that these religions tend to overestimate their strength, it is clear that they are able to attract a sizeable number of adherents. Estimates vary as to the precise extent of their influence: some surveys suggest that as few as 10 per cent of the population belong to new religions,[7] while more generous evaluations have gone as high as 30 per cent.[8]

The enormous numbers of new religions preclude giving more than a general overview of them as a phenomenon. I shall in this chapter largely focus on one very contemporary new religion, Agonshū, dealing with it particularly as an example of a religious movement that has become prominent in the 1980s. I have chosen this approach not least because of the broad literature that already exists on the slightly older new religions[9] but also because the 'new' new religions themselves are such a contemporary phenomenon exemplifying many of the major religious issues of concern in Japan at present. Moreover, Agonshū exemplifies many of the characteristics of new religions in general, especially when in the first flush of youth before they settle into religious middle age and become systematised and, frequently, lose their initial impetus. Consequently, to examine it will provide a picture of a religion in its early and most expansive phases of dynamism.

RENOVATIONS OF TRADITION IN A MODERN SETTING

Before describing Agonshū in detail I shall make a few general comments about some of the common characteristics of the new religions. The first point to make is that their sheer numbers, their continuing emergence and the masses of followers, some temporary like the young man mentioned in Chapter 1 who joined and left Risshōkōseikai, others fervent and long term like the Sōka Gakkai girl described in Chapter 1, all point to a powerful undercurrent of constant renewal and religious dynamism in Japan. In Chapter 2 I described the new religions as renovations of traditional Japanese religious ideas, as restatements and contemporary expressions of Japanese religious sentiment relayed within a relevant, modern context. They are very much products of the Japanese religious environment, taking elements from the various interpenetrating traditions, Shinto, Buddhist and folk, that form the framework of the Japanese religious world. Some have exhibited more distinctly Shinto nuances (as with Tenrikyō, whose rituals and religious centres borrow extensively from Shinto) and others such as Reiyūkai, Risshōkōseikai and Sōka Gakkai, which all base their teachings on interpretations of the Lotus Sūtra and consider themselves to be reawakenings of the true essence of Buddhism, are more clearly Buddhistic in nature. However, they all tend to share similar sets of characteristics, especially with regard to their adherence to core Japanese religious concerns such as the import-ance of ancestors and spirits of the dead, concepts of spiritual causation and the emphasis on *genze riyaku* and on the goal of finding meaning and ultimate happiness in this life.

Their syncretic tendencies exhibit many of the culturally assimila-tive qualities of Japanese society in general, taking also influences and ideas from outside the Japanese system and absorbing them, usually at the same time giving them a distinctly Japanese stamp. Besides the incorporation of Christian figures such as Jesus and Mary, mentioned in Chapter 2, some of the most recent new religions have assimilated aspects of Western occultism and trans-formed them into Japanese entities. For instance, the myth of the lost continent of Mu so beloved of Western occultists has surfaced in the teachings of Mahikari, albeit with strongly Japanese nuances which place Japan in primaeval times at the centre of Mu, from where it once ruled the entire globe.[10]

In terms of teaching and background, then, the new religions are not really new at all. Nor can many of them really be described as all that new in historical terms: Tenrikyō, for example, is over 150 years old, tracing its beginnings to the 1830s, although this still makes it comparatively new when compared to the histories of Shinto and Buddhism. Besides this question of relative age, their 'newness' is relative in another sense too: they are new because they represent a contrast to the established (*kisei*) religions of Japan, Shinto and Buddhism, that have historically formed the mainstream and official religious structure.

The new religions are organisations that have crystallised from the Japanese religious tradition distinct from this official mainstream and from its priestly establishments. As a generic phenomenon they represent a departure from, and an alternative to, the idea of a religious establishment with its close ties to government, state and social norms. The term 'new' is thus more clearly a contrast with 'established' and 'mainstream' than with 'old', a point that is further emphasised by the fact that while Protestantism and Catholicism, themselves closely associated with establishment and mainstream traditions in general, are *not* regarded as new religions in the Japanese context, it is common nowadays for Japanese academics to treat non-mainstream Christianity (for example the Jehovah's Witnesses, the Mormons and the Unification Church (the Moonies), all of which proselytise in Japan) as new religions.[11]

As we saw in Chapter 4 with the ignorance of Sōtō Zen members of their sect's teachings, people have belonged to the established traditions largely through inertia, remaining unaware of their doctrines and concerned mostly with the social framework they provide. This lack of understanding has been compounded by a general failure of the established traditions to put across their message in accessible terms. The priesthood has operated far more as a class of ritual functionaries than as a proselytising medium for religious teachings, a point emphasised by the attitudes of Sōtō Zen members reported in Chapter 4, who clearly did not regard the priest as someone to visit for spiritual advice, counselling or teaching. To some extent this tendency to ritualised formalism has left a spiritual vacuum, especially in the cities and recently developed urban areas where the traditional community underpinnings of Buddhism and Shinto have been least effective.

In many ways the new religions have flourished in response to such weaknesses, filling this spiritual vacuum and providing a sense of community in urban areas where the traditional community structures upheld by Shinto/Buddhist belonging either do not exist or have been marginalised by rapid change, and giving on an individual level relevant and accessible teachings and practices to help the individual find meaning in his/her life. They are also by and large lay-focused, giving their members (rather than a professional priesthood) an active role in guiding development, in spreading their teachings and in controlling their rituals.

Their newness is also contained in the ways in which they have assumed modern forms and exteriors that contrast with the traditions and age of the established religions. Their modern buildings and external forms imply a dynamic modernism that provides them with an up-to-date image and, concurrently, makes the established religions appear less relevant for the times. This external modernism combines with the internal traditionalism of their cosmologies and teachings to make these more acceptable in modern society, enabling these two apparently contrasting elements, the modern exterior and the highly traditional interior, to form a potent combination relevant to the needs of contemporary Japanese society.

In their methods of teaching they have shown an activism until recently lacking in the inertial nature of established religion: unable to rely on a virtually captive audience they have had to go out and get followers. Members of the new religions spread the word of their faith by going out on the streets, knocking on doors and handing out leaflets at stations and in shopping thoroughfares. This active proselytisation has been at the core of their development and growth. Conversely it has also given them a rather negative image amongst large segments of the population, who more than anything else see them as intrusive and annoying. The negative image of religion mentioned in Chapter 1 as something associated with being interrupted on Sunday mornings by ladies ringing one's doorbell and asking intrusive questions is largely a product of the vigorous activities of the new religions, including the Jehovah's Witnesses, who have in recent years conducted door-to-door campaigns in Japan, meeting with the same mixture of success and anathema as they have achieved in other parts of the world.

As a rule, their main channels of recruitment have been through personal contacts with close family and friends: Tani Fumio, surveying Mahikari members in the Osaka region in 1986, found that over 90 per cent were recruited by someone they knew, 40 per cent of these being close family members.[12] Earhart's survey of Gedatsukai members shows a similar pattern with most recruited by immediate family (37.8 per cent), relatives (14.5 per cent), friends (21 per cent) and neighbours (15.5 per cent).[13] These recruitment processes, whereby one is drawn through personal contacts into the movement, extend also to the structures of the religions themselves, for they tend to operate through close membership networks that provide support and counselling for their members and give them a place to feel at home, a sense of belonging and identity that existed in traditional village communities but that has largely been eroded by urbanisation.

Many new religions are also active on university campuses, especially attracting those who are living away from home in student accommodation. The student from Sōka Gakkai cited in Chapter 1 told me that she had been lonely and isolated in her first year at university because she was living away from home and had few friends in the area. She was eventually befriended by two members of Sōka Gakkai living in the same student residence who took her to Gakkai meetings and introduced her to others in the movement. Her original involvement, then, grew out of social contacts which provided her with a sense of friendship and belonging that countered her earlier isolation, and was the first stage along her road to active commitment. Non-mainstream Christian movements such as the Mormons and the Unification Church have also been especially active on many campuses, frequently benefiting from the growing empathy among the educated young towards Christianity in general and transforming this, through their own active proselytisation coupled with an active social organisation that encompasses would-be members in a network of support and friendship, into a small but growing membership.

As was noted earlier, the new religions are principally an urban phenomenon: while some of the earlier movements like Tenrikyō did develop in rural areas among farming communities, most that have flourished in this century have done so in urban contexts. In contrast, in rural areas where social networks have remained strongest the new religions have been comparatively less successful. A Sōka Gakkai official, discussing both its comparative strength in cities and weakness in rural areas, once described the Gakkai to me as a *toshigata no shūkyō*, a city-centred religion.[14] In earlier decades the major source of recruitment to Sōka Gakkai and the other new religions was amongst those who had moved to the cities and who had thus lost their traditional community ties but who had not found anything to replace them in their new environment. This pattern is now nowhere near as prevalent, however, for, besides second- and third-generation members who are born into these religions, a large proportion of those who join now come from urban backgrounds. Tani's Mahikari survey shows that 60 per cent of the 1001 adherents questioned were born, brought up and educated in cities, and that 80 per cent of its adherents in the Osaka region had been brought up there.[15]

Until recently it has been fairly standard for analyses of the new religions to assume that, since they found a ready constituency amongst those uprooted from rural society and from the unsettled urban masses, their membership largely consisted of an under-educated, impoverished and alienated underclass.[16] Because new religions were, in their formation, movements diverging from, and hence antithetical to, the establishment, they rarely gained a balanced press: the media (itself identifying with the establishment) largely portrayed them as fallacious, peddling superstitious ideas to under-educated, weak and gullible people on the fringes of society, and centred much of its attention on the occasional scandals that occurred within them.[17]

Contemporary research has shown a somewhat different picture: Japanese academics and the media in general have become far more ready to accept new religions as legitimate,[18] a process enhanced by the realisation that these old pictures — of marginal, uneducated and gullible people — are either no longer true or have been misleading from the beginning. Gedatsukai, according to Earhart's research, appears to attract a high proportion of clerical workers, sales personnel and farmers, while also attracting some from the upper, professional and technically skilled groups: conversely it had a very low (1.2 per cent) proportion of students.[19] Davis's Mahikari respondents covered a broad spectrum, with 14 per cent being high-level white collar workers, 11 per cent skilled workers, 46 per cent lower-middle-class white collar, 20 per cent unskilled workers and 8 per cent farmers.[20] Tani shows a very high level of students, either at school or college, amongst the Mahikari members he surveyed: 10 per cent were classified as blue collar, 60 per cent as white collar and skilled workers, while 30 per cent were students.[21]

Educational levels tend to be relatively high: Davis found that the Mahikari members he surveyed had slightly higher than average educational backgrounds,[22] while Tani shows that over 50 per cent of his Mahikari respondents above college age had graduated from university or junior college — a rate appreciably above the national average.[23] In the light of these statistics it can, I think, be safely said that members of new religions do not really, at least in contemporary Japan, constitute a deviant or lumpen underclass: rather they tend to vary very little from national norms, to the extent that Tani concluded that his Mahikari interviewees were 'average Japanese' if somewhat conservative politically.[24]

NEW TRUTHS, PERSONAL VERIFICATIONS AND THE IMPORTANCE OF MIRACLES

There is another area in which the new religions lay claim to a newness that is lacking in the established traditions, and this is in their claims to have discovered a new or previously hidden truth, as well as a means of implementing and making that truth available for the direct benefit of all. Many of the Buddhist new religions, for example, have found within the Buddhist canon messages and understandings that bring their innate power to all who recite them. As we shall see later in this chapter, one of the basic foundations of Agonshū's teaching is its claim to have discovered the true means to Buddhahood for both the living and the spirits of the dead in a Buddhist text that had previously barely been studied in Japan. Shinnyoen's teaching is centred on the discovery by its founder, Itō Shinjō, of the essential and inner truths of Buddhism within another text, the Nirvana Sūtra (Japanese: *Nehangyō*). There are several new religions, prominent among them Sōka Gakkai, Risshōkōseikai and Reiyūkai, that have found new meanings within the seminal Buddhist text, the Lotus Sūtra.

Similar patterns are found in the Shintoesque and folk-orientated new religions, where the source of new or hidden truth is generally a powerful *kami*, often portrayed as the source of original creation who has been neglected by mankind ever since with the result that the world has slid into disaster and chaos. Hence the deity has come forward again to reveal itself through an individual religious figure in order to right these troubles. Various religious founders have had such visitations and become the mouthpieces and mediators for the words and power of such deities: in the nineteenth century the previously overlooked *kami* Ushitora no Konjin spoke through the impoverished peasant woman Deguchi Nao, leading her to found Oomoto, while the creator deity God the Parent revealed himself and his powers to another woman of farming stock, Tenrikyō's foundress, Nakayama Miki. In recent decades others have revealed themselves to specially chosen figures: Su-god, ruler of Mu and creator of the human race, revealed himself to Okada Kōtama, entrusting him with the mission of purifying the world and repairing all its ills, while the deity Ōyama Nezunomikoto descended on and entrusted a similar mission to Inai Sadao, a public bathhouse owner in Yokohama who subsequently founded Ōyama Nezunomikoto Shinshikyōkai.[25]

The discovery of new truths provides the new religion with a vitalistic dimension, entrusting it with the power to overturn contemporary upheavals and ruin: this sense of world renewal (*yonaoshi*) forms an intrinsic part of the mission and message that many new religions bring to the world, often giving them a universal and internationalist dimension that serves to transcend their localised origins within the Japanese religious tradition. By finding new truths in Buddhist texts or through a newly revealed (or rediscovered) deity, the new religion mediates this power to its members and places in their hands a means and a technique (for example, the *okiyome* or spirit purification methods used by Mahikari or the recitation of passages of the Lotus Sūtra in Sōka Gakkai) through which they can combat and control problems at both personal and wider levels. This gives them a personally verifiable path of action in which — as was discussed in Chapter 1 — they can discover for themselves the truths of the teaching and the efficacy of the technique.

This path of personal action and verification based on experience and efficacy certainly democratises the accessibility of power, placing it within the realm of all, and opens up a channel of hope to all who are beset by problems, offering them potential paths for solutions. The problem/hope of solution interplay is a central motive for many who join the new religions, and is especially prevalent in connection with issues of health. Davis has shown that 52 per cent of his respondents in Mahikari cited sickness as their motivation for joining, while similar reasons were cited by 35 per cent of the members of Ōyama Nezunomikoto Shinshikyōkai in a survey conducted by a Japanese newspaper in 1986.[26]

The means and techniques used to counter such problems vary from religion to religion, but they invariably centre on the identification and treatment of spiritual root causes, of which the problem, be it illness or some other misfortune, is regarded as just an external manifestation. Tenrikyō, for example, considers that all problems stem from spiritual dust that accumulates on the mind because of one's bad actions: if one does not take steps to clear away this dust (that is, does not polish one's soul), it will accumulate and gradually cloud the mind, causing further aberrations and giving rise to problems such as illness. Problems are thus warning signs indicating that one's life is unbalanced and spiritually incorrect: thus patients in Tenrikyō's hospital receive not just the best modern medical care possible but also visits from Tenrikyō priests offering the spiritual guidance and counselling deemed necessary to deal with fundamental spiritual dimensions implicit in their illness and recovery.[27]

Many of the older new religions such as Reiyūkai and Risshōkōseikai offer a path of reform and renewal through self-reflection and counselling, often running special discussion groups through which members air problems and, with the guidance of other members and group leaders, discover the source of a fault or problem and, by performing appropriate actions such as memorial services for a neglected ancestor, eradicate it.[28] The 'new' new religions frequently have a more dramatic approach, preferring to place the processes of therapy within a framework of identification, analysis, confrontation and exorcism that expresses a concern for spiritual healing and miraculous interventions. Mahikari, for example, often locates the fault in a polluting or possessing spirit that necessitates either placatory ritual performances, purification or exorcism through the powerful technique of *okiyome* passed to members by Su-god through Okada's mediation.

This is not to say that these techniques alone are used. Agonshū, which performs fire rites to transform the unhappy and afflicting spirits that are the cause of problems into protective and benevolent ones, also has spiritual counsellors on hand at its centres to talk to members, discuss, give advice and help solve personal problems and illnesses. Besides its focus on ritual techniques it also emphasises that there is a close relationship between lifestyle and problems, and encourages moderation, promoting health foods such as brown rice and advocating the eradication of unhealthy habits such as smoking and eating lots of meat. Although illnesses may be produced by germs and other discernible physical causes, for which one might need to go to hospital, their root causes are spiritual: one's actions cause spiritual blockages and hindrances and make one prone to the attentions of unhappy spirits, which cause illnesses to occur. To avoid such problems involves removing these blockages on both the physical and spiritual planes, by living well and healthily and by performing spiritual activities prescribed by Agonshū that utilise both one's own power and that of the spiritual world.

While spiritual healing is thus a major element in the world of the new religions this does not mean that modern Western medicine is wholly rejected. Rather, it is criticised for dealing with only a part of the problem, dealing with the surface and failing to confront the heart of the matter. Thus, when Davis asked a Mahikari teacher whether Western medicine was wrong in saying that sickness is caused by germs and bacteria he was told: 'It isn't wrong. It's just not a complete explanation. The question remains, why did we pick up the germs in the first place?'[29]

By focusing on what they see as the spiritual causes of such problems new religions such as Mahikari and Agonshū provide their members with a very vital sense of self-awareness and identity that stands in sharp contrast to the rationalised and often coldly impersonal processes of modern society. Modern medicine, for example, has a tendency to treat the patient impersonally: a germ is general, random and arbitrary, affecting everyone in much the same way, and its treatment is predetermined and clinical. It thus has no personal dimension, and in its arbitrary randomness can offer no answers, meanings or lessons to the 'why me?' question that always comes to mind when any misfortune strikes. Being cold, random and impersonal, the germ and illness typify vicarious and disturbing malice that exists outside of human control, and hence have an implicitly irrational nature. In contrast, the identification of a cause in a personalised context, which points to a problem that is specific and unique to a particular individual, as with interference from a long-dead ancestor seeking redress for previous neglect, is direct, specific and innately bound up with that particular person's fate, karma and being in the world. It thus answers why that person has been afflicted, thereby placing the problem of illness within a controllable and understandable human framework. Simultaneously it provides lessons for living, and hence gives meaning to the problem, reminding those involved of their duties to the network of relationships in which they live while allowing the afflicted person to play an active role in the therapeutic religious rites that are intrinsic to the solution itself.

Because such solutions are personalised and involve action and results on a spiritual level they are frequently hailed as miracles. The incidence of miracles, which has been mentioned previously in this book as an active dynamic in Japanese religion, is perhaps nowhere more strongly expressed than in the new, and especially the 'new' new religions. Miracles come from an immanent, vibrant and dynamic religion, reflecting the caring nature of its deities and the alive and active force of its techniques and practices: a religion that can perform miracles and that can place their power in the hands of its members is thus a living and vital entity. The importance of such active and demonstrable solutions has been widely expounded by many new religious groups in Japan. Thus Goi Masahisa, the founder of Byakkō Shinkōkai, has written:

A religion that offers no miracles cannot attract people and will hardly spread among them. A religion that only preaches and has no miracles to show may eventually fall back into mere collection of dead formalism.[30]

while a Mahikari teacher quoted by Davis has stated that:

We are critical only of religions that perform no miracles.[31]

Miracles affirm a caring deity who is concerned to intervene directly to help individuals; they affirm the direct viability and efficacy of a technique that is accessible to individuals. Thus they serve to tell individuals that they are not forgotten or overlooked within the impersonal nature of contemporary society: rather, there exists a direct and immanental interventionist dynamic working just for them. Here again there is a contrast between the established and the new: as the above statements powerfully imply, those religions that have departed from this direct immanentalism have lost their meaning as religions and hence are faded, worn out and useless.

By making miracles accessible and by affirming the individual nature of religious intervention the new religions offer a means through which each person may assert control over their environment and thus enhance their own self-esteem and confidence. By giving people another way to stand out, by allowing them to perform or experience miracles, these religions also help them affirm and re-emphasise their own sense of individuality. Indeed, it is not uncommon for the apparent source of a problem itself to be part of this process of self-expression, individuality and self-esteem. The person who is afflicted by an unhappy ancestor of several generations past is also the person who has been chosen to redeem that distress. In such terms the Agonshū woman mentioned in Chapter 2 who married into a family and was then tormented by one of its ancestors is in effect affirming her belonging to that new lineage. It is *she* who that family ancestor has selected to save it from its sufferings, and it is she who is the vehicle through which it will be redeemed from the neglect and failures of its kin. Her possession, then, can be read as a means of professing not just that she is part of her husband's family, but further as a means of asserting that she has a vital role to play in it, and hence should not herself be neglected or treated as subservient.

Mahikari members appear, according to Davis's research, to be rather prone to possession by the spirits of samurai killed in battles in the sixteenth century or thereabouts: clearly being possessed by, and hence associated with, the romance and drama of the warrior class provides them with some sense of status.[32] I first became aware of this phenomenon at first hand in 1982 when I was taken to a Mahikari centre in Sendai by a rather quiet, shy and nervous young man, who confided in me as we entered that he was possessed by the spirit of a samurai, which came out under *okiyome*. When we arrived he underwent purification from another Mahikari member and was soon stamping around the centre, uttering ferocious war cries, drawing an imaginary sword and slaughtering fictitious foes. When the *okiyome* was over he reverted to his normal, subdued and subservient manner, a warrior no more. The spirit, he told me, was a very powerful and stubborn one that would not readily yield to *okiyome*, hence involving him in frequent visits to the centre. For him it seemed that possession was not just a means of explaining and working out a problem but also a means of self-expression, of stepping outside his normal reticent self and the impositions and restrictions society placed upon him. Mahikari thus gave him the medium through which he could unleash his pent-up emotions, act out his fantasy and acquire the confidence and power of a samurai warrior within a controlled environment that could give meaning to and place that fantasy within an acceptable cosmological frame-work. Possession and exorcism allowed him an avenue through which to experience the world of the warrior in safety and in a way that caused others to take notice of him when perhaps otherwise they might not. While this meant that he had no immediate and vested interest in the 'solution' to his problem (that is, in the final exorcism of the troublesome spirit) he clearly was greatly concerned with the therapy whereby this took place, finding in it a way to stand out and find meaning in his life.[33]

THE IMPORTANCE OF VITALITY

This general overview has set out several characteristics found in the world of the new religions, showing their vitality, dynamism and the energies expressed within them. These are crucial to their general popularity and to their image of newness, providing a general contrast with the more staid and less miraculous orientations of the established religious traditions. This does not mean that all new religions express such a vitality: as they grow older and as more members are born rather than converted into them they tend to lose their dynamism, to be threatened and to have their constituencies eroded by newer and more vigorous groups. In recent years many of the older, large-scale new religions such as Sōka Gakkai and Risshōkōseikai have ceased expanding, and there is some suggestion that they are entering periods of stagnancy and even some decline.[34] As they have done so, the mantle of contemporary vigour has shifted to the 'new' new religions and it is one of these movements, Agonshū, that I shall now describe so as to provide a more comprehensive picture of the new religions especially as they develop and operate in Japan at present.

KIRIYAMA SEIYŪ AND THE DEVELOPMENT OF AGONSHŪ

Agonshū has become widely known in Japan through its aggressive use of media techniques and for its massive festival, the *hoshi matsuri* or Star Festival, held outside Kyoto on 11 February each year, which annually attracts over half a million visitors.[35] It exhibits many of the characteristics of other new religions, from its focus on a charismatic founder figure, Kiriyama Seiyū, and a cosmology rooted in Japanese folk religious traditions of unhappy spirits of the dead afflicting the living and causing spiritual hindrances and pollution (*tatari*), to its claims to an inherent universalism and message of salvation for mankind, its provision of a framework and support system through which its members can find meaning and solace in contemporary life, and its aggressive proselytisation. Although much of its cosmology derives from the folk tradition, it claims to be spearheading a return to pure Buddhism in Japan and in this mirrors many other new religions with their restatements of ancient truths and their revival of a pristine past as a means to counteract contemporary ills and renew the world around it.

Agonshū was founded as recently as 1978 and has come to prominence largely since the beginning of the 1980s although its roots trace back to an earlier religious group founded by Kiriyama in 1954. It remains, however, a relatively young religious movement closely associated with the charismatic figure of its founder and as such has undergone many rapid developments and changes typical of religions in their early growth. Agonshū's development and Kiriyama's path to awareness as they are narrated in various Agonshū publications make interesting reading because they are full of miraculous and extraordinary happenings, visitations and other occurrences that create a sense of dramatic vigour and expectation around the religion and its leader, endow them with a legitimacy and suggest that they possess a special, chosen nature. There are distinct similarities here with the histories and biographies produced by other new religions about their origins and founders: they also call to mind the tales of formation of temples and shrines and the deeds of other figures from Japanese religious tradition such as Kōbō Daishi.

Kiriyama exemplifies many of the characteristics of the powerful individual figures discussed in Chapter 5, for it is his dynamic teaching, spiritual power and charisma, coupled to his talent for proselytisation, organisation and development that have been at the core of Agonshū's contemporary prominence. His experiences also provide the foundations for Agonshū's teachings. Like many founders of new religions and charismatic figures he has had his share of difficulties, being impelled into a religious path in despair after failing in just about everything he had done in his life. Born in 1921 under the name Tsutsumi Masao (Kiriyama Seiyū is a name he adopted in 1955 after undergoing a lay ordination in the escteric Shingon Buddhist sect), he appears to have had a rather nondescript youth, subject to various illnesses and poverty, followed by an unsettled adulthood in which he tried and failed to make a living in various ways, including writing novels and running businesses. Eventually he fell foul of the law and went to prison for six months in 1953 for tax offences connected with the illegal brewing of alcohol. Soon after this débâcle compounded by further business failures he determined to commit suicide: according to his own account, subsequently transcribed into Agonshū lore, he went to throw a noose over a beam in order to hang himself, only to find a copy of the *Kannongyō*, the short Buddhist text outlining the compassions and mercies of Kannon, resting there. He read the text and underwent a religious conversion: realising he had been selected for salvation by Kannon's grace he established a Kannon-worshipping religious movement, the Kannon Jikeikai, and embarked on a path of austerities to develop his own awareness.[36]

By undergoing a long period of ascetic practice, standing under waterfalls, meditating, fasting, reciting Buddhist prayers and making offerings to Kannon, he came to realise that he had been surrounded by karmic hindrances (specifically, unhappy ancestral figures) that were the root cause of his failures. His religious practice served to eradicate these hindrances and, at the same time, to build up a small group of followers. In 1970 Kannon appeared to him in a dream and told him he had eradicated the encumbrances of the past (in Agonshū terminology he had 'cut his karma' – *karuma o kiru*):

henceforth he was no longer a seeker but a guide for others and was to go out and help others 'cut their karma' and find salvation. That this certification of power had occurred in a dream was quite in keeping with Japanese religious traditions: dreams are common vehicles for the transmission of spiritual messages, commands and powers throughout Far Eastern Buddhism, occurring, for example, with great regularity in temple *engi*, as in the dream of Enchin of Kiyomizudera cited in Chapter 6.

Agonshū's cosmology, founded in Kiriyama's experiences, is based on the central premise that all problems and misfortunes are the result of spiritual hindrances caused by unhappy spirits of the dead who are suffering because they have failed to achieve liberation after death. This failure comes about for a number of reasons, because of an unhappy and unfulfilled life, a violent death, or (most commonly of all) because the correct memorial services have not been performed to transform the dead into Buddhas (*jōbutsu*). Everyone, and every household, inherits karmic debts from the past, from their ancestors: if these have died content and been properly cared for in the past then the fortunes of the household in the present will be good; if not, misfortunes will accrue. The causes of the problems of the two Agonshū members mentioned in Chapter 2 were of such a sort, the one from an unhappy ancestor and the other from the angry spirit of an aborted baby. Until these issues were recognised and until their existence was overtly acknowledged through ritual performances the women themselves could not be freed from their sufferings and pain or, in Agonshū terms, their karma could not be cut.

Viewed through this lens of interpretation, Kiriyama's own transgressions are the result of bad karma inherited from the past, and hence not his fault as an individual. His weakness and susceptibility to the ills that afflict ordinary people, and his subsequent exertions of his will as an individual over this collective and inherited fate so as to cut his own karma and grasp his own destiny are lessons providing a role model for his followers. In his frequent lectures Kiriyama repeatedly comes back to this point, instilling into Agonshū members the importance of positive thinking, telling them that they can be like him, breaking free from all their problems to lead a positive, happy life. His failures of earlier years and his period in prison combined with his subsequent religious leadership work together as a model of the potential salvation syndrome of Agonshū and testify to its transformative powers. In addition, they testify to the importance of and legitimate the desire for leading a happy and successful life, for this is the surest way of dying content and thus not becoming an unhappy spirit who afflicts subsequent generations.

In the dream Kannon also told Kiriyama that he should henceforth perform the *goma* rites of esoteric Buddhism and Shugendō, using his mediating powers to liberate the wishes and needs of others through the intercessionary powers of these fire rituals. From this point he began to write prolifically, producing book after book on spiritual matters, including, in 1971, *Henshin no genri* ('The Principles of Transformation'), which became something of a bestseller. In this he claimed to have acquired extraordinary powers through his mastery of esoteric Buddhist practices, and stated that, under his guidance, others also could acquire the power to achieve high levels of activity, the power to change the environment through their thoughts, and the development of great powers to realise their own, and others', wishes.[37]

His following remained small, despite a general if passing interest in this expression of potential esoteric power. In 1978 he changed the name of the organisation to Agonshū after 'finding' new, hidden truths that form the core of Agonshū's subsequent growth in the 1980s. This discovery came through reading the Āgama (Japanese: *Agon*) sūtras, early Buddhist texts that pre-date Mahāyāna and esoteric Buddhism and that had been accorded little importance in Japan, especially when compared to major Mahāyāna texts such as the Lotus Sūtra. By reading the Āgamas in the light of his esoteric training Kiriyama was able to 'see' their inner truths that had long been overlooked and find in them a direct and rapid path to Buddhahood not just for the living but for the spirits of the dead as well. Kiriyama saw a powerful fusion between the essential truths hidden in the Āgamas (which are proclaimed by Agonshū as the essence of original Buddhism) and the esoteric knowledge that had evolved since they were transcribed and that he had mastered through his austerities and command of ritual performances. The two in tandem could be synergised into a potent structure through which to overcome all spiritual hindrances, release unhappy spirits from their turmoil and liberate the living from the karmic hindrances that were blocking their own happiness.

In reality the Āgamas have little to do with ancestors, nor are they studied in any real systematic way in Agonshū. As with Japanese Buddhism in general and with the new religions that have focused their attentions on particular Buddhist texts, the importance of the texts is located in their efficacy as ritual implements far more than it is in any philosophical nuances they might contain. The Āgamas are important for Agonshū in that they provide a vehicle through which Agonshū can claim the discovery of a quintessential truth that it alone may unlock the light of new, contemporary circumstances. Because they are early Buddhist texts Agonshū can portray itself as being a return to original Buddhism and thus criticise established Buddhism for having lost or missed its real essence.

Kiriyama's new interpretations, based not so much on the word as read but the inner meanings as 'seen' by the esoterically trained mind, manage to incorporate them within the basic orientations of Japanese religion and of the perceived role of Buddhism in Japan. The Japanese people primarily see in Buddhism a means of dealing with the spirits of the dead: it is this role that they have historically asked it to perform, and this is what they both want and expect it to do. From such a perspective, then, it would appear quite logical for the content of the texts of original Buddhism to be concerned with this issue. Certainly, in various discussions with Agonshū members in Tokyo and Kyoto I have been assured repeatedly that the basic aim of all Buddhism is to look after and transform the spirits of the dead into Buddhas. This does not give it an other-worldly orientation, however; for the purpose of transforming and making the spirits of the dead happy is so that they will protect and help rather than afflict and hinder the living, and thus will contribute to the development of happiness and prosperity in this life. Agonshū therefore provides a framework of interpretation which sees Buddhism as essentially concerned with both the spirits of the dead and the joyous and positive life of the living: in other words, as a very Japanese religion indeed.

A MESSIANIC OPTIMISM

Agonshu's basic teaching is that it alone, because of the unique configuration of understanding and teaching that it has acquired through the marriage of the hidden truths of the Āgamas and the ritual performances of esotericism, is able to perform the correct rites to liberate the souls of the dead. This, it asserts, is a vital role because of the vast numbers of households tainted with some spiritual misfortune from the past. If unchecked these will cause people in the present to suffer, with the result that they will die unfulfilled and angry, leading to a greater escalation of problems and further turmoil for future generations, not just on personal or household levels but on a broader, national and world scale. Political violence and upheaval, and all sorts of cataclysms stem from the multiple threats of unfulfilled and angry spirits, especially those killed in wars and never properly recognised or cared for. Having died a violent and often unmemorialised death and having been torn away from this life abruptly, these spirits remain chained to the world and hence are unhappy, unable to attain solace in death and forever seeking to remind the living of their plight through malevolent interference.

It is only through recognising this plight via the enactment of religious rituals that eradicate the sufferings of the dead and lead them to Buddhahood (*jōbutsu*), a role only Agonshū is fully capable of performing, that the roots of spiritual interference, and hence of contemporary problems on all levels, can be dealt with. Through the purificatory powers of its fire rites Agonshū can liberate the souls of the dead and transform them into benevolent spirits, thus removing these potential dangers. Because it sees this problem as a world-wide one (which, if not dealt with, will lead to universal destruction) it performs such rites not just in Japan but elsewhere, most notably in areas where large numbers of Japanese died fighting in the Second World War: in recent years such rituals have been performed at numerous battle sites in the Pacific and also, in 1986, at Harbin in China. These rituals form an important element in what Agonshū sees as its mission to the world, a mission that involves universal salvation, renewal and the search for world peace.

In talking about the fears of potential destruction if action is not taken Agonshū has, along with many other new religions, picked up on and articulated, in a religious sense, the fears and worries of many, especially young, Japanese who display an appreciable degree of pessimism concerning the future, especially because of increasing environmental pollution and their concern about nuclear weapons.[38] The Japanese in general, according to various surveys carried out by the Prime Minister's Office, have rather pessimistic views of the future: in 1984 50 per cent of those polled considered that the future would bring increasing instability and chaos in Japanese society.[39] Tani records that many of the young Mahikari members he surveyed felt that a cataclysm might occur by the end of the century and that human beings had created but lost control of various threats to their future well-being: again, nuclear proliferation and environmental pollution were prominently mentioned. For many of his Mahikari respondents this was a situation now beyond normal, rational human control: miracles alone could save humankind from these impending disasters.[40] This apparent pessimism has been fuelled by a general feeling that politicians and the political process have failed to find any solutions and, moreover, are incapable of doing so, a cynicism towards politics that has been heightened by the recurrent bribery and sexual scandals of the late 1980s that drove successive Prime Ministers and other leading politicians from office.

The coming end of the millennium has if anything heightened such messianic sentiments, persuading many people that the coming of the twenty-first century, or the ending of the twentieth, will see some crucial and major change in world fortunes. When in 1973 the prophecies of Nostradamus were translated into Japanese their forebodings of impending doom found a ready audience amongst many Japanese, and have ever since been widely read. To some extent Agonshū and others of the new religions (including the Jehovah's Witnesses, whose prophecies of Armageddon clearly fit in to some degree with the contemporary attitudes of pessimism expressed by many Japanese) have stoked up these fears by reiterating such forecasts of disaster if nothing is done, but at the same time they have held out a branch of hope to those fearing for the future by providing an accessible and coherent framework of action that offers an immanent religious, emotionalist interpretation and solution on personal and universal levels to these problems and fears.

Like many new religions Agonshū expresses a messianic view of world doom underpinned by assertions that such an ending will be averted through its own salvific powers. Just as Kiriyama himself, and all members, can escape their impending fate and cut their karma so too can society, through Agonshū's actions. These role models of regeneration, renewal and the overcoming of all problems provided by the founder apply to the world in general and show that pessimism and messianism are not complete sentiments in themselves, but incorporate also a sense of potential renewal, transformation and salvation. In other words, it, like many new religions, expresses what can best be described as a messianic optimism.

Agonshū argues that only by going to the heart of the problems through looking at their spiritual causes rather than toying with superficial political answers that have, in any event, failed, can any solution to the crisis of contemporary society be found. A dramatic Agonshū video based on Kiriyama's book *1999 nen: karuma to reishō kara no gedatsu* ('1999: Salvation from Karma and Spiritual Hindrances') expounds these themes dramatically, suggesting that the ruin foretold by Nostradamus could come by the end of the century as a result of the escalating hordes of unhappy spirits unless a *religious* answer is found that gets to the core of the problem by dealing with the souls of the dead themselves. The video makes it clear that such a solution may be found in Agonshū's methods of pacifying these spirits and enabling people to live positive and fulfilled lives: hence it can, and will, save the world. It further affirms Agonshū's chosen role by describing how Kiriyama, while visiting the site of the first Buddhist monastery at Sahet Mahet in India, received a 'vibration' directly from the Buddha himself. This transmission confirmed his sense of purpose and made him realise that his mission was to revive Buddhism for the modern world: thus he was to build a 'new Sahet Mahet' in Japan, at Agonshū's headquarters at Yamashina near Kyoto, from which Agonshū will spread peace across the globe. Since then Agonshū has set in motion the construction of a vast new temple network at Yamashina for this purpose. The video ends by stating that the Buddha has come from India to Japan through the offices of Agonshū, and that through his power which will henceforth emanate from Japan to the rest of the world the catastrophes predicted by Nostradamus will be averted.

VISITATIONS, LEGITIMATIONS AND NEW POWERS

The vibration felt at Sahet Mahet was but one of a series of visitations and events that have both heightened Agonshū's own self-legitimation and affirmed its mission to the world. The Yamashina site was acquired in 1976 after Kiriyama had had a vision convincing him it was holy: since then it has been the setting for the *hoshi matsuri*, in the flames of which various apparitions and visions have appeared to further emphasise the sanctity of the site. In 1978 a dragon king from Buddhist mythology, Nanda, appeared announcing that he would be the guardian of the site; in 1979 Dainichi (the Cosmic Buddha of the esoteric tradition), Kannon and the Buddha appeared in a triad; and in 1980 the Buddha in meditation and surrounded by a pantheon of figures including Fudō, Kannon and Bishamonten. Since then other celestial apparitions (visible to those with the right level of spiritual awareness, according to Agonshū spokesmen, and demonstrated in photographs taken of the event and shown in Agonshū books and at its centres[41]) have appeared with great regularity.

In 1986 President Jayawardene of Sri Lanka presented to Agonshū a casket said to contain a genuine bone relic of the Buddha. This relic (known in Agonshū as *shinsei busshari*, 'true relic of the Buddha', but generally shortened to *busshari*) was, according to Agonshū, given by the government of one Buddhist country as recognition of its work to revive original Buddhism: in reality the reasons behind the presentation remain unclear. The donation, collection and trading (whether for financial, diplomatic or other reasons) of Buddhist relics have a long history throughout Asia, for relics have traditionally been viewed, perhaps even more so than statues, as symbols and manifestations of holy power, representations of the living transcendence of holy figures. There are certainly many hundreds of reputed relics in Japan alone, some being relics of Japanese religious leaders (Kōbō Daishi's body in the mausoleum at Kōyasan being perhaps the prime example) and others ascribed to figures such as the Buddha, including, as we saw in Chapter 4, the relic used to sanctify and promote the graveyard at Myōshinji in Kyoto. Many such relics have been presented to Japanese institutions, as ways of promoting diplomatic friendship, as gestures of Buddhist solidarity and bridge building, and as recognition of the economic support that has been given by many Japanese Buddhist organisations to the poorer Buddhist countries of Southern Asia. In the past various relics (usually said to be of the historical Buddha) have been presented to Japanese temples and organisations by the Indian, Thai and Sri Lankan governments: President Jayawardene himself gave a further relic to a temple in Tokyo in 1987.[42] The new religion Shinnyoen received in 1965 a donation from Thailand of ashes said to be the Buddha's: like Agonshū, Shinnyoen has expressed surprise at this donation, reasoning it to be a recognition of *its* adherence to true Buddhism.[43]

None the less, the donation has been widely publicised by Agonshū as a major legitimation of its teachings and as the only true relic that is properly venerated in Japan. Perhaps more important still, the *busshari* or relic has become the main image of the religion, interpreted as the Buddha incarnate, containing immense power that has been unlocked by Kiriyama via his performance of esoteric rituals and his use of the 'true essence' of the Āgamas. According to Agonshū an unique confluence has occurred with the arrival of the *busshari*: the true manifestation of Buddha's power (the relic), the true method of transforming spirits into realised Buddhas via the fire rituals and the Āgamas, and the true teacher who has learnt these methods via a direct transmission from the Buddha.[44] Taken together they represent a coalition of tremendous power that can benefit the lives of all.

The *busshari* has become the main focus of worship in Agonshū, considered to contain the powers to transform the spirits of the dead and liberate the wishes of the living. Members acquire their own versions of this relic in a casket that is a scaled-down model of the one holding the *busshari*. The casket contains a stone, sacralised by rituals performed before the 'real' relic and thus transformed into manifestations of the relic itself: the process is similar to that through which *o-mamori* and *fuda* become the essence of a Buddha or *kami*. Until the acquisition of the relic members used to perform a 1000-day-long practice that involved reciting a set series of prayers each day before an image of Kannon: this practice gradually transformed their ancestors into Buddhas and released the members themselves and their families from all but the most serious spiritual hindrances (for example, a *mizuko* spirit); for this they would need to seek help from a leading Agonshū counsellor or Kiriyama himself. Now this 1000-day practice has been given up in favour of the simple veneration of the relic whose superior power, according to Agonshū, facilitates a swifter transformation of unhappy spirits into contented Buddhas who will then act as guardians, helping one towards increased happiness. Thus as signs have appeared to legitimate Agonshū its practices themselves have become more efficacious and direct.

PUBLICITY, TECHNOLOGY AND RITUAL DRAMAS

The developments of Agonshū have been fast in the 1980s: at the start of the decade it had probably 30,000 members and by the end was claiming over 300,000 (although private estimates put it somewhat lower).[45] In many ways its development has taken on something of the air of a media event in itself, full of dramatic twists and turns, with the events themselves dressed up to create messages, as with the acquisition of the *busshari* and Kiriyama's prison sentence. There have been suggestions that this latter was originally kept quiet until journalists began probing and uncovered the truth.[46] Now the fact is loudly trumpeted and has become central to Agonshū's message of salvation.

Its intensive use of the mass media to advertise its teachings is by no means unique: most new religions have their own printing presses, and several place advertisements in the media. Shinreikyō, for example, sponsors full-page articles in the Japanese press advertising the miraculous cures experienced by its followers. Agonshū is, however, almost certainly the most dynamic and technology-conscious of them all, exhibiting an essential modernism in this respect which works in tandem with its traditionalist cosmology. It is ever-vigilant to keep up with and utilise the latest means of technology to transmit its messages: officials at its centres in Tokyo and Kyoto have expressed a deep sense of pride to me that their religion is, in their view, the most technologically advanced and innovative in the country, even telling me on one occasion that they had nothing to learn from American tele-evangelists on this matter.[47] Agonshū rituals are advertised in the mass media and on the television, and are presented in skilful ways with specially composed and dramatic music blasted from huge banks of amplifiers, as well as special lighting effects. They are also broadcast simultaneously live across the country via the NHK telecommunications satellite so that members in Agonshū centres throughout the Japanese archipelago can participate along with Kiriyama in events in Kyoto or Tokyo without having to travel. Each year after the *hoshi matsuri* a 30-minute film of the rite is broadcast on regional commercial television channels, paid for by Agonshū. It also produces countless videos and films that both reiterate and expound its messages, and has installed video machines at all its centres so that anyone visiting may watch them: this was how I came to learn of the contents of the *1999* video cited earlier.

Besides these electronic means it also uses mass leafleting, delivering colourful broadsheets through millions of letterboxes to advertise Kiriyama's books, the *hoshi matsuri* and other rituals. Whether this use of advertising and technology has really brought members to it is questionable: as we have seen, it is largely through personal contact that people are drawn into most new religions, and as Numata Kenya has pointed out, other of the 'new' new religions such as Shinnyoen, which work more through personal channels of contact and do not advertise in the Agonshū way, have actually grown faster.[48] It is reasonable to say, however, that many of those who go to the fire festival have been intrigued by the promise of the grand and spectacular event depicted in its advertising. Indeed, I first became aware of Agonshū through a leaflet pushed through my letterbox which intrigued me enough to make me go to the *hoshi matsuri*.

Agonshū's use of technology and the media shows that it is a religious movement very much at home in the modern world, despite an apparently traditionalist cosmology and teaching. The sense of modernity it displays has given it an up-to-date image that makes the traditional cosmological teachings it propounds appear in tune with the times rather than outworn or antiquated. This apparent straddling of traditionalism and modernity is exemplified clearly by Kiriyama himself who is able, according to Agonshū, to 'see' the unhappy spirits of the dead that are afflicting people, to exorcise them and release them from their pain, and to have visions of the spirit world, yet who is equally at ease in front of a microphone in a skilfully managed religious ritual-cum-media event, at a press conference or delivering a talk on positive thinking to Agonshū members. His ability to put messages across in an accessible fashion has certainly won him followers: commenting on the youthful nature of those listening to one of his talks a Japanese newspaper wrote:

> Kiriyama Seiyū consciously interprets Buddhism into a language that young people can relate to — thus the satellite broadcasts, the modern temple building, his friendly sermon and his approachable manner. All this adds up to a user-friendly religion appropriate to the needs of the modern Japan.[49]

THE USER-FRIENDLY RELIGION IN ACTION

The use of a term from the vocabulary of the computer age, 'user-friendly', in this context in many ways captures the ethos Agonshū is attempting to put across to its potential members. It points to its inherent modernity that in many ways balances and reinforces the intrinsic traditionalism of its teachings, and also implies the relaxed, open and accessible style that Agonshū, like other new religions, wishes to maintain so as to allow its members to feel at home in it.

Its accessibility is emphasised by the fact that, like many new religions, it does not demand absolute adherence from its followers. Despite its apparent messianism and despite Kiriyama's criticisms of established Buddhism, there is no prohibition on Agonshū members taking part in religious activities outside Agonshū, for it is recognised as perfectly acceptable and normal for members to have funerals and memorial services performed by their traditional *bodaiji*. Members are reminded that such services are not completely efficacious and that truly to transform the spirit of the dead person Agonshū rites should be performed, but there is no suggestion that members should break with their traditional social orientations.[50]

This relaxed structure pervades Agonshū's religious centres throughout the country. Members come and go as they wish, performing their own private obeisances to the *busshari* and the other objects of worship on the altar, speaking to counsellors and receiving advice about problems, and looking at Agonshū videos. They may also browse through the various magazines and books, many written by Kiriyama, on sale, or pick up some of the many pamphlets and leaflets outlining current activities of the movement on local, national and international levels.

They are likely also to perform what they call *shugyō*, religious practice, which can involve all manner of activities concerned with the smooth running of the centre, from cleaning the floor and helping in the office to talking to visitors. As in many other new religions such as Tenrikyō great emphasis is placed on joyfully and gratefully performing simple voluntary acts that benefit oneself and others: such activities are in themselves religious practice, *shugyō*.

This concept of voluntary action is not directed solely at and for the benefit of Agonshū, for it expresses a concern for others as well, not just on the rather lofty level of saving the world through religious rituals but in more direct ways as well. Like many other new religions it is actively involved with various social welfare activities, and sponsors and carries out various organised campaigns of voluntary public service in Japan. For example, members go out in teams to clean up public areas such as parks on a regular basis. This sense of charity and giving extends beyond Japan as well, for Agonshū has been active in various charitable activities, sponsoring in particular the United Nations Food and Agriculture Organization's well-digging project in Sudan and Chad through the donation of equipment and funding.

Such voluntary activity helps foster a sense of happiness and joyful participatory positivism that makes members feel they are wanted, are very much part of, and playing a vital role in, the religion. In my conversations with members at the Tokyo and Kyoto centres I have been impressed by the amount of time they appeared to put into it: many came in every day on the way to or from their jobs. By working together and by contributing in such ways, of course, members develop a sense of belonging which heightens their positivism and makes the centres alive and vibrant (and thus more attractive to potential converts). Members are — as is invariably so in the new religions — ready, indeed keen, to share their own feelings, to tell their own stories of how they have been helped by Agonshū and to express their gratitude to Kiriyama for the benefits he has brought to their lives. All those I have talked to have been extremely positive on this last point.

TWO AGONSHŪ RITES: RELIGIOUS MEDIA EVENTS IN ACTION

This sense of positivism is expressed throughout Agonshū's activities, but comes most vividly to the fore in its organised rites and festivals. Since these also manifest most clearly the ways in which Agonshū has utilised media resources to create events of intense drama and spectacle and to show the religion in action, I shall here describe the two major ritual events in the Agonshū calendar. The first is the *hoshi matsuri*, held outdoors at Yamashina near Kyoto on 11 February each year, and the second is a fire rite, held indoors at its Tokyo centre on the first day of every month, known as the *tsuitachi goma* (literally, 1st of the month fire rite). Each is presided over by Kiriyama and performed in front of the *busshari*, and each is broadcast by telecommunications satellite so that members across Japan can participate 'live'. My descriptions of each are based on attendance, twice at the Yamashina site for the *hoshi matsuri* and twice for the *tsuitachi goma*, once in Tokyo and the other time watching it with several hundred Agonshū members on a screen in the Kyoto centre as it was being performed in Tokyo.

The Hoshi Matsuri

The *hoshi matsuri* (Star festival) is an outdoor fire ritual of the type traditionally performed by *yamabushi* in which *gomagi*, wooden sticks on which requests have been written, are burned to liberate those wishes. Similar forms of *goma* rite are also performed by Shinto priests (including a large and colourful rite at Fushimi Inari in Kyoto on 8 November every year) and by several other new religions including Bentenshū and Shinnyoen. Agonshū's, however, is the biggest, most dramatic and — in line with everything else Agonshū does — the most spectacularly orchestrated and publicised, presenting an awesome spectacle of drama and colour that has, for the past several years, attracted more than half a million visitors each year and acted as a potent advertising rite for the movement. According to an Agonshū spokesman I interviewed, on average 3000 people a year join Agonshū because of their attendance at the festival.[51] Its scale also means it is reported in the national press and on television, thus drawing further attention to Agonshū.

The whole performance is smoothly run by a veritable army of Agonshū volunteers in the cheerful displays of mass participation that are found prominently in the new religions.[52] Volunteers are on hand at major railway stations in Kyoto to guide visitors on to the fleets of buses that transport them to the Yamashina site, where they are met by blue-jacketed Agonshū members who line the steps from the bus park up the hillside to the ritual setting itself. The members greet everyone with the words *o-kaerinasai* ('welcome back'), a greeting used in many new religions, including Shinnyoen and Tenrikyō, to transmit the message that, rather than going somewhere, one is returning to an original source, to the roots of belief.

The festival incorporates many eclectic features from various parts of the Japanese religious world. It has in particular assimilated motifs from the world of Shugendō: Kiriyama is, according to Agonshū, an adept of *yamabushi* practices because of his years of asceticism and has developed Agonshū's own *yamabushi* order for lay members who participate actively in the fire rites themselves, performing roles once the preserve of religious specialists. At the festival Kiriyama and a large number of these members are dressssed in the traditional costume of the *yamabushi*, in white robes with various tassels and adornments that symbolise aspects of Buddhist teaching, small skull caps that represent the crown of wisdom, deer skins tied around the waist which are the symbol of Monju the Buddha of wisdom whose mount is a lion (the skin traditionally was used by *yamabushi* as a blanket when they slept in the mountains), and straw sandals.[53]

The festival takes place on a large, flat piece of land cordoned off by ropes festooned with white paper, Shintoesque markers traditionally used in Japan to denote sacred space. At one side of this area, which is well over 100 metres long and almost as wide, is a huge Buddhist-style altar, in the centre of which is the *busshari*. Before it are two huge pyres of pine branches each several metres high and over ten metres across on which the *goma* sticks are piled. Each pyre represents a separate yet related function: one is for *gedatsu* or liberation of the afflicted souls of the dead who are causing hindrances to the living, and the other for *hōshō*, giving life to people's inner wishes. Those who wish to make requests on either pyre can write on the sticks provided (these cost 100 yen each), and deposit them in collection boxes at the site: the two types are sorted and stacked to the sides of the pyres in massive but well-ordered piles. The two pyres thus represent two basic and vital themes of Japanese religion: the achievement of wishes and personal welfare (that is, *genze riyaku*), and the pacification of the souls of the dead and the veneration of the ancestors, and as such can be said to have specifically Japanese orientations.

The festival starts at 7 a.m. with a large procession of *yamabushi* into the cordoned-off arena. This is followed by the recitation of prayers and a series of invocations and dedications in which, amongst other things, the spirits of past Emperors are invoked and various references are made to the Japanese spirit. These strongly nationalist connotations are reinforced by the fact that the date on which the festival is held, 11 February, is National Foundation Day, a public holiday with nationalistic undertones proscribed after the war but since restored. Despite these apparently nationalistic nuances the festival has a further overarching theme that goes beyond the more specialised and Japanese dimensions of the ancestors and personal welfare: the attainment of world peace. According to Agonshū spokesmen at the site, this aim is implicit in every request made on the *gomagi*. Agonshū also sponsors interfaith dialogues on world peace, and in 1988 a delegation of Islamic leaders from Egypt was in attendance at the festival to lend their presence (and an international touch) to this theme.

After the invocations a signal is given and the pyres are lit, throwing up clouds of smoke and eventually bursting into flames. From then until the early evening the Agonshū *yamabushi* work in teams, throwing the inscribed wooden sticks in bundles on to the fire, and also ferrying buckets of water from tanks on either side to keep the fires under control. Throughout the rite there are always several hundred members in *yamabushi* clothing in the enclosed space around the pyres. As the *gomagi* burn, all hindrances blocking the wishes of those who write them are, according to Agonshū, swept away, while malevolent and unhappy spirits are transformed through the power of the flames into benevolent ones. Kiriyama presides over the whole affair, at times seated before the fires chanting invocations and performing esoteric rituals, and at others marching around giving blessings to the crowd.

The scale is immense: the first Agonshū *hoshi matsuri* took place in 1970 with an attendance of 200 people, with 100,000 *gomagi* burnt. In 1979 the number topped one million for the first time and has risen each year since. In 1988 30 million sticks were burned and over 500,000 visitors came.[54] The pyres are rapidly transformed into masses of flame, the heat of which can be felt 60 or so metres away in the temporary stands erected around the site for the benefit of visitors, who are a mixture of members and casual visitors. Some pray fervently to the fire, others buy and inscribe *gomagi*, and still others appear to be there largely to watch the spectacle. There are stalls throughout the site where one can buy Agonshū *o-mamori* and other talismans, as well as magazines and books on Agonshū teaching and events.

The influence of modern technology is everywhere: the helpers wear headphones and have two-way radios (including many of those dressed as *yamabushi*, making a rather interesting cameo picture of the traditional costume of the mountain ascetic topped off with the technology of the modern age) to keep things co-ordinated. Cameras film every action from helicopters and overhead cranes while huge television screens and banks of loudspeakers are on hand to transmit every event as it occurs throughout the site. Teams of *yamabushi* take turns in beating great rows of drums and chanting through microphones, to accompany the activities of those hurling *gomagi* on to the fire, and specially composed dramatic music is played through the banks of loudspeakers to add to the overall effect. The entry and exit of the teams of *yamabushi* from the heat of the arena is carefully regulated and theatrically staged, each group marching in and out as a phalanx under a banner depicting the regional branch of Agonshū from which they come.

All in all, the *hoshi matsuri* is a spectacular ritual drama that transmits, on a gigantic scale and in ringing tones, Agonshū's messages and themes. For casual visitors it may serve to draw them into Agonshū, or alternatively provide them with yet another means through which to express their wishes, even on a casual basis, for peace, happiness and for the salvation of their ancestors: besides these it of course provides for a colourful day out. For members it serves as an affirmation of the vitality and prominence of their religion, and enables them to play an active part in this, helping and transmitting their feelings of joy to visitors or, dressed as a *yamabushi*, helping to pacify the angry spirits and bring about world peace. The *hoshi matsuri* is Agonshū's major event of the year. Besides this huge outdoor fire rite, however, Agonshū conducts indoor ones as well, the most important of which is the *tsuitachi goma* which will be described next.

The Tsuitachi Goma

The *tsuitachi goma* was inaugurated in April 1987 and since then has been held on the first day of each month. There are two parts to the rite: the first, a fire rite performed by Kiriyama in which he burns a number of *gomagi* before the *busshari* so as to liberate members' wishes, and the second, a short discourse by Kiriyama. It takes place at 6.30 a.m. but manages to draw large crowds: when I went to the Tokyo centre on 1 July 1987 the road from the nearest subway station was lined with Agonshū volunteers greeting people and directing them to the centre. Inside the large modern building about 2000 people crowded into the main hall, kneeling on the *tatami* floor and quietly praying before a raised dais in the centre of which was an altar containing Buddhist accoutrements and the silver casket of the *busshari*. At other centres throughout Japan members were doing likewise before a screen depicting the scenes in Tokyo. Before the service began there was an announcement stating that its aims were for world peace, for good fortune and for improving everyone's luck.

At precisely 6.30 a.m. the lights were dimmed and Kiriyama's entrance was announced over the public address system. He entered the hall, sombre and dressed in brown Buddhist robes, to the accompaniment of a reverberating drum beat and a quiet and controlled chanting from the audience. He took his place in front of the altar, his back to the crowd, and began the ritual performance of the *goma*, reciting *mantras* and performing other actions such as special hand movements that, in esoteric Buddhism, symbolise religious power while consigning a small number of sticks to the flames. During this, various prayers were chanted by the audience, including the *Hannya Shingyō* and a short section from the Āgamas. The rite lasted barely fifteen minutes, after which the fire was extinguished and Kiriyama quietly rose and left the dais.

A few moments later he returned, this time dressed not in brown but in bright yellow. His face was transformed from the serious, stern look of the *goma* into a smiling, friendly, even avuncular expression. Whereas, in the fire rite his back had been to the audience, now he faced them. Holding a microphone he began a dialogue which started as follows:

> Kiriyama: *O-genki desu ka* [Are you well?]
> Audience: *Hai, genki desu* [Yes, we are.]

At this Kiriyama shook his head a little and said that they did not sound as if they really were well: he wanted them to say it again, but this time with feeling. They did, shouting loudly and in unison. On both occasions I attended this same procedure took place: the members in Kyoto, watching on the screen, responded in very much the same way as those in the 'live' performance in Tokyo. After this Kiriyama began a short monologue on positive thinking: both addresses that I heard contained similar messages centring on the pitfalls of harbouring negative and pessimistic attitudes, for these only lead to frustration and unhappiness. He urged everyone to develop the will to succeed in all things, using himself as an example of someone who had had problems but who had overcome them: everyone else could do the same. If one had the correct spirit and confidence and put all one's force into things one could do anything, and by so satisfying oneself one could have a happy life. At the end he asked the audience to chant in unison a series of five exhortations ('Let's do it! I will certainly succeed! I am blessed with very good luck! I will certainly do well! I will definitely win!') that are regularly used in Agonshū meetings, and then left the dais to rapturous applause.

The whole performance from the start of the *goma* had taken exactly 30 minutes: Agonshū in fact rents 30 minutes' transmission time on the NHK satellite for this ritual, and this forms the temporal framework for the performance. The restrained esotericism of the religious rite and the positive joy of the sermon provided a striking combination of religious ritual tinged with awe and mystery and a sales seminar devoted to positive and secular advancement. Yet there was a sense of unity, in Kiriyama's own persona which seemed equally at home in either situation, in the *busshari* which is revered because it provides the spiritual power necessary to achieve one's wishes and which was displayed prominently throughout, and in the ritual symbolisation and legitimation, through the *goma*, of these wishes on a spiritual level coupled with their direct expression and externalisation on the practical level. At the end of the rite members left to go to their jobs or to put in some voluntary work at the centre, clearly buoyed up by the atmosphere of intense positivism.

IMPLICIT MEANINGS: THE HARMONISING DYNAMIC

Agonshū encapsulates and restates many of the basic themes of religion in Japan (the concerns for this-worldly peace and happiness, and for the ancestors) within a modernised exterior. It helps and serves, like so many religious activities do in Japan, to legitimate success and emphasise the importance of leading a happy and positive life which will benefit not only the individual but his/her surroundings and future generations. It instills positive feelings into its members and makes them 'feel good', thus helping them to encounter and gain the confidence to overcome problems that face them on personal and wider levels. Despite the messianic undertones it espouses one certainly does not feel, when watching crowds of perspiring *yamabushi* who have just spent their time hurling stacks of *gomagi* into the *hoshi matsuri* fires, or at Agonshū centres being greeted by joyful members ready to share their positive feelings with all who walk through the door, that these are pessimists waiting for the end of the world.

Nor does one feel that they are merely dupes led astray by ignorance, drama and the lure of fancy clothing. While dressing up as *yamabushi* is appealing and allows members temporarily to become powerful religious figures from Japanese tradition, and while the events in Agonshū are presented in ways that emphasise their intrinsic entertainment value, it would be wrong to see Agonshū just as an 'entertainment and event religion' pandering to the gullible. In many ways, Agonshū's interfusions of messianism and optimism, of traditional themes and modern expressions, of Japanocentric particularisms and universalising motifs, and of arcane esoteric ritualism and of sales-convention techniques of confidence-raising offer a sense of meaning and emotional support suitable for and relevant to their members as they live in contemporary Japanese society, and especially in its cities, trying to cope with the rapidly changing patterns of life around them. Through these interfusions, and through Agonshū's processes of problem explanation and ritualised solution, members have a viable framework through which to express and vanquish, on numerous levels, the fears and insecurities that they face in contemporary society both in terms of their personal life and in the wider social context, and can attain the confidence to confront them, and thus to place themselves in control of their destinies.[55]

The messianic/salvationist interplay that Agonshū expresses works on the microcosmic level to provide the individual with a coherent framework for dealing with his/her own life: the individual beset by personal problems is given a therapeutic and personalised process of explanation, identification and solution to deal with those worries. Individuals, because of the power mediated from the spiritual world through the founder, can perform or acquiesce in the performance of techniques that enable them to surmount, or at least make meaningful, such problems. Thus they can attain some sense of control over their lives and environment. The same pattern occurs on the macrocosmic level as well, with the whole of society and humanity as the focus of salvation. The assertion that the religion can save the world through its special techniques and teachings is in reality an extension and universalisation of the salvation of the individual, with the individual given a renewed sense of worth, becoming not just a cog in an industrial society, a humble office-worker or a bright university student, but rather an active contributor to the whole process of world salvation. In place of the fear that things have got out of hand and that society has gone beyond human control, then, the member is given an assurance that this can be rectified and is provided with an emotionalist channel through which it can be made manageable.

One can see, again, the model of the founder (in Agonshū's case, Kiriyama) as a paradigm not just for the individual but for the wider society and for the world at large: by solving his problems and attaining salvation, by eradicating the disturbing influences around him, he serves as a role-model in microcosm for the world as a whole. Indeed, one could argue that Japan itself, like the individual founder who has conquered his hardships, serves as a paradigm of revival, renewal and salvation. Having collapsed, less than half a century ago, into defeat, destruction and occupation, its cities in ashes and its people impoverished and dejected, it now stands as one of the richest and most advanced technologies in the world, an economic giant.

This motif of renewal helps affirm Japan's place in the peace cosmologies prevalent in Agonshū and other new religions, in which peace is depicted as spreading across the world from Japan. Byakkō Shinkōkai, for instance, promotes the erection of peace poles bearing the words 'May Peace Prevail on Earth' and incorporates prayers for world peace into its rituals, giving Japan a central position in this process.[56] New religions such as Risshōkōseikai and Sōka Gakkai sponsor peace conferences, hold exhibitions depicting the evils of nuclear warfare, and assert that religions have a vital role in creating the climate whereby people may be able to live without fear of war. The established religions too have been involved in articulating these feelings, with the Tendai Buddhist sect hosting a Peace Summit at Mount Hiei in 1987 attended by representatives of religious groups from across the world.

These peace initiatives articulate the desire for peace felt by millions of ordinary Japanese and enable them to feel they are doing something to contribute to its progress. Frequently such initiatives, especially when expressed in the new religions, also manage simultaneously to incorporate themes of Japanocentricism and universalism and issues of Japanese cultural identity especially in relation to the growing pressures of internationalisation in contemporary Japanese society. These are issues of major concern in a country which closed itself off to the outside world for over 200 years, only opening up again rather reluctantly to external trade and influences in the middle of the last century, and which has constantly striven to see itself as different, somehow unique, apart from and even threatened by the rest of the world. Contemporary changes, including Japan's growing place as an international trading nation dependent on external contacts coupled with the tide of Western influences that have become commonplace in Japan since the end of the war, have opened (at times somewhat forcibly) the doors, certainly made it impossible for Japan to retreat from the outside world, and at times appear even to threaten and undermine the roots of Japanese cultural traditions, belonging and identity.

New religions such as Agonshū (and indeed the religious world in general) offer a means through which to deal, at least on an emotional level, with such problems of cultural identity in relationship to the processes of internationalisation, and also with the continuing problem, which is irrevocably bound up with the issue of identity and internationalisation, of the relationship between tradition in general and the modernising processes that are altering Japanese lifestyles. In the face of rapid change that at times appears to be sweeping away the old and threatening to undermine Japan's cultural stability, a religious movement such as Agonshū provides a network of ritual actions and emotional images and responses through which its members can relate and rationalise these seemingly opposite themes and synthesise them into a manageable and understandable unity.

In terms of peace, the assertion that Japan has a message for and is going to save the whole world (in Agonshū's case through such distinctly Japanese religious practices as the fires of the *goma*), especially when underlined by the nationalistic undertones and images of the *hoshi matsuri*, helps to reaffirm Japanese integrity and centrality. Yet Agonshū's apparently narrow nationalism is at the same time transcended through the fires of the *goma* which allow members to go beyond the limits of particularism and express a concern for the world at large, for *world* peace: they can thus assert their Japanese cultural identity through the form and cosmological perspectives of the ritual and yet emotionally express their internationalism through its idealistic aims. There is a similar parallel and interplay with Agonshū's expression of particularist Japanese religious perspectives (spiritual causation and malevolent spirits) that are universalised via the Āgamas and the *busshari*. Members can thus transcend the particularisation of their situation and be part of a world religion, yet need not forsake the emotional comfort of their own particularist perspectives which are reaffirmed and even strengthened by being universalised.

A similar interplay exists between the images of tradition and modernisation: while overtly the former (and hence Japanese culture) appears to be threatened and eroded by the latter, in reality the two work in tandem, each reaffirming the other. The traditionalism of the rituals is emphasised by the ways they are highlighted and projected via modern media, while the emotional appeal of traditionalist ceremonies, cosmologies and images is enhanced by the surrounding modernity of the society in which they occur. In such terms the *yamabushi*'s clothing and two-way radio form a logical whole rather than an aberrant contrast. On one level the reaffirmations of traditional cosmology in Agonshū and the other 'new' new religions do represent an innate desire to reaffirm Japanese cultural traditions as a counterbalance to the encroachments of external influences and modernisation. By placing the roots and solutions of all problems within a traditionalist framework Agonshū asserts the values of Japanese cultural belonging and identity and implicitly suggests that solutions to Japanese problems must take note of these factors. The spirits of the dead and the ancestors serve as symbols of tradition and of Japan's cultural past: they are also the cause of problems if neglected. Implicitly there is a message here that to neglect or jettison cultural values and traditions will in itself bring problems, and that contemporary unease stems in part from a failure to pay enough attention to the past and to cultural traditions. The search for cultural and emotional security requires that the values of the past are recognised and valued as factors essential in the fruitful development of the present.

This does not, however, mean that the modern world is rejected. The Japanese are, in general, fascinated by newness, and live in what is, on the surface at least, an extremely modern, highly technologised world, in which they have eagerly assimilated every possible modern convenience. They are extremely reluctant to leave these behind or reject them, at least on a physical level. They are, however, ready to do so on an emotional one, with the image of tradition providing a cathartic yet safe and temporary escape route from the modern world. They may, through the medium of the religious world, its rites and practices and the emotive nuances they imply, enter, in a controlled way, the world of tradition without committing themselves to it, and can afterwards return, renewed, to the modern. The modern setting of the Mahikari centre and its *okiyome* allowed the man cited earlier to become a samurai, safely untroubled by any need actually to endure the pains, strife and danger of a real warrior's life, and to step outside his everyday life for a while, after which he could return, imbued with his warrior's strength, for the continued struggles of the present. The Agonshū *yamabushi* can enter the world of the mountain ascetic without enduring the austerities of standing under waterfalls, sleeping out in the mountains and other such inconveniences. There are parallels too with the pilgrims mentioned in previous chapters, who can perform their emotional pilgrimages through the image of traditionalism and asceticism contained in the garb they put on of the wandering pilgrim, but who can retain the modern comforts of luxury buses and pleasant hotels to cocoon their physical journey.

In reality, neither the pilgrim nor the adherent of the new religion wants to go back to the inconveniences and hardships of the past: by restating their ideals in an emotional and controlled environment they can reap the benefits of traditionalism without its encumbrances. This is emphasised in the individually assertive rites of Agonshū such as the *tsuitachi goma* and in the importance of cutting one's karma. When Agonshū members, at the end of Kiriyama's sermon, get up and shout that they will succeed, that they can win, they are in effect stating personalised desires in line with the growing influences of individualism in Japanese society. They are hence saying that they will not be hindered and bound by the restrictive nature of traditionalist social ethics: after all, cutting karma equals freeing oneself from the chains of the collective past. The individual in seeking liberation from the harmful influences of unhappy ancestors is also escaping from the culturally stifling limitations of traditional value systems.

New religions such as Agonshū exemplify the continuing problems that perceptions of tradition and the cultural past hold for many Japanese. On the one hand these are affirmations of Japanese identity and strength, helping stabilise Japanese society during times of rapid social change, yet they are also, for many people, weak and limiting for they appear to stand in the way of progress and development. Modernisation, too, is similarly both welcomed for its fruits and admired as a symbol of progress (few Japanese take other than pride in their country's achievements since the end of the war and in its technological progress). It is also feared for the disturbances it poses and for its inherent rationalisations and structuralisations that are seen as tending to categorise life and denude it of its meaning and vitality.

Agonshū, like other new religions, provides its followers with a nexus of identity and self-confidence on many levels through which they can deal, on individual and social levels, with all these major problems. It provides them with a means through which to remain true to their cultural roots and surmount their own worries while feeling comfortable with the shifting patterns of modernity. Through Agonshū's unified structure the local is universalised, the past is glorified and cultural belonging is reintensified in such ways as to provide contemporary Japanese with a path through which to come to terms with and feel at home with the processes of internationalisation, modernisation and rapid change.

Agonshū thus enables its members to reap psychologically the benefits of the society they live in, taking the best of both tradition (especially its emotional comforts) and modernity (especially its conveniences and physical comforts) while freeing them of the negative aspects of both. In such respects they are offered a path through which they can 'definitely win' and experience a bright, happy life in which they can feel that they are in control of their own destinies and are playing an important, even vital, and valid role in the world. Thus Agonshū, like other contemporary religious movements in Japan, gives its followers a sense of personal value and confidence, and a framework of cultural and emotional security through which to deal with the various strains, problems and turbulences inherent in the changing patterns of Japanese society. It thus provides them with a religious frame of meaning relevant to contemporary life.

Conclusion: Mystery, Nostalgia and the Shifting Sands of Continuity

The 'new' new religions have clearly demonstrated that many Japanese remain interested in causal explanations centring on the miraculous, and are actively concerned with the incidence of religious dynamism in their lives. This interest in miracles, mystery and spiritual power is not limited just to the 'new' new religions but extends beyond them into a healthy publishing industry focusing on such issues as spirit possession, UFOs, the myths of Mu and Atlantis, and other such phenomena that appear to be a mixture of 'new age' concepts and extremely traditional Japanese folkloric ones. Nowadays in Japan there are many magazines, the best-known of which is called *Mū*, devoted to accounts of the supernatural, visitations, UFOs and the like, which sell several hundred thousand copies a month.

Most Japanese bookshops have special sections to accommodate the large and expanding tide of books offering methods for avoiding spiritual pollution and for exerting one's control over ghosts and wandering spirits so as to turn them into protective benefactors, as well as chronicles of meetings with UFOs and aliens, and stories of miracles and power. To name but a few examples, Fujii Hōen's *E de miru kyofu no shinreikai* ('The Terrifying World of Spirits Seen Through Pictures') asserts that all sorts of spirits exist in the world and that they can be seen and, where necessary, exorcised by spiritually endowed people, while Kumamoto Akira's *Daireikai* ('The Great Spirit World') series focuses on such matters as spiritual healing (Volume 1), the existence of spirits (Volume 6) and gods and miracles (Volume 9). Other authors have produced voluminously on similar themes: Ōkawa Ryūhō has written profusely about UFOs, miracles, spiritual power and psychic experiences while Kondō Kazuo has, for the benefit of those interested in the contemporary activities of the spirits of samurai warriors, documented the messages relayed by samurai spirits of centuries past who have returned to speak through the mouths of young Japanese today.[1]

234

This apparent interest in miracles and the mysterious has been documented widely by Japanese academics in recent years. Nishiyama Shigeru's survey on 363 university students from Tokyo that produced such a negative response concerning established and organised religion (see p. 14) found at the same time that they were extremely interested in such things as UFOs, miracles and the existence of spirits. Sixty-two per cent expressed interest in the subject of UFOs, 53 per cent believed in their existence and 10 per cent had direct experience of them. Sixty-six per cent of the students not only believed in premonitions but had personally experienced them; 56 per cent expressed great interest in the existence of superhuman spiritual powers, although only 5 per cent had actual experience of them; and 60 per cent expressed an interest in the concept of miracles, with 50 per cent believing that they occurred.[2] I became very much aware of this preoccupation when teaching a seminar group of twelve Japanese students in the late 1980s. When asked to comment on the above survey all expressed interest in these various phenomena and several claimed to have experienced premonitions of some sort or to know others who did. Their fascination with miracles, UFOs and other psychic phenomena constituted not so much a positive belief in their existence as a general inclination not to rule it out.

Miracles and mystery are of course an enduring theme of Japanese religious history. The early Japanese myths of the *kami*, the rich history of *engi*, the purple clouds guiding ascetics to holy places where Kannon might appear in trees, the miraculous events surrounding statues of Fudō, and the various legends concerning Kōbō Daishi that have been encountered in this book are but a sample of the rich tradition of extraordinary events that punctuate Japanese religious history. There is, besides, a rich literary tradition of collections of tales of the miraculous, extraordinary events with religious undertones and divine interventions to save people from disasters and illness, dating back at least to the eighth century.[3]

The contemporary fascination for miracles and for events beyond the ordinary parameters of life that give it added excitement and colour is a direct extension of this tradition and of this perennial concern with a direct and immanent religious world. Bearing in mind also the tendency we have seen with, for example, the content of prayers and the form of *o-mamori*, for religious phenomena frequently to keep pace with the modernising and changing patterns of the surrounding environment, it might be feasible also to suggest that UFOs in many ways could be twentieth-century equivalents of miraculous clouds. The innate Japanese penchant for assimilating external influences and placing them within Japanese frameworks is also evident in the recent interest in Mu.

That so much attention is paid to them at present (and to the traditional cosmological attitudes that underpin them) is at least in part related to the increasing structuralisations and rationalisations of contemporary society, and in many ways represents an emotional counterbalance and response to and escape from them. In particular, too, it reflects an unease concerning the roles of science and technology: recent surveys (notably those by the NHK) have indicated large majorities (in 1981, 76 per cent) of people of all ages expressing either their distrust of science or their feelings that science cannot find solutions to all issues.[4] This is especially, as was noted in the previous chapter, associated with the deep worries many people have about the negative effects (for example, pollution) that are seen as concomitants of science and technology. It is also, perhaps even more so, associated with the feeling that the apparently increasing rationalisations of society are limiting the scope for human action and imagination. For young people caught up in the pressures of the heavily structured Japanese education system with its strong inclinations towards facts and rote learning and its inherent bias against personal expression and analytical discussion, the world of miracles, spirits and mysterious happenings provides a ready means of mental escape, of self-expression and of emotional solace otherwise denied them.

The processes of modernisation, rationalisation, scientific development and increased education thus tend to stimulate rather than diminish interest in spiritual matters and the world of the irrational.[5] Indeed one of the major themes that has surfaced in this book has been the continuing and even increasing levels of activity across the religious spectrum in contemporary Japan. This has not been uniform for, as we have seen, the established traditions of Shinto and Buddhism continue to face the threat of decline due to changes in their traditional constituencies, while some of the older and larger new religions are also beginning to face similar problems as they become more closely identified with the establishment and lose their earlier dynamism. None the less, many of the phenomena that I have introduced, such as the rising numbers participating in festivals, *shichigosan*, *hatsumōde* and the various occasions which memorialise the ancestors, the current interest in pilgrimages, the large numbers who acquire amulets and talismans and visit religious centres to pray for benefits, the small but growing interest in meditation mentioned in Chapter 4, the contemporary focus on ascetic and charismatic figures of power, and the seemingly endless emergence and growth of new religions, are indicative of the energies inherent in the religious world of Japan today. While there are economic factors in much of this, with increased affluence clearly stimulating activity in such areas as pilgrimage and festivals, there is more behind it than that. As the current interest in miracles and the growing numbers of adherents of the 'new' new religions amply testify, the religious arena remains a vital and alive element in contemporary Japanese life, and one that grows in importance as social pressures and tensions increase.

NOSTALGIA AND THE IDEALISED SPIRITUAL HOMELAND

The growing interest in traditionalist cosmologies exhibited in the 'new' new religions and the increasing desires for some route of emotional release from the pressures and structuralisations of contemporary society have been mirrored also by a powerful interest in the traditions of the past — or, to be more precise, in images of the traditional past that are in many ways idealised and thus 'inventions of tradition' more than anything else. We have already encountered this sense of nostalgia and tradition in Chapter 3, with festivals in contemporary Japan being described as representations of the spiritual homeland (*kokoro no furusato*) of the Japanese people and as counterweights to the encroachments of modern society; and in Chapter 4, where the Sōtō Zen sect used the same imagery to encourage its members to participate in the *o-bon* rites.

This inherent sense of idealised traditionalism and nostalgia also came out in Chapter 5 in the remarks made by two Japanese commentators on the image of the ascetic of Hiei against the modern background of contemporary Japan, and in Chapter 6 in the contemporary imagery of pilgrimage. Such images of revival and nostalgia are far more widespread than this: the *Jinja honchō*, the organisation uniting most of Japan's Shinto shrines, has described its most important religious centre, the shrines of Ise, as 'the spiritual homeland of the Japanese people' (*nihonjin no kokoro no furusato*).[6] The next rebuilding of the Ise shrines (this is done in a traditional and unchanging style every twenty years) which will take place in 1993 has been widely publicised on banners erected by the *Jinja honchō* throughout Japan proclaiming that this rebuilding represents and symbolises a 'revival of the Japanese spirit'.[7]

The author Kino Kazuyoshi, in a book itself entitled *Kokoro no furusato* ('The Spiritual Homeland'), which is largely a travelogue of famous Japanese religious places such as Kōyasan, Ise and the like, has described the Shikoku pilgrimage as a 'spiritual homeland of the Japanese people',[8] while the Awaji island tourist board, in publicising two pilgrimage routes around the island, has also appropriated the same words, describing Awaji as a Japanese spiritual homeland.[9]

This use of the image of the *furusato*, the homeland, and of the *kokoro no furusato*, the spiritual homeland, is redolent with emotive nuances of tradition, of unsullied life, peace and harmony, and acts as (and is intended to act as) an idealised contrast to the realities of contemporary, especially urban, life.[10] These images (and hence the idealised *furusato*) stand as bastions of Japanese culture and tradition and as bulwarks against, and escapes from, the increasing disharmonies of contemporary life, and as representations of a peace that has been lost in the processes of modernisation. In other words, the images are restatements and reaffirmations of Japanese ideals in the modern world that serve as a means of enabling Japanese people to maintain or reawaken contact with the cultural and, indeed, spiritual roots that help to formulate Japanese identity and provide them with a sense of peace of mind, *anshin*, and a sense of feeling at ease and at home that is lacking in modern life. There is *anshin*, peace of mind, and a sense of belonging in tradition, in the structures of the *furusato*, the native village with its social ties of belonging cemented by the shrine, temple, ancestors and festivals, far more than there is in the modern city with its crowded apartments and commuter trains.

This is, of course, an imagery that has grown in strength as the traditional village *furusato* with its inherent images of peace, tranquillity, rice fields, thatched farmhouses, streams and mountains[11] has, for most people, become more remote, lost or never experienced. A large percentage of contemporary urban dwellers have lived all their lives in the cities: accordingly they have never experienced the *furusato* as it really was. This loss, and the demise of the traditional *furusato* which itself is irrevocably tied to the changing structure of Japanese society with its shift from agriculture to manufacturing, high technology industries and international finance, has been balanced by the creation of the fictionalised *furusato* of the emotions, the *kokoro no furusato* with its implicit cultural warmth and sense of belonging and identity specific to the Japanese. The *furusato*, in a spiritual sense, has thus become national, rather than regional or localised, implying identification not with a particular village but with the wider Japanese spiritual and cultural homeland.

This invented and pristine *furusato* (in the imagery none of the problems of traditional rural life, with its occasional periods of famine and lower life-expectancy, intrude) stands in contrast to the (by implication) westernised chaos, tensions and problems of the city, and in many respects represents a contemporary extension and development of the Japanocentric and, especially, the nationalistic traits within the Japanese religious world. By reiterating the mythic images of Japanese cultural uniqueness and homogeneity depicted in the stories of early Shinto texts it creates an emotional national-ism within a religious framework, and an idealisation in a religious context of Japanese cultural traditions and identity.

CONFIDENCE AND UNCERTAINTY

To some extent these reaffirmations of cultural strength that provide focuses of peaceful harmony as a counterbalance to the present turmoil of society can be seen, as can the reassertions of traditional-ist causation over and against the rationalist explanations of modern science, as expressions of a Japanese confidence, cultural strength and assuredness in the contemporary world. The powerful focus on miracles and the innately revivalist tendencies of nostalgia exhibit — as do the attentions paid to the ancestors and spirits of the dead by the growing numbers who perform *haka mairi* and memorial rites for *mizuko* spirits, and the increasing crowds visiting shrines and temples and performing pilgrimages — the extent to which the contemporary focus of activity in the religious sphere reflects not only a search for individual meaning but also a powerful contempo-rary interest in aspects of Japanese tradition, identity and cultural belonging.

One of the major impetuses to this revival of interest in Japanese tradition has come about as a result of Japan's growing economic prevalence in the world. Until the mid-1970s (in fact, until the time of the 'oil shocks' of 1973–4) Japan had been involved in rebuilding and catching up with the industrialised world. Although the 'oil shocks' brought to a close a period of extremely high growth they affected the rest of the world at least as much as Japan and marked the real beginnings of Japan's emergence as not a follower but an economic leader and technological innovator. As Japan has over-taken many of her Western counterparts in technological development and economic power this has led to a growth of internal self-confidence and to a powerful sense of cultural assurance. As Japanese people have gained this confidence they have been able to look again at their own traditions with a deep sense of pride. Technological success has thus in many ways validated Japanese customs and outlooks over and against those from the outside, has helped reaffirm the respectability of traditional views of causation and has reminded the Japanese that they should not lose sight of their own roots. At the same time their increased wealth has provided them with the means with which to return to those traditions in some way, a factor that has played its part in the contemporary growth of pilgrimage, festivals and the like.

None the less, there is perhaps a defensiveness about all this as well. Japan is, as I noted in the previous chapter, tied in to the modern world, and the pulls towards nostalgic longing and tradi-tionalism do not suggest a real desire to abandon the riches won through participating in the modern world. No one really wishes to go back to the apparent idylls of the *furusato*: people are still moving to, not from, the cities. Yet, as with all aspects of nostalgia, there is an inherent sense of loss involved in this: the processes of modernisation require the inevitable and irrevocable disappearance of many aspects of life and traditional culture prevalent in earlier times and give rise to a deep-seated unease about the extent to which participation in the wider world is eroding, and will continue to erode, Japan's own cultural heritage. The rather dualistic approaches to modernisation expressed though the 'new' new religions are expressions of this unease, just as are the motivations of those who, even while ardently studying and seeking success in the rationalised and fact-oriented structure of the education system are looking for emotional solace in the world of spirit possessions and miracles.

The problem centres on the extent to which the fruits gained from modernisation and from becoming deeply involved with the rest of the world (which, in Japanese terms constitutes something of a success story) can be balanced against the external influences and changes brought upon Japanese society as a result. In this nexus of confidence and anxiety (and, like so many of the apparently conflicting themes I dealt with at the end of the last chapter, they clearly do fit together in many respects) the religious world has been brought into play, providing a means of escape from the pressures of contemporary society which allows the scope for return and renewal rather than rejection. It also provides a renewed sense of belonging and identity in Japanese terms through a restatement of Japanese attitudes, outlooks and traditionalist interpretations.

In reality, the tensions that exist between change and preservation, between expressions of Japanocentric confidence and the innate fears of cultural erosion, are not much different from the frequently conflicting tensions and interpenetrating dualities we have encountered not just in the constantly fraught relationship between Japan and the outside world, exhibited both in the assimilation of Buddhism and in later attempts to reassert the ethnic powers of Shinto over it, but elsewhere. The tensions between group and individual that both attempt to enforce conformity yet stimulate and indeed demand individualism and the development of religious charisma, the tense dualities in the nature of *kami* and ancestors who can cause malevolent problems and beneficial protection, and the problematic attitudes towards the dead exhibited by Izanagi who could not face separation yet had to take measures to enforce it, all manifest these same latent tensions. Indeed, there is an inherent tension between the ideals of *anshin*, peace of mind, feeling at home, belonging and hence being warm and secure, all of which are expressed within the image of *furusato* and are central elements within the social parameters of Japanese religion, and the wish for excitement and encounters with the mysterious found in the enduring role of miracles and spiritual intercessions.

The Japanese religious world balances these seeming tensions and contradictions, providing a means through which they can be contained and expressed within an overall framework relevant to contemporary needs. When a new religion such as Tenrikyō affirms the importance of encountering the spiritual nature of an illness through religious means, it is not denying the advances of modernity but is stating that these are not alone enough. Metaphorically, this, along with the statements of nostalgia and the importance placed by many contemporary Japanese on the incidence of miracles, shows that to live happily in the contemporary world requires a fusion of its benefits with the stabilising forces of cultural tradition.

CONCLUDING REMARKS: CHANGING CONTINUITIES

In Chapter 1 I quoted the businessman who said that there was no longer such a thing as Japanese religion. I also suggested that in reality the Japanese did have high levels of religious activity and suggested that religiosity was especially concerned with expressive action. In Chapter 2 I showed that there was a unifying nature to the world of religion largely shared by the various traditions extant in Japan. In subsequent chapters I have shown that unity in action, and have described various aspects and manifestations of that religiosity as it occurs in contemporary Japan. As I have done so I have drawn attention to the ways in which the forms of religion are expressed tend to keep pace with the changing patterns of society: thus the contemporary modes of pilgrimage, the prayers at shrines and temples that reflect contemporary needs and the dynamism of the 'new' new religions that espouse modern technologies and address the needs and worries of people living in a modern urban society.

Yet, within the fluidities of the Japanese religious framework that enable it to respond to and remain in line with contemporary change and needs, there are remarkable continuities and consistencies. The parameters of religion set out in Chapters 1 and 2, from the importance of situational needs and the emphasis on a happy present life to the centrality of concepts of causation and the interrelationship of humans and spiritual entities, are as relevant as they ever were. When Mahikari followers raise their hands so as to purify fellow-believers and drive out spiritual pollutions to allow them to lead a fuller and more fruitfully productive life, they are not far, in underlying meanings, from Izanagi bathing to wash away the pollutions of the world of the dead and to give life to renewed hopes and wishes in the form of new *kami*. The sense of regeneration and renewal in Izanagi's bathing, and the statements of world renewal implicit in his optimistic counteraction to the threats of messianic doom posed by Izanami's pledge to kill 1000 people a day, are restated in contemporary form in the context of the present fear and threat of environmental depredation and nuclear war by new religions such as Agonshū. The continuing worries about the potential threats posed by the dead to the living inherent in the myth of Izanami and Izanagi, and which surface in the ninth-century story of Sugawara Michizane, are expressed in the present age by the Agonshū members who seek, through the powers of the Buddha relic or in the fires of Agonshū rituals, the pacification of angry ancestors who they think are causing them trouble.

As we have seen in Chapter 7, the inner meanings of prayers remain remarkably constant, even if the spheres within which they are expressed may change. In the contemporary age people are less likely to pray for such economically marginal things as the prosperity of horse-rearing. Stock market transactions are, however, relevant, and consequently, as we saw in Chapter 3, we find contemporary securities companies asking the *kami* for help. In doing so they are acting in the same way, under the same parameters, with the same motives, and expressing the same psychological needs of reassurance as the horse-farmers of Kisogawa or, indeed, as Japanese farmers and peasants over a thousand years ago. The same is true for those praying for safe travel in automobiles or entering a prestigious university. The point, which has already been made in the last chapter, is that religion is not now (nor ever has been) out of date or step with contemporary society in Japan.

As such it is clear that religious matters, and religiosity, are very much part of Japanese life, relevant in social terms and playing roles on personal individual levels simultaneously, providing avenues through which Japanese people may express themselves and through which they may find meaning and a source of identity as well as help and support whenever they need it. Religion is thus not, in the final analysis, something that is out of date or irrelevant to a modern and changing society like Japan. Rather, as has been shown in this book, it remains an essentially contemporary phenomenon, with a constantly modernising internal dynamic that keeps in line with and relevant to the changing needs of the people themselves and to those of the society in which they live. As such it also provides a medium through which people can come to terms with social change while giving them a framework of meaning, vitality, reassurance and cultural belonging. The religious activities of the 1980s demonstrate the continuing validities of the Japanese religious world in the rapidly changing context of contemporary Japanese society. In coming decades and in the next century it will no doubt continue to change in step with society while preserving and updating its inherent continuities so as to remain as relevant and responsive to Japanese needs on social and individual levels as it is at present.

Notes

Notes to the Introduction

1. For historical background Kitagawa (1966); Hori *et al.* (1972); Earhart (1974) and (1982); and Murakami (1980) are all useful, as is Sasahara (ed.) (1977) vols 1 and 2.

Notes to Chapter 1: Turning to the Gods in Times of Trouble

1. Shūkyō shakaigaku no kai (ed.) (1985) pp. 134–6.
2. Reader (1989) p. 8.
3. Bunkachō (ed.) (1988) p. 13.
4. Sōtōshū shūseichōsa iinkai (ed.) (1984), esp. Appendix pp. 1–40; Sasaki (1984) p. 365; see also Reader (1986), esp. p. 12.
5. Davis (1980a) p. 264.
6. These figures and discussions on them are given in Yanagawa (1988) p. 11: further comments on these and other figures cited in this section can be found in Swyngedouw (1986) pp. 2–5; Iida (1986) pp. 182–203; Miyake, Kōmoto and Nishiyama (eds) (1986) pp. 282–5; Kaneko (1988) pp. 33–76; and Kōmoto (1988) pp. 77–117.
7. Iida (1986) pp. 183–4.
8. Miyake, Kōmoto and Nishiyama (eds) (1986) p. 282.
9. Graphs depicting these changes are given in Kaneko (1988) p. 99; and in *Shūkyō jōhō*, no. 26 (1987) pp. 16–17.
10. Ibid., p. 17.
11. There are a number of groupings under which religious organisations can be classified, including Buddhist, Shinto, Christian and miscellaneous: many new religions are classed under Buddhist (as with Reiyūkai and Risshōkōseikai) or Shinto (e.g. Tenrikyō), while a few remain under the miscellaneous label. Agonshū is one of these, although it regards itself as Buddhist.
12. Bunkachō (ed.) (1988) p. 13.
13. Kajimura (1988) pp. 4–6.
14. Swyngedouw (1986) pp. 4–5; Yanagawa (ed.) (1988) p. 12.
15. Earhart (1989) pp. 2–12: later he provides a statistical outline of how joining Gedatsukai appears to promote participation in various traditional religious activities connected with Shinto and Buddhism (pp. 112–20).
16. See, for example, Kitagawa (1966) pp. 145–9, 201–4, 221–5.
17. Bunkachō (ed.) (1988) pp. 95–129, gives a long although not exhaustive list of registered religious organisations in Japan that runs into several hundreds.
18. There has been something of a growth in very recent years of more aggressively exclusive groups, including imported religions such as the Jehovah's Witnesses: for a discussion of the growth of the Jehovah's Witnesses in Japan see Numata (1988) pp. 136–55.

19. These figures were cited by officials of Sōka Gakkai during interviews at the Gakkai headquarters in Tokyo, 2 July 1987, and various interviews with officials at its Kansai headquarters in Osaka during the period between January and December 1988. In both places the estimate made to me was around 60 per cent.
20. Kaneko (1988) pp. 104–5, 113–5.
21. Bunkachō (ed.) (1987) pp. 76–7: the figures in the 1988 edition are slightly up, at 6,933,817 (Bunkachō (ed.) (1988) pp. 70–1).
22. Sōtōshūshūmuchō (ed.) (1987) pp. ii and 137–9.
23. Bunkachō (ed.) (1987) p. 2.
24. The figure of 3–4 per cent came in the 1981 NHK survey: Reid (1984) p. 379, suggests that this 3–4 per cent largely consists of members of new religions with Shintoesque themes.
25. Kōmoto (1988) p. 40.
26. See, for example, Iida (1986); Kaneko (1988); and Kōmoto (1988).
27. Kōmoto (1988) p. 51, gives a graph showing the growth in numbers of those taking part in *hatsumōde* over the past decades.
28. *Shūkyō jōhō*, no. 26 (1987) p. 17.
29. Swyngedouw (1986) p. 5.
30. Iida (1986) p. 184.
31. Ibid., p. 185.
32. Kōmoto (1988) p. 61.
33. Dore (1958) p. 307, notes that 'children are taught to bow to the *kami-sama* as they are taught to bow to visitors, and they grow up with an idea of the *kami-sama* as important beings to whom deference must be shown without ever receiving explicit instruction concerning the nature, abode or function of the *kami*'.
34. There is an interesting discussion on this point in the editorial columns of the religious newspaper *Chūgai Nippō*, 12 August 1987, p. 3.
35. Ōmura (1988) p. 1.
36. Nishiyama (1988a) p. 206.
37. Ōmura (1988) pp. 17–19.
38. Amongst many such published in the last few years are Bukkyō bunka kenkyūkai (ed.) (1987a) and (1987b) (both of which had by 1988 gone through several new reprints); Ikeguchi Ekan (ed.) (1987); and Saeki (1986).
39. Hardacre (1986) pp. 26–7.
40. Shūkyō shakaigaku no kai (ed.) (1985) pp. 125–36. I am grateful to Professor Iida Takafumi of Toyama University, one of the team who carried out this survey, for bringing this to my attention.
41. This Sōtō Zen leaflet, entitled *Anata no bodaiji*, is undated and without pagination: it is cited in Reader (1989) p. 16. In Reader (1985), (1986) and (1989) I have given a fuller analysis of contemporary Sōtō Zen writings that focus on this process of developing empathy and transforming it into commitment and belief.
42. Hattori (1977) pp. 59–63: see also Reader (1985). The points made here have been reiterated to me by various officiants of the Sōtō sect in interviews at the Sōtō Zen Headquarters in Tokyo on various occasions between 1985 and 1988.

43. Davis (1980b) p. 212.
44. Numata (1988) pp. 76–82, has a short discussion of Shinnyoen's teachings, as does Shinshūkyō kenkyūkai (1987) pp. 56–61: the cosmology outlined here is as reported by my student.
45. Davis (1980b) p. 229.
46. Ibid., pp. 2–5, 72–9, gives a more detailed description of the earlier parts of this process of secession and fragmentation: for the subsequent secession within the Sekiguchi branch of Mahikari see *Chūgai Nippō*, 25 March 1988, pp. 10–11.
47. Hokutoumi's comments were reported in the *Sankei spōtsu* newspaper on 5 January 1989.

Notes to Chapter 2: Unifying Traditions, Cosmological Perspectives and the Vitalistic Universe

1. Miyake (1981) p. 122. For a fuller discussion see Miyake (1974) pp. 89–148 and 166–74; and also Hori (1968) esp. pp. 1–48.
2. Herbert (1967) pp. 389–459, has a comprehensive compilation of historical *kami* (i.e., people who came to be regarded as *kami* or *kami* who were once people). Whether Ōjin was an historical figure is a matter of some question, although Herbert, pp. 426–38, treats him as such.
3. Hardacre (1986) pp. 23–5, also discusses Japanese social dynamics in her discussion of religion and of religious relationships in Japan: all I would add is that, while the relationships so created are hierarchical, there is frequently also a degree whereby they may be exploited by the lower ranking figure (as, perhaps, with humans in their relationship with *kami*) who plays on the social responsibilities implicit in the position of the higher-ranking figure.
4. See Reader (1987a), esp. pp. 294–8.
5. On Byakkō Shinkōkai's world perspective see Pye (1986).
6. Davis (1980b) pp. 64–72, outlines Mahikari's views of world history and cosmology, which has Japan in ancient times ruling over the entire world and in which Jesus not only came to Japan at the age of eighteen but returned again after falling foul of the authorities in Israel (where his younger brother was crucified in his place) and died in Japan at the age of 118 (p. 69).
7. Young (1988) discusses the process of self-universalisation in Oomoto, showing how it has interpreted various world religious figures as *kami*: elsewhere, Young (1989) has shown how another religious group, Megami no Umi, led by the shamanic and visionary woman Fujita Himiko, has incorporated Jesus as a *kami*.
8. See Swyngedouw (1986) p. 4.
9. This item was broadcast during one of the news programmes on the Asahi television channel in Osaka on the evening of 7 January 1989.
10. On the influence of Confucianism in Japanese religion see Tomikura (1981) pp. 105–20.

11. This is clearly an expression of the doctrine of *upāya* (Japanese: *hōben*) or skilful means, using the means and teachings appropriate to the circumstances to propagate Buddhism. For a full discussion of this major Buddhist concept see Pye (1978).

12. Technically Buddhas and Bodhisattvas are at different stages of the path (Bodhisattvas basically have vowed not to enter full Buddha-hood until they can aid all others to attain this state), but in reality little if any differentiation is made by the vast majority of Japanese people, who are more concerned with how these figures can help them rather than with what level of status they possess. Since, in general everyday practice, few people appear to see much status difference between, for example, the Bodhisattva Kannon and the Buddha Yakushi, I have not dwelt on the technical differences between them.

13. See Daitō Shuppansha (ed.) (1965) p. 143; also for separate entries on the concepts of *jōgu bodai* and *geke shujō* see Inagaki (1984) pp. 60 and 143. Hattori (1977) is basically a discussion of the concept both in theory and what it means in practical terms for a Buddhist sect in contemporary Japan.

14. On the general developments of Buddhism in Japan, especially to the fourteenth century, the best available work in English is D. and A. Matsunaga (1974). Saunders (1972) gives a generalised history that concentrates mostly on doctrinal developments and major person-alities; while Kitagawa (1966) incorporates Buddhist developments and changes into his overall study of Japanese religious history. Sahashi (1978) is a general outline of the relationship between the Japanese and Buddhism from a contemporary perspective.

15. Kannon, who usually appears in female form in Japan, although as male in India, Tibet and China, makes this vow in the 25th chapter of the Lotus Sūtra, which is a popular Buddhist text in its own right in Japan. For a translation see Hurvitz (1976) pp. 311–19.

16. The ninth-century collection of tales, the *Ryōiki*, translated by Nakamura (1973), is but one of many collections of miracle stories that can be found in Japanese religious history containing stories of Kannon's infinite mercy, intercessory actions and compassion. Hay-ami (1983) is the best general work on beliefs and stories concerning Kannon, while both Maeda (1987) and Shimizutani (1983), esp. pp. 1–36, are contemporary works extolling the virtues of Kannon and her compassion.

17. On the Buddhist origins of *riyaku* see Fujii (1972) pp. 184–6. Among the various manuals and guidebooks that I have seen in the past few years in Japan are Kōdansha (ed.) (1981) and Satō (1982).

18. On the topic of *genze riyaku* see Miyake (1974) pp. 129–48, which is a little dated but provides a good outline of the ways in which it operates; and Fujii (1972).

19. On the importance of this seminal Buddhist text see Pye (1977), and Blacker (1975), esp. pp. 95–6. Many expositions of the text exist in Japanese, usually emphasising its virtues and powers: see for example Miyazaki (1981), and Hashimoto (1982).

20. Morris (trans.) (1975) p. 31.

21. Chōkokuji publishes a leaflet which says that the statue has such powers, while *Chūgai Nippō*, 23 December 1987, has an article about the Nagoya statue. The pages of *Chūgai Nippō* often carry articles about new statues: I have used these two examples simply because they are temples I have stayed at and know well.

22. An advertisement for these pendants appear in the *Mainichi shinbun*, 18 October 1983.

23. The popular nature of Jizō has been discussed in Yoritomi (1984) pp. 93–158. I have been given numerous reasons when asking people why they put bibs on Jizō, but like most folk-orientated practices there seems to be no single one.

24. For a detailed account of this process see Matsunaga (1969).

25. Okada (1988) p. 261; Miyamoto (1984) pp. 170–3.

26. For example, the university I worked for in Japan had such ceremonies carried out when constructing its new library and other facilities.

27. My remarks are based on numerous visits to Toyokawa and to Toyokawa Inari itself between June 1981 and December 1986.

28. Miyake (1981) p. 123.

29. There is, technically, a difference between *senzo* who are ancestors of the household and are thus implicitly benevolent, and *hotoke*, referring to all who have died and thus are not necessarily benevolent. In general, though, few people make much distinction between them. For further discussion, including the relationship of *hotoke* to *senzo*, see Guthrie (1988) pp. 65–8.

30. These issues will be dealt with in Chapter 4.

31. I saw this in March 1982 and referred to it also in Reader (1989) p. 11.

32. Sakai (1980) p. 22.

33. Kamata (1977) p. 4.

34. Davis (1980b) p. 30.

35. These ideas are particularly strongly expressed by the new religion Reiyūkai and discussed throughout Hardacre (1984), and summarised in Hardacre (1986) pp. 29–31.

36. My views are based on several years of observing religious behaviour and discussing such issues in Japan. Despite the importance placed on ancestors in Japan I do not think that this indicates an other-worldly orientation or concern with the state of being of the ancestors so much as a continued valuation of this one.

37. Buddhism's involvement with the rites of death is dealt with by Mace (1985); see also Goodwin (1989a), and Tamamuro (1963).

38. Hoshino and Takeda (1987) pp. 309–10.

39. I have dealt with this issue also in Reader (1988a) pp. 247–8.

40. This issue has been dealt with by Brooks (1981); Hoshino and Takeda (1987); and Smith (1988), and is currently the subject of a major research project conducted by Smith with Elizabeth Harrison of the University of Chicago.

41. The information in this section comes from the Revd Oda Baisen, head-priest of Tōganji in Nagoya, and from the Revd Nishiyama Kōsen, head-priest of Daimanji in Sendai. Both were kind and

patient enough to allow me to stay for several months at their temples during 1981–2 and to answer my questions on these issues.

42. *Chūgai Nippō*, 22 September 1987, p. 14.
43. Ibid., 4 September 1987, p. 16: this newspaper often carries reports of memorial services for objects of all sorts.
44. Davis (1980b) gives detailed descriptions both of the way this is performed and what occurs at Mahikari centres when this is done.
45. This film was shown at an Agonshū meeting I attended at Hirakata in Osaka prefecture on 6 November 1988.
46. Davis (1980b) pp. 201–9.
47. See the comments made by Numata (1988) pp. 279–80.
48. The importance of *yōkigurashi* is emphasised in many Tenrikyō publications; for example, Tenrikyō (ed.) (1985) pp. 75–81; and Moroi (1972) pp. 58–61. Hardacre (1986) pp. 14–21, examines the 'bright' outlooks of Shintoesque new religions such as Tenrikyō and Kurozumikyō.
49. According to the figures in Bunkachō (ed.) (1987) p. 94, until 1980 the numbers of those classified as members of Christian religious groups was under one million. Although there has been some growth since, most of this has been among non-mainstream Christian groups such as the Jehovah's Witnesses, the Mormons and the Unification Church.
50. This is according to the 1981 NHK survey reported by Swyngedouw (1986) p. 3.
51. Miyake (1974) p. 89.
52. *Chūgai Nippō*, 29 August 1988, p. 14.
53. These observations are based on occasional forays into this area and some of its bars.
54. This story is related in Shūkyō shakaigaku no kai (ed.) (1985) pp. 104–5.

Notes to Chapter 3: 'Born Shinto . . .'

1. *Mushi okuri* and *mushi kuyō* are virtually the same; on the former see Ono *et al.* (eds) (1985) pp. 308 and 627–8, and on the latter, Miyake (1974) pp. 191–2.
2. Obviously this is a fairly perfunctory description of the situation in pre-modern Japan. For further information see Ueno *et al.* (1978), esp. pp. 78–108 and 142–61, and Miyake (1974) pp. 184–202. Uno (1988) pp. 348–52, gives brief outlines of *kami* involved with agriculture, sericulture and fishing.
3. Kōmoto (1988) p. 40.
4. Inoue *et al.* (1979) p. 165.
5. On the relationship between *ujiko* and local society see Sonoda (1988a) pp. 266–82.
6. Okada (1988) pp. 252–3.
7. Kyburz (1987) pp. 91–2.

8. This figure of 80,000 refers to those shrines registered under the *Shūkyō hōjinhō* (Religious Juridical Persons Law) and is given in Bunkachō (ed.) (1988) pp. 58–9: it does not include wayside and unattended shrines.

9. *Pachinko* is a popular game in Japan played on machines similar to an upright bagatelle board and arrayed in garishly illuminated arcades which emit an enormous amount of noise, of music and of the metal *pachinko* balls as they tumble through the machines.

10. Ono (1962) pp. 68–9.

11. Ueda (1981) pp. 42–5; Ono (1962) p. 50.

12. This, for instance, is the case at the *yutate* rituals carried out at Ishikiri shrine.

13. Sonoda (1975) p. 103.

14. The interpretation and analysis of this rite here is based on my observations at Katano and at several other shrines, including Ishikiri shrine in Osaka, Iwashimizu Hachimangū in Yawata near Kyoto, and Minatogawa and Rokkō Yahata shrines in Kōbe and on discussions with the priests of all of these shrines. I am especially grateful to the Revd Miya of Iwashimizu Hachimangū and the Revd Kobayashi of Ishikiri for patiently answering my questions on the meanings of the rite.

15. For a further description of a somewhat less active (because of depopulation) local shrine see Guthrie (1988) pp. 95–114.

16. This phrase (in Japanese: *kutōten*) is used by Sonoda (1988b) p. 355.

17. Kurrehayashi (1984) p. 11, also pp. 217–28.

18. For a fuller description of the implications of this term, and of nostalgia in a religious context, see Reader (1987a); while Robertson (1988) discusses the meanings of *furusato* and of nostalgia in cultural and political contexts.

19. Kōmoto (1988) pp. 36–7, further discusses these shifts of pattern.

20. These words (in Japanese: *shūkyō fudō jinkō*) are used by Fujii (1974) p. 91. In ibid., pp. 91–144, he discusses this issue at some depth with regard especially to Buddhist temples.

21. Matsudaira (1983) pp. 23–46, 255–91; also Kōmoto (1988) pp. 58–9.

22. Uno (1978) pp. 66–82.

23. This point is made very effectively by Sonoda (1975) pp. 132–6.

24. Uno (1978) pp. 66–82, discusses the development of this festival, including the machinations that occurred to correlate the shrine and city festivals.

25. Inoue *et al.* (1979) pp. 163–85.

26. See, for example, Rohlen (1974).

27. Rohlen (1973), esp. pp. 1544–7, describes such spiritual training for company employees at Zen temples.

28. *Mainichi shinbun*, 12 December 1987, p. 1.

29. Uno (1985) p. 265.

30. Swyngedouw (1986) p. 8.

31. Ono (1988) pp. 10–11, gives this and many more examples of the shrine–company relationship.

32. Dobbelaere (1986) p. 140; for a description of religious rituals within a Japanese factory in Japan see Lewis (1986).

33. I should like to thank Ruta Noreika of the Scottish Centre for Japanese Studies, University of Stirling, for bringing this information to my attention.

Notes to Chapter 4: '. . . Die Buddhist'

1. For a more thorough description of these sects, especially in philosophical terms, see D. and A. Matsunaga (1974).
2. See, for example, Suzuki (1959).
3. I spent one year in 1981–2 doing fieldwork at Sōtō Zen temples, in all staying at twelve different temples for periods ranging from three days to six months.
4. Yokoi (1976) has translations of some of the later sections of Dōgen's major work, the *Shōbōgenzō*, as well as an introduction to his life and thought. Nishiyama Kōsen and John Stevens have produced a translation of the whole work in four volumes (Nishiyama and Stevens (1975–83)), while Kim (1975) discusses his thought and the ways he applied it to monastic life.
5. Sometimes read as *shinjin darraku*, this term was widely used by Dōgen in the *Shōbōgenzō* and remains in use in monastic situations in Sōtō today.
6. Sōtōshūshūmuchō (ed.) (1987) pp. 93–5.
7. See Reader (1986), esp. pp. 16–21.
8. I have discussed these issues at some length in ibid., pp. 7–27.
9. Okazaki *et al.* (eds) (1982) pp. 406–8.
10. Weatherall (1989) p. 67.
11. My articles (Reader, 1985 and 1989) demonstrate how Sōtō literature focuses on the continued existence of the soul by talking about the return of the souls of the dead to this world at *o-bon* and the continued role of the ancestors.
12. Marcure (1985) provides a good outline of the workings of the *danka* system; while Kyburz (1987) pp. 133–81, details its history and workings in a mountain village: he also makes it clear (pp. 139–46) that the priest was generally regarded as something of an outsider.
13. See Collcutt (1988) on this failed attempt to destroy Buddhism.
14. Maeda (1976) pp. 151–2. Kaneko (1988) pp. 104–5 relates a 1978 survey which showed similar patterns for worship at the grave, with 47 per cent of the 16–24 age group and 72 per cent of the over-60s performing *haka mairi*.
15. Guthrie (1988) p. 64, states that 74 per cent of the income of the temple in the village where he did his fieldwork came from such services.
16. Sōtōshūshūmuchō (ed.) (1987) p. 53, suggests that in all about 40 per cent of priests have second jobs, although I think this is a conservative figure: officials at the sect's headquarters have suggested to me that the figure might be nearer 80 per cent. Certainly this latter figure is closer to the mark for the numbers who marry and inherit their temples (ibid., pp. 24–6).

17. The obligation to train a priest to succeed one is inscribed in Article 28 of the sect's rules: making one's son that successor is the easiest (and for many the only) feasible option in an age where there are few outsiders entering the priesthood. The question of the hereditary priesthood is a contentious one that cannot easily be resolved. I have friends who are priests who condemn the system because they think it weakens the vocational elements and makes priesthood into a business, while others who have grown up in temples consider it to be a good system because it means the priest will have been raised in a temple environment and thus be extremely suited to the position.
18. See Reader (1986) pp. 14–5.
19. Sōtōshū shūseichōsa iinkai (ed.) (1984) Appendix, pp. 23–7.
20. Ibid., Appendix, p. 18. Kyburz (1987) p. 135, notes that none of the villagers that he asked (some 50 or so) knew what sect they belonged to.
21. For a full description of this process see Ooms (1967) pp. 271–8; and Smith (1974) pp. 69–114.
22. Ooms (1967) pp. 275–6, suggests that the one left at the grave to decay symbolises the body and the one at the *butsudan* symbolises the soul.
23. Smith (1974) p. 85.
24. Sōtōshūshūmuchō (ed.) (1987) p. 106. The percentage discrepancy is because a small number (just under 4 per cent) went on beyond 100 years and about 24 per cent ceased before the 33rd.
25. *Mainichi Daily News*, 9 March 1989.
26. *Shūkan Asahi*, no. 11/4 (1988) pp. 13–5.
27. I am aware this is something of an oversimplification as the practices of ancestor worship and the customs of the household itself vary from region to region, and also because many of these customs themselves are in a state of flux in contemporary Japan. None the less, this description, which is based on Takeda (1976) pp. 119–27, is useful in that it serves to show the extent and nature of the changes that are taking place.
28. Smith (1974) pp. 152–86, esp. p. 174.
29. Kōmoto (1988) pp. 39–50.
30. Wisewell (1988) pp. 373–4.
31. I have commented on some of these themes in Reader (1985) and (1989) pp. 10–15.
32. See Smith (1974) pp. 115–46, esp. p. 140–6.
33. *Asahi shinbun*, 15 February 1987, p. 1.
34. See, for example, Bukkyō bunka kenkyūkai (ed.) (1987a).
35. The Revd Oda Baisen of Tōganji in Nagoya informed me of a temple parishioner whose illness was divined as being the result of spiritual hindrances caused by an inappropriately sited ancestral grave: the family concerned had a new grave constructed as a result. I have been told of many similar cases by friends and acquaintances, and have since the mid-1980s picked up several leaflets from diviners and from gravestone manufacturers asserting that misfortunes may accrue from wrongly sited or constructed graves.
36. Kōmoto (1988) pp. 43–7.

37. On graveyard problems see Kōmoto (1988) pp. 43–7; Weatherall (1989) pp. 66–8; Matsumoto (1989) pp. 39–41.
38. Information taken from a pamphlet published by the Hanshin Company and put through my letterbox when I lived in Japan.
39. For instance, Rokugatsu Shobō publishes the quarterly magazine called *Reien gaido* ('Cemetery Guide') which gives information on the latest cemeteries, has short articles about aspects of caring for the grave, advertisements for graveyards and other such information.
40. The article was by Rick Kennedy in the *Japan Times*, 15 March 1987, p. 15.
41. Sōtōshūshūmuchō (ed.) (1987) pp. 2–3.
42. In Reader (1986), esp. pp. 12–4 and 24–5, I have discussed this issue, basing my remarks on the findings of the comprehensive survey published in Sōtōshū shūseichōsa iinkai (ed.) (1984).
43. The principal of these is *Zen no kaze* (subtitled in English *Zen Forum*, although no English appears in the text), an annual magazine which was first published in Sōtō in 1981. I have described this and other such publications in Reader (1985) pp. 44–5.
44. This short tract has been included in various Sōtō publications, including Sōtōshūshūmuchō (ed.) (1981a) p. 4, and (1981b) pp. 28–9 (the latter with an added commentary).
45. For a fuller exposition of the nostalgic imagery in Sōtō literature see Reader (1987a) pp. 294–8.

Notes to Chapter 5: Individuals, Ascetics and the Expression of Power

1. Sugimoto and Mouer (1986) pp. 199–200.
2. Hardacre (1986) pp. 11–21.
3. Tenshō Kōtai Jingūkyō (ed.) (1954) emphasises how she polished her own soul and encouraged others to do likewise: see, for example, p. 19.
4. The interrelated themes of ascetic practice, the powers that accrue from this and the ways in which these are used are discussed thoroughly by Blacker (1975), which remains very much the best account of the whole topic of individual practice and shamanism in Japan.
5. Gojō (1983) p. 47.
6. Goodwin (1989b) pp. 137–49.
7. Blacker (1984) p. 596.
8. See Reader (1988b), esp. pp. 53–8.
9. On the development, practices and activities of the *Kōya hijiri* see Gorai (1984).
10. See Reader (1987b).
11. See Imai (1981) pp. 131–44, where she, a journalist sent by her newspaper to travel some of the Shikoku route and write about it, relates miracle stories told her by fellow pilgrims. Shikoku hachijūhakkasho reijōkai (ed.) (1984) is a collection of experiences of the

pilgrimage, including numerous miracle stores, told by various pilgrims, pilgrim guides and priests.

12. Blacker (1975) (see above, note 4) provides a comprehensive description of the richness of this tradition in historical and practical terms.

13. Few people go all the way from the first station now as a new road and regular bus service convey people up to the fifth. On the issue of mountains in general see Hori (1968), esp. pp. 141–79.

14. A good description of this pilgrimage is to be found in Swanson (1981), while the summer 1989 edition of the *Japanese Journal of Religious Studies* concentrates on Shugendō, especially in historical terms, and contains many useful articles. Miyake (1971) is a standard reference work on Shugendō rituals in which he describes (pp. 110–20) a Shugendō version of the *yutate* rite described in Chapter 3. Miyake (1983) is a short and clear general outline of Shugendō rites and pilgrimage accompanied by an excellent photo-essay by Yano Takehiko (pp. 91–126).

15. Blacker (1975) pp. 248–51, describes various Shugendō ascetic feats including *hiwatari*.

16. See the devastating comments in Blacker (1975) pp. 295–7.

17. Numata (1988) pp. 4–86.

18. Davis (1980b) p. 302.

19. Shūkyō shakaigaku no kai (ed.) (1985) pp. 27–30.

20. Tanigame (ed.) (1986) pp. 104–5.

21. Descriptions and photographs of this austerity can be found regularly in *Chūgai Nippō*, for example 15 and 24 February 1988. Blacker (1975) pp. 302–3, also describes such Nichirenist asceticism, while an illustrated commentary on such practices is given in Tanigame (ed.) (1985) pp. 95–106.

22. Blacker (1975) pp. 301–14 describes such exorcistic practices at two separate Nichirenist temples.

23. Nagamura's comments are reported in Tanigame (ed.) (1985) pp. 104–5.

24. One full length film, *Yomigaeru: Tōtō*, directed by Tabata Keiichi in 1983, and one major documentary, *Gyō*, by Wazaki Nobuya in 1979, have been shown in recent years in Japan: each follows the path of one of the ascetics through the practice. TVC Yamamoto (ed.) (1983) is a collection of essays on the practice and the film itself. Books by the ascetics about the practice and their experiences include Hagami (1971) and Mitsunaga (1973), while those about the practitioners include Wazaki (1979), Shima (1983), and Hironaka (1985) pp. 70–92. In English, Stevens (1988) contains general information on the practice, short biographies of some of the ascetics and some good photographs, while Rhodes (1987) provides a thorough discussion of the practice and its meanings.

25. For historical details I have based my remarks on Rhodes (1987).

26. The description of the practice given here is based on the sources and films cited in note 24 and on my own visits to Hiei.

27. Stevens (1988) p. 126.

28. When I talked to Sakai in September 1984 he spoke along these lines: similar words were used in the documentary *Gyō* (see note 24).

29. Gojō (1983) pp. 36–43, describes this fast.
30. Yamada (1988) is a description of austerities, including the 1000-day practice, performed at Mount Kubote.
31. Ibid., p. 218.
32. Sōtōshū shūseichōsa iinkai (ed.) (1984) Appendix, p. 31.
33. Ōishi (1987).
34. Blacker (1975) pp. 160–1.
35. This estimate is given in Fitzpatrick (1989) p. 43.
36. Nakamura (1983) p. 6; Matsumoto (1983) pp. 32–3: see also my comments on these remarks in Reader (1987a) pp. 287–303.

Notes to Chapter 6: Sites and Sights

1. See Grapard (1988) and (1982).
2. Though there is a Buddhist bias to the origins and nature of *engi* their nature, structures and themes have been assimilated also by Shinto: see Sonoda (1988c).
3. This myth, an English version of which is found in Rugola (1986) p. 144, is described in pamphlets available at the temple.
4. My account here is based on leaflets obtained at the shrine.
5. This simplified version of the legend is given in Rugola (1986) pp. 138–40; a far longer and more complex version is given in Enkyōji (ed.) (1968) pp. 1–11.
6. Naritasan (ed.) (1981) pp. 87–91.
7. This information is based on an interview with the Revd Yoshii at the Kōrien temple on 28 October 1988. The *engi* and the story of the transmission of the statue are described on a large billboard at the temple.
8. The advertisement cited in Chapter 2 concerning the Kannon in Mie is a good example of this, as are the posters displayed throughout Kyoto by Jishu shrine (which will be discussed later in this chapter as a centre for would-be lovers).
9. Kōdansha (ed.) (1981).
10. Jishu shrine leaflet (undated but available at the shrine). Interestingly the shrine publishes an English leaflet which does not contain these words.
11. These remarks are based on several visits to the temple between 1986 and 1988. An outline of this temple appears in Ohnuki-Tierney (1984) pp. 138–42.
12. Ibid., p. 182.
13. This comment is based on a brief survey of the *ema* there on 15 November 1987.
14. See Reader (1988b) and also below, Chapter 7.
15. Rugola (1986) and Sawa (1970) both discuss the art treasures of Saikoku in some detail.
16. See Foard (1982).
17. These remarks are based on observations and interviews at Saikoku temples between November 1986 and October 1988: many people appear to have taken several years to do the whole route.

18. See, for example, Maeda (1971), esp. pp. 57–71.
19. These and other preliminary figures are given in Leavell and Reader (1988) pp. 116–8.
20. The primary work on all matters relating to the relationship between religious centres and economic issues such as travel and trade is Shinjō (1964).
21. Cited in Reader (1987b) p. 134.
22. See my article, Reader (1987a), for further comments on this issue.
23. Shūkyō shakaigaku no kai (ed.) (1985) pp. 104–15.
24. Ibid., pp. 85 and 99–100.
25. On the numbers and proliferation of *shichi fukujin* pilgrimages see Ōishi (1989).
26. On the Awaji route see ibid., pp. 189–91.
27. See Reader (1987b) pp. 139–40.
28. *Chūgai Nippō*, 1 July 1987, p. 12.
29. Ibid., 6 April 1988. p. 12.

Notes to Chapter 7: Actions, Amulets and the Expression of Meaning

1. For a fuller discussion of this phenomenon see Reader (1988b).
2. The observations are based on several visits to Sumadera between April 1985 and March 1987.
3. Hirahata (1982) pp. 140–2.
4. For a fuller discussion of styles and types of *o-mamori* see Swanger (1981).
5. I should like to thank the Revd Shiratori at Shinshōji for describing this process to me in detail.
6. On the development of *ema* see Iwai (ed.) (1983), esp. pp. 14–77.
7. Holtom (1938) pp. 161–3.
8. Shūkyō shakaigaku no kai (ed.) (1985) pp. 54–68.
9. These figures are given in Kōmoto (1988) p. 40.
10. Swyngedouw (1986) p. 4.
11. I should like to thank Ms Kathy Scott of Kansai University of Foreign Studies for submitting these questions to two classes there in October 1988.
12. This conversation took place on 24 September 1986 at Daisenji.
13. See *Asahi shinbun*, 25 May 1986.
14. These figures come from an undated and anonymous article translated from the *Asahi shinbun* and printed in the *Journal for Popular Culture*, no. 17 (1983) pp. 149–51.
15. These remarks are based on interviews with the Revd Shiratori (see above, note 5) and other officiants at the temple, 29 June 1987, and on further comments by the Revd Yoshii at the Kōrien temple, 28 October 1988.
16. Further information from the Revd Shiratori, 29 June 1987.
17. Zenpōdō (ed.) (1985) p. 5.
18. Kyburz (1987) pp. 189–228.

Notes to Chapter 8: Spirits, Satellites and a User-Friendly Religion

1. In English the best-known works are by Thomsen (1963); Offner and van Straelen (1963); McFarland (1967); Davis (1980b); Hardacre (1984) and (1986); and Earhart (1989). Recent works in Japanese include Numata (1988); and Nishiyama (1988a) and (1988b). Earhart (1983) is a comprehensive Western-language bibliography, while Inoue *et al.* (1981) pp. 259–306, gives an extensive bibliography largely in Japanese.

2. McFarland (1967) deals with the new religions specifically as responses to social crisis: although he tends to place too much emphasis on this interpretation it is clear that social unrest does help to create a ready climate for new religions to grow in.

3. The term 'new' new religion seems to have come into use around 1980: see Numata (1988) pp. i–ii.

4. Kanagawa Shinbunsha (ed.) (1986) pp. 12–32.

5. Numata (1988) p. 57.

6. Hori *et al.* (1981) pp. 207–8.

7. Kanagawa Shinbunsha (ed.) (1986) p. 226, gives a survey carried out in Yokohama which suggests that the active membership of new religions was around 9 per cent, with a further 2 per cent who were formerly active (p. 241).

8. Hardacre (1986) p. 3, estimates around 30 per cent, although I think this is rather over-generous, especially in the light of the figure produced by the Kanagawa survey (note 7).

9. See above, note 1.

10. Davis (1980b) pp. 67–8.

11. Numata (1988) pp. 128–60, covers these movements as new religions.

12. Tani (1987) p. 110.

13. Earhart (1989) p. 100.

14. Interview, Tokyo, 2 July 1987.

15. Tani (1987) p. 108.

16. Ibid.

17. This tendency still persists to some extent, especially among some of the weekly magazines in Japan that largely focus on scandals of all types.

18. See the comments made by Numata (1988) pp. ii–iii.

19. Earhart (1989) p. 85.

20. Davis (1980b) p. 282.

21. Tani (1987) p. 108.

22. Davis (1980b) p. 285.

23. Tani (1987) p. 108.

24. Ibid., p. 109.

25. On Okada's revelation see Davis (1980b) pp. 3–5; and on Inai's see Kanagawa Shinbunsha (ed.) (1986) pp. 12 and 124–8.

26. Davis (1980b) p. 103; Kanagawa Shinbunsha (ed.) (1986) p. 239.

27. On Tenrikyō's teaching on this matter see Tanaka (1982).

28. Numata (1988) pp. 243–250.

29. Davis (1980b) p. 37.

30. Goi (1983) p. 43.
31. Davis (1980b) p. 31.
32. Ibid., p. 122.
33. For a fuller discussion of the psychological framework of Mahikari possession see Davis (1980b) pp. 126–60.
34. Byōdō (1987) pp. 14–6.
35. The following discussion of Agonshū is based on my article in the *Japanese Journal of Religious Studies* (Reader, 1988a): I am grateful to the Editor of the Journal for allowing me to use this material. I have supplemented it with works by Kiriyama (1971, 1983, 1987) and by two uncritical biographies: Yajima (1985) and Murō (1987).
36. Kiriyama (1983) pp. 77–84.
37. Reader (1988a) pp. 248–9; Murō (1987) p. 51.
38. Nishiyama (1988b) p. 221; Nishijima (1988a) pp. 156–65.
39. These figures are given in Robertson (1988) p. 506.
40. Tani (1987) p. 113.
41. Murō (1987) pp. 33–7.
42. These figures were given by Agonshū spokesmen on the day itself and later reported in the media.
43. Shinnyoen (ed.) (1977) p. 82.
44. Agonshū (ed.) (1986) pp. 26–7.
45. Numata Kenya considers the figure to be closer to 100,000 (personal communication).
46. See, for example, Kakida (1984) pp. 62–4.
47. This information was given in an interview with a member of Agonshū's publicity department in Tokyo, 1 July 1987.
48. Numata (1988) pp. 56–86.
49. *Mainichi Daily News*, 15 October 1987.
50. This information was given to me in an interview on 1 July 1987 (see above, note 47).
51. Ibid.
52. See, for example, McFarland (1967) pp. 71–96.
53. Swanson (1981) pp. 66–8, reports a *yamabushi* dialogue where the symbolism of the clothing is given.
54. For further details see Reader (1988a) p. 241.
55. Although I am speaking of Agonshū here I think that this assessment is valid for all the new religions.
56. On Byakkō Shinkōkai's peace campaign see Pye (1986).

Notes to the Conclusion

1. Fujii (1985); Kumamoto (1981 onwards). Ōkawa's books are published by Shinrei Books, Tokyo, and Kondō's by Chōbunsha, also of Tokyo. These are but a selection of a vast and burgeoning market.
2. Nishiyama (1988a) pp. 203–4.
3. For a fuller exposition of these themes see Picone (1986) pp. 157–65.
4. Iida (1986) pp. 187–8.
5. This point has been well argued by Kaneko (1988) pp. 106–7.

6. The *Jinja honchō* publishes a broadsheet entitled *Jinja shashin jihō* which frequently carries this statement.
7. Such banners had certainly begun to appear by 1988: I first saw one in Nara prefecture in that year, and later saw others at Ise and in various locations in the Kyoto–Osaka region.
8. Kino (1985) p. 65.
9. See Reader (1987a) p. 292.
10. For a fuller exposition of this issue see Reader (1987a).
11 Robertson (1988) p. 494, outlines the images conjured up by the image of *furusato*: she also discusses how the image is extended to cities and the ways in which it has been used in cultural and political terms.

References Cited

Agonshū (ed.) (1986), *Senzo kuyō* (Tokyo: Agonshū).

Blacker, Carmen (1975), *The Catalpa Bow: A Study of Shamanistic Practices in Japan* (London: George Allen and Unwin).

Blacker, Carmen (1984) 'The Religious Traveller in the Edo Period', *Modern Asian Studies*, vol. 18, no. 4, pp. 593–608.

Brooks, Anne Page (1981), '*Mizuko kuyō* and Japanese Buddhism', *Japanese Journal of Religious Studies*, vol. 8, no. 3, pp. 119–47.

Bukkyō bunka kenkyūkai (ed.) (1987a), *Bochi erabi haka zukuri* (Osaka: Hikarinokuni).

Bukkyō bunka kenkyūkai (ed.) (1987b), *Butsuji no shikitari* (Osaka: Hikarinokuni).

Bunkachō (ed.) (1987) and (1988), *Shūkyō nenkan* (Tokyo: Gyōsei).

Byōdō Fumihiro (1987), 'Shūkyō "kaiki" genshō o yomu — shakai ishiki chōsa no bunseki', in Yamamoto Harugi (ed.), *Gendai nihon no shūkyō* (Tokyo: Shinsensha) pp. 11–30.

Collcutt, Martin (1988) 'Buddhism: the Threat of Eradication', in Marius B. Jansen and Gilbert Rozman (eds), *Japan in Transition: From Tokugawa to Meiji* (Princeton, N.J.: Princeton University Press, pp. 143–67.

Daitō Shuppansha (ed.) (1965), *Japanese–English Buddhist Dictionary* (Tokyo: Daitō Shuppansha).

Davis, Winston (1980a), 'The Secularization of Japanese Religion: Measuring the Myth and the Reality', in Frank E. Reynolds and Theodore M. Ludwig (eds), *Transitions and Transformations in the History of Religions* (Leiden: E. J. Brill) pp. 261–85.

Davis, Winston (1980b), *Dojo: Magic and Exorcism in Modern Japan* (Stanford, Cal.: Stanford University Press).

Dobbelaere, Karel (1986), 'Civil Religion and the Integration of Society: a Theoretical Reflection and an Application', *Japanese Journal of Religious Studies*, vol. 13, no. 3, pp. 127–46.

Dore, Ronald P. (1958), *City Life in Japan: A Study of a Tokyo Ward* (Berkeley, Cal.: University of California Press).

Earhart, H. Byron (1974), *Religion in the Japanese Experience* (Belmont, Cal.: Wadsworth).

Earhart, H. Byron (1982), *Japanese Religion: Unity and Diversity* (Belmont, Cal.: Wadsworth).

Earhart, H. Byron (1983), *The New Religions of Japan: A Bibliography of Western-Language Materials* (Ann Arbor, Mich.: Centre for Japanese Studies).

Earhart, H. Byron (1989), *Gedatsukai and Religion in Contemporary Japan* (Bloomington, Ind.: University of Indiana Press).

Enkyōji (ed.) (1968), *Banshū Shoshasan engi* (Himeji: Enkyōji).

Fitzpatrick, Christopher (1989), 'Letter from Aomori', *Far Eastern Economic Review*, 30 Nov. 1989, vol. 143, no. 11, pp. 42–3.

Foard, James (1982), 'The Boundaries of Compassion: Buddhism and National Tradition in Japanese Pilgrimage', *Journal of Asian Studies*, vol. 16, no. 2, pp. 231–51.

Fujii Hōen (1985), *E de miru kyōfu no shinreikai* (Tokyo: Hōyū Shuppansha).

Fujii Masao (1972), 'Genze riyaku', in Tamaru, Muraoka and Miyata (eds) op. cit., pp. 179–238.

Fujii Masao (1974), *Gendaijin no shinkō kōzō* (Tokyo: Hyōronsha).

Goi Masahisa (1983), *God and Man* (Ichikawa: Byakko Press).

Gojō Junkyō (1983), *Shugendō no kokoro* (Osaka: Toki Shobō).

Goodwin, Janet R. (1989a), 'Shooing the Dead to Paradise', *Japanese Journal of Religious Studies*, vol. 16, no. 1, pp. 63–80.

Goodwin, Janet R. (1989b), 'Building Bridges, and Saving Souls: the Fruits of Evangelism in Medieval Japan', *Monumenta Nipponica*, vol. 44, no. 2, pp. 137–49.

Gorai Shigeru (1984), *Kōya hijiri* (Tokyo: Kadokawa Sensho).

Grapard, Alan (1982), 'Flying Mountains and Walkers of Emptiness: Toward a Definition of Sacred Space in Japanese Religions', *History of Religions*, vol. 21, no. 2, pp. 195–221.

Grapard, Alan (1988), 'Institution, Ritual and Ideology: the Twenty-Two Shrine–Temple Multiplexes of Heian Japan', *History of Religions*, vol. 27, no. 3, pp. 246–69.

Guthrie, Stewart (1988), *A Japanese New Religion: Risshō Kōsei-kai in a Mountain Hamlet* (Ann Arbor, Mich.: Centre for Japanese Studies).

Hagami Shōchō (1971), *Dōshin: kaihōgyō no taiken* (Tokyo: Shunjūsha).

Hardacre, Helen (1984), *Lay Buddhism in Contemporary Japan: Reiyūkai Kyōdan* (Princeton, N.J.: Princeton University Press).

Hardacre, Helen (1986), *Kurozumikyō and the New Religions of Japan* (Princeton, N.J.: Princeton University Press).

Hashimoto Tetsuma (1982), *Hannya Shingyō kōwa* (Tokyo: Shiunsō).

Hattori Shōsai (1977), *Jōgu to geke* (Tokyo: Sōtōshūshūmuchō).

Hayami Tasuku (1983), *Kannon shinkō* (Tokyo: Hanawa Sensho).

Herbert, Jean (1967), *Shinto* (New York: Stein and Day).

Hirahata Ryōyū (1982), *Shikoku hachijū hakkasho*, 2 vols (Chiba: Manganji Kyōkabu).

Hironaka Heisuke (1985), *Kagaku no chie, kokoro no chie* (Tokyo: Kōsei Shuppansha).

Holtom, Daniel C. (1938), 'Japanese Votive Pictures: the Ikoma Ema', *Monumenta Nipponica*, vol. 1, no. 1, pp. 154–64.

Hori Ichiro (1968), *Folk Religion in Japan* (Chicago, Ill.: University of Chicago Press).

Hori Ichiro et al. (eds) (1981), *Japanese Religion* (Tokyo: Kodansha).

Hoshino Eiki and Takeda Dōshō (1987) 'Indebtedness and Comfort: the Undercurrents of *Mizuko kuyō* in Contemporary Japan', *Japanese Journal of Religious Studies*, vol. 14, no. 4, pp. 305–20.

Hurvitz, Leon (1976), *Scripture of the Lotus Blossom of the Fine Dharma (The Lotus Sūtra)* (New York: Columbia University Press).

Iida Takafumi (1986), 'Gendai shūkyō no shakai shinri', in Manba Hisaichi (ed.), *Shakai shinrigaku o manabu hito no tame ni* (Tokyo: Sekaishisōsha) pp. 182–203.

Ikeguchi Ekan (ed.) (1987), *Shingonshū no butsuji* (Tokyo: Sekaibunkasha).

Imai Mimisako (1981), *Oyako henro tabi nikki* (Tokyo: Tōhō Shuppan).

Inagaki Hisao (1984), *A Dictionary of Japanese Buddhist Terms* (Kyoto: Nagata Bunshodo).

Inoue Nobutaka *et al.* (1979), 'A Festival with Anonymous Kami: the Kōbe Matsuri', *Japanese Journal of Religious Studies*, vol. 6, nos 1–2, pp. 163–85.

Inoue Nobutaka *et al.* (1981), *Shinshūkyō kenkyū chōsa handobukku* (Tokyo: Yūzankaku).

Iwai Hiromi (ed.) (1983), *Ema hisshi* (Tokyo: NHK Books).

Kajimura Noboru (1988), *Nihonjin no shūkyō* (Tokyo: Chūōkōronsha).

Kakida Mutsuo (1984), 'Hoshi matsuri no himitsu', *Bunka hyōron*, no. 280, pp. 56–66.

Kamata Shigeo (1977), *Zen no ningenkan* (Tokyo: Sōtōshūshūmuchō).

Kanagawa Shinbunsha (ed.) (1986), *Kami wa orita* (Yokohama: Kanagawa Shinbunsha).

Kaneko Satoru (1988), 'Gendaijin no shūkyō ishiki', in Ōmura and Nishiyama (eds), op. cit., pp. 77–117.

Kim Hee-Jin (1975), *Dōgen Kigen, Mystical Realist* (Tucson, Ariz.: University of Arizona Press).

Kino Kazuyoshi (1985), *Kokoro no furusato: tabi to nihonjin* (Tokyo: Kōsei Shuppan).

Kiriyama Seiyū (1971), *Henshin no genri* (Tokyo: Kadokawa Bunsho).

Kiriyama Seiyū (1983), *Gense jōbutsu* (Tokyo: Rikifu Shobō).

Kiriyama Seiyū (1987), *Hito wa donna innen o motsu ka* (Tokyo: Agonshū).

Kitagawa, Joseph M. (1966), *Religion in Japanese History* (New York: Columbia University Press).

Kōdansha (ed.) (1981), *Fuku o yobu jisha jiten* (Tokyo: Kōdansha).

Kōmoto Mitsugu (1988), 'Gendai toshi no minzoku shinkō — kakyō saiken to chinkon', in Ōmura and Nishiyama (eds) op. cit., pp. 33–76.

Kumamoto Akira (1981 to date), *Daireikai*, 9 vols to 1989 (Tokyo: Kōbunsha).

Kurehayashi Shōji (1984), *Matsuri no kōzō* (Tokyo: NHK Books).

Kyburz, Josef (1987), *Cultes et croyances au Japon: Kaida, une commune dans les montagnes du Japon Central* (Paris: Maisonneuve et Larose).

Leavell, James, and Reader, Ian (1988), 'Research Report on the Saikoku Pilgrimage in Japan', *Studies in Central and East Asian Religions*, vol. 1, no. 1, pp. 116–18.

Lewis, David (1986), 'Religious Rites in a Japanese Factory', *Japanese Journal of Religious Studies*, vol. 13, no. 4, pp. 261–75.

Mace, François (1985), *La Mort et les funerailles dans le Japon ancien* (Paris: Presses Orientalistes de France).

McFarland, H. Neill (1967), *The Rush Hour of the Gods: A Study of New Religious Movements in Japan* (New York: Macmillan).

Maeda Kōdō (1987), *Kannon shinkō nyūmon* (Osaka: Toki Shobō).

Maeda Takashi (1971), *Junrei no shakaigaku* (Kyoto: Minerva Books).

Maeda Takashi (1976), 'Ancestor Worship in Japan: Facts and History', in W. H. Newell (ed.), *Ancestors* (The Hague: Mouton) pp. 139–61.

Marcure, Kenneth (1985) 'The *Danka* System', *Monumenta Nipponica*, vol. 40, no. 1, pp. 39–67.

Matsudaira Makoto (1983), *Matsuri no bunka* (Tokyo: Yuhikaku).

Matsumoto Kenichi (1983) 'Nihonteki fūkei e no chakuchi', in TVC Yamamoto (ed.), op. cit., pp. 31–3.

Matsumoto, Nancy (1989), 'A Grave Affair', in *PHP Intersect*, January, vol. 5, no. 1, pp. 39–41.

Matsunaga, Alicia (1969), *The Buddhist Philosophy of Assimilation* (Tokyo: Sophia University).

Matsunaga, Daigan and Alicia (1974), *Foundation of Japanese Buddhism*, 2 vols (Los Angeles, Cal.: Buddhist Books International).

Mitsunaga Chōdō (1973), *Tada kono hito to nare* (Tokyo: Yamanote Shobō).

Miyake Hitoshi (1971), *Shugendō girei no kenkyū* (Tokyo: Shunjūsha).

Miyake Hitoshi (1974), *Nihon shūkyō no kōzō* (Tokyo: Keiō Tsūshin).

Miyake Hitoshi (1981), 'Folk Religion', in Hori *et al.*, op. cit., pp. 121–43.

Miyake Hitoshi (1983), 'Shugendō: sono rekishi to shugyō', in Satō Shinji (ed.), *Mikkyō to sei naru yama*, Taiyō no. 36 (Tokyo: Taiyō) pp. 127–31 (plus photo-essay by Yano Takehiko, pp. 91–126).

Miyake Hitoshi, Kōmoto Mitsugu and Nishiyama Shigeru (eds) (1986), *Shūkyō*, vol. 19 of *Riidingsu — nihon no shakaigaku* (Tokyo: Tōkyō Daigaku Shuppankai).

Miyamoto Kesao (1984), 'Inarigami to bukkyō, *Daihōrin*, vol. 51, no. 10, pp. 170–3.

Miyazaki Ninshō (1981), *Shakyō to Hannya Shingyō* (Osaka: Toki Shobō).

Moroi Yoshinori (1972), *Contemporary Thought and Tenrikyō* (Tenri: Tenrikyō Overseas Mission Department).

Morris, Ivan (trans.) (1975), *As I Crossed a Bridge of Dreams* (trans. of the *Sarashina nikki*) (Harmondsworth, Middx.: Penguin).

Murakami Shigeyoshi (1980), *Japanese Religion in the Modern Century*, trans. H. Byron Earhart (Tokyo: University of Tokyo).

Murō Tadashi (1986), *Wakamono wa naze shin shinshūkyō ni hashiru no ka* (Tokyo: Tokino Keizaisha).

Murō Tadashi (1987), *Agonshū: sekai heiwa e no michi* (Tokyo: Seiunsha).

Nakamura Hajime (1983), 'Yomigaeru nihon no tamashii', in TVC Yamamoto (ed.), op. cit., pp. 6–9.

Nakamura Kyoko Motomochi (1973), *Miraculous Tales from the Japanese Buddhist Tradition: The Nihon Ryōiki of the Monk Kyōkai* (Cambridge, Mass.: Harvard University Press).

Naritasan (ed.) (1981), *Naritasan kyokā tokuhon* (Narita: Daihonzan Naritasan Shinshōji).

NHK Seiron chōsabu (ed.) (1986), *Gendai nihonjin no ishiki kōzō*, 2nd edn (Tokyo: NHK Books).

Nishijima Takeo (1988), *Shinshūkyō no kamigami* (Tokyo: Kōdansha).

Nishiyama Kōsen, Stevens, John, *et al.* (trans.) (1975–83), *Dōgen Zenji: Shōbōgenzō*, 4 vols (Tokyo: Nakayama Shobo).

Nishiyama Shigeru (1988a), 'Gendai no shūkyō undō', in Ōmura and Nishiyama (eds), op. cit., pp. 169–210.

Nishiyama Shigeru (1988b), 'Gendai shūkyō no yukue', in Ōmura and Nishiyama (eds), op. cit., pp. 211–28.

Numata Kenya (1988), *Gendai nihon no shinshūkyō* (Osaka: Sōgensha).

Offner, Clark B., and van Straelen, Henry (1963), *Modern Japanese Religions, with Special Reference upon their Doctrines of Healing* (Tokyo: Enderle).

Ohnuki-Tierney, Emiko (1984), *Illness and Culture in Contemporary Japan* (Cambridge: Cambridge University Press).

Ōishi Mahito (1989) *Zenkoku shichifukujin meguri* (Tokyo: Midori Shoten).

Ōishi Ryūichi (1987), *Nihon no reinōryokusha* (Tokyo: Nihon Bungeisha).

Okada Shōji (1988), 'Ryōijin to sūkeikō', in Sonoda (ed.), op. cit., pp. 252–65.

Okazaki Jōji *et al.* (eds) (1982), *Butsugu daijiten* (Tokyo: Kamakura Shinsho).

Ōmura Eishō (1988), 'Gendaijin to shūkyō', in Ōmura and Nishiyama (eds), op. cit., pp. 1–32.

Ōmura Eishō and Nishiyama Shigeru (eds) (1988), *Gendaijin no shūkyō* (Tokyo: Yuhikaku).

Ono Masaaki (1988), 'Kigyō to jinja', *Chūgai Nippō*, 21 April 1988, pp. 10–11.

Ono Sokyo (1962), *Shinto: The Kami Way* (Rutland, Vt: Tuttle).

Ono Yasuhiro *et al.* (eds) (1985), *Nihon shūkyō jiten* (Tokyo: Kōbundō).

Ooms, Hermann (1967), 'The Religion of the Household: a Case Study of Ancestor Worship in Japan', *Contemporary Religions in Japan*, vol. 8, Nos 3–4, pp. 201–333.

Picone, Mary (1986), 'Buddhist Popular Manuals and the Contemporary Commercialization of Religion in Japan', in Joy Hendry and Jonathan Webber (eds), *Interpreting Japanese Society: Anthropological Approaches* (Oxford: JASO) pp. 157–65.

Pye, Michael (1977), 'The Heart Sutra in its Japanese Context', in Lewis Lancaster (ed.), *Praj'naparamita and Related Systems: Essays in Honor of Edward Conze* (Berkeley, Cal.: University of California and Berkeley Institute of Buddhist Studies) pp. 123–34.

Pye, Michael (1978), *Skilful Means* (London: Duckworth).

Pye, Michael (1986), 'National and International Identity in a Japanese Religion (Byakkō Shinkōkai)', in V. Hayes (ed.), *Identity Issues and World Religions: Selected Proceedings of the XVth Congress of the International Association for the History of Religions* (South Australia: Australian Association for the Study of Religion), pp. 234–41.

Reader, Ian (1985), 'Transformations and Changes in the Teachings of the Sōtō Zen Buddhist Sect', *Japanese Religions*, vol. 14, no. 1, pp. 28–48.

Reader, Ian (1986), 'Zazenless Zen? The Position of Zazen in Institutional Zen Buddhism', *Japanese Religions*, vol. 14, no. 3, pp. 7–27.

Reader, Ian (1987a), 'Back to the Future: Images of Nostalgia and Renewal in a Japanese Religious Context', *Japanese Journal of Religious Studies*, vol. 14, no. 4, pp. 287–303.

Reader, Ian (1987b), 'From Asceticism to the Package Tour: the Pilgrim's Progress in Japan', *Religion*, vol. 17, no. 2, pp. 133–48.

Reader, Ian (1988a), 'The Rise of a Japanese "New New Religion": Themes in the Development of Agonshū', *Japanese Journal of Religious Studies*, vol. 15, no. 4, pp. 235–61.

Reader, Ian (1988b), 'Miniaturization and Proliferation: a Study of Small-Scale Pilgrimages in Japan', *Studies in Central and East Asian Religions*, vol. 1, no. 1, pp. 50–66.

Reader, Ian (1989), 'Images in Sōtō Zen: Buddhism as a Religion of the Family in Contemporary Japan', *Scottish Journal of Religious Studies*, vol. 10, no. 1, pp. 5–21.

Reid, David (1984), 'Japanese Religions', in John R. Hinnells (ed.), *Handbook of Living Religions* (Harmondsworth, Middx.: Penguin) pp. 365–91.

Rhodes, Robert F. (1987), 'The *Kaihōgyō* Practice of Mt Hiei', *Japanese Journal of Religious Studies*, vol. 14, nos 2–3, pp. 185–202.

Robertson, Jennifer (1988), '*Furusato* Japan: the Culture and Politics of Nostalgia', *Politics, Culture and Society*, vol. 1, no. 4, pp. 494–518.

Rohlen, Thomas P. (1973), '"Spiritual Education" in a Japanese Bank', *American Anthropologist*, vol. 75, pp. 1547–62.

Rohlen, Thomas P. (1974), *For Harmony and Strength: Japanese White Collar Organization in Anthropological Perspective* (Berkeley, Cal.: University of California Press).

Rugola, Patricia (1986), *Japanese Buddhist Art in Context: The Saikoku Kannon Pilgrimage Route*, unpublished PhD thesis, Ohio State University.

Saeki Kaishō (1986), *Butsuji, hōyō no jōshiki* (Osaka: Toki Shobō).

Sahashi Bunju (1978), *Nihonjin to bukkyō* (Tokyo: Jitsugō no Nihonsha).

Sakai Daigaku (1980), *Kaze no naka o aruku* (Tokyo: Sōtōshūshūmuchō).

Sasahara Kazuo (ed.) (1977), *Nihon shūkyōshi*, vols 1 and 2 (Tokyo: Yamakawa Shuppansha).

Sasaki Kōkan (1984), 'Kaisetsu — shuyō na mondai o megutte', in Sōtōshū shūseichōsa iinkai (ed.), op. cit., pp. 363–73.

Satō Tsuneharu (1982), *Nippon goriyaku kikō* (Tokyo: Arachi Shuppansha).

Saunders, E. Dale (1972), *Buddhism in Japan* (Rutland, Vt: Tuttle).

Sawa Ryūken (1970) *Saikoku junrei: sanjūsankasho kannon meguri* (Tokyo: Shakai Shisōsha).

Shikoku hachijū hakkasho reijōkai (ed.) (1984), *Shikoku hachijū hakkasho reigenki* (Sakaide: Shikoku hachijū hakkasho reijōkai).

Shima Kazuharu (1983), *Gyōdō ni ikiru* (Tokyo: Kōsei Shuppansha).

Shimizutani Kōshō (1983), *Kannon junrei no susume* (Osaka: Toki Shobō).

Shinjō Tsunezō (1964), *Shaji sankei no shakaikeizai shiteki kenkyū* (Tokyo: Kaku Shobō).

Shinnyoen (ed.) (1977), *Shinnyoen: The Way to Nirvana* (Tachikawa: Shinnyoen).

Shinshūkyō kenkyūkai (ed.) (1987), *Shinshūkyō gaidobukku* (Tokyo: KK Best Books).

Shūkyō jōhō (ed.) (1987), 'Sūgaku ni miru nihonjin no shūkyō ishiki', *Shūkyō jōhō*, no. 26, pp. 16–17.

Shūkyō shakaigaku no kai (ed.) (1985), *Ikoma no kamigami: gendai toshi no minzoku shūkyō* (Osaka: Sōgensha).

Smith, Bardwell (1988) 'Buddhism and Abortion in Contemporary Japan: *Mizuko kuyō* and the Confrontation with Death', *Japanese Journal of Religious Studies*, vol. 15, no. 1, pp. 3–24.

Smith, Robert J. (1974), *Ancestor Worship in Contemporary Japan* (Stanford, Cal.: Stanford University Press).

Sonoda Minoru (1975), 'The Traditional Festival in Urban Society', *Japanese Journal of Religious Studies*, vol. 2, nos 2–3, pp. 103–36.

Sonoda Minoru (1988a), 'Ujigami to kakyō shakai', in Sonoda (ed.), op. cit., pp. 266–82.

Sonoda Minoru (1988b), 'Matsuri to seikatsu kankaku', in Sonoda (ed.), op. cit., pp. 355–62.

Sonoda Minoru (1988c), 'Jinja engi', in Sonoda (ed.), op. cit., pp. 103–20.

Sonoda Minoru (ed.) (1988), *Shintō: nihon no minzoku shūkyō* (Tokyo: Kōbundō).

Sōtōshū shūseichōsa iinkai (ed.) (1984), *Shūkyōshūdan no ashita e no kadai* (Tokyo: Sōtōshūshūmuchō).

Sōtōshūshūmuchō (ed.) (1981a), *Sōtōshū no nenjūgyōji* (Tokyo: Sōtōshūshūmucnō).

Sōtōshūshūmuchō (ed.) (1981b), *Sōtōshū hōreki* (Tokyo: Sōtōshūshūmuchō).

Sōtōshūshūmuchō (ed.) (1987), *Sōtōshū shūsei sōgōchōsa hōkokusho* (Tokyo: Sōtōshūshūmuchō).

Stevens, John (1988), *The Marathon Monks of Mount Hiei* (London: Rider).

Sugimoto Yoshio and Mouer, Ross (1986), *Images of Japanese Society: A Study in the Structure of Social Reality* (London: Kegan Paul International).

Suzuki Daisetz (1959), *Zen and Japanese Culture* (New York: Pantheon Books).

Swanger, Eugene R. (1981), 'A Preliminary Examination of the *Omamori* Phenomenon', *Asian Folklore Studies*, vol. 40, pp. 237–52.

Swanson, Paul (1981), 'Shugendō and the Yoshino–Kumano Pilgrimage: an Example of Mountain Pilgrimage', *Monumenta Nipponica*, vol. 36, no. 1, pp. 55–79.

Swyngedouw, Jan (1986), 'Religion in Contemporary Japanese Society', *Japan Foundation Newsletter*, vol. 13, no. 4, pp. 1–14.

Takeda Chōshū (1976), '"Family Religion" in Japan: *Ie* and its Religious Faith', in W. H. Newell (ed.), *Ancestors* (The Hague: Mouton), pp. 119–27.

Tamamuro Taijō (1963), *Sōshiki bukkyō* (Tokyo: Daihōrinkaku).

Tamaru Noriyoshi, Muraoka Kū and Miyata Noboru (eds) (1972), *Girei no kōzō* (*Nihonjin no shūkyō*, vol. 2) (Tokyo: Kōsei Shuppansha).

Tanaka Kikuo (1982), *Dust and Innen* (Tenri: Tenrikyō Overseas Mission Department).

Tani Fumio (1987), 'Shinpi kara shūkyō e', in Hatakenaka Sachiko (ed.), *Gendai no kokoro: Sūkyō Mahikari* (Tokyo: Ōbundō) pp. 107–16.

Tanigame Riichi (ed.) (1985), *Nichiren to hokekyō shinkō* (Tokyo: Yomiuri Shinbunsha).

Tanigame Riichi (ed.) (1986), *Kyūshū Sasaguri reijō no tabi* (Tokyo: Yomiuri Shinbunsha).

Tenrikyō (ed.) (1985), *The Doctrine of Tenrikyō* (Tenri: Tenrikyō Church Headquarters).

Tenshō Kōtai Jingūkyō (ed.) (1954), *The Prophet of Tabuse* (Tabuse: Tenshō Kōtai Jingūkyō).

Thomsen, Harry (1963), *The New Religions of Japan* (Rutland, Vt: Tuttle).

Tomikura Mitsuo (1981), 'Confucianism', in Hori *et al.* (eds), op. cit., pp. 105–20.

TVC Yamamoto (ed.) (1983), *Yomigaeru: Tōtō* (Tokyo: TVC Yamamoto).

Ueda Kenji (1981), 'Shinto', in Hori *et al.* (eds), op. cit., pp. 29–45.

Ueno Kazuo *et al.* (1978), *Minzoku kenkyū handobukku* (Tokyo: Furukawa Kōbunkan).

Uno Masato (1978), 'Toshi no matsuri e no shikaku', in Shūkyō shakaigaku kenkyūkai (ed.), *Gendai shūkyō e no shikaku* (Tokyo: Yūzankaku) pp. 66–82.

Uno Masato (1985) 'Kigyō ni okeru jinja saishi', *Shūkyō kenkyū*, vol. 58, no. 3, pp. 264–6.

Uno Masato (1988), 'Kamigami to seigyō', in Sonoda (ed.), op. cit., pp. 348–54.

Wazaki Nobuya (1979), *Ajari no tanjō* (Tokyo: Kōdansha).

Weatherall, William (1989), 'A Nation's Dying Industry', *Far Eastern Economic Review*, 16 March, vol. 146, no. 48, pp. 66–8.

Wisewell, Ella (1988), 'Suye Mura Fifty Years Later', *American Ethnologist*, vol. 15, no. 2, pp. 369–79.

Yajima Teruo (1985), *Agonshū to Kiriyama Seiyū* (Tokyo: Akimoto Shobō).

Yamada Ryūshin (1988), *Aragyō* (Tokyo: Gendai Shorin).

Yanagawa Keiichi (ed.) (1988), *Seminaa shūkyōgaku kōgi* (Tokyo: Hōzō Sensho).

Yokoi Yūho (1976), *Zen Master Dōgen* (New York: Weatherhill).

Yoritomi Motohiro (1984) *Shomin no hotoke* (Tokyo: NHK Books).

Young, Richard (1988), 'From *Gokyō-dōgen* to *Bankyō-dōkon*: a Study in the Self-Universalization of Ōmoto', *Japanese Journal of Religious Studies*, vol. 15, no. 4, pp. 263–86.

Young, Richard (1989), 'The Little-Lad Deity and the Dragon Princess: Jesus in a New World Renewal Movement', *Monumenta Nipponica*, vol. 44, no. 1, pp. 31–44.

Zenpōdō (ed.) (1985), *Boke fūji sanjūsan kannon reijō annai* (Kyoto: Zenpōdō).

NEWSPAPER AND MAGAZINES CITED

Chūgai nippō (thrice weekly religious newspaper).
Sankei spōtsu (daily sports paper).
Shūkyō jōhō (monthly religious news magazine).
Mainichi shinbun (daily newspaper).
Asahi shinbun (daily newspaper).
Shūkan Asahi (weekly magazine).
The Japan Times (English language daily).
Mainichi Daily News (English language daily).

Index

abortion 45, 47, 152–3
   see also mizuko
advertisements 145, 148, 164,
   218–19
Āgama sūtras 211–12, 226, 230
Agonshū xiv, 44–5, 49, 119, 195,
   196, 202, 204–5, 206,
   208–233, 242
   film: *Reishō o toke* 44–5, 47
   video: *1999 nen no karuma to
      reishō kara no
      gedatsu* 215, 218
Amaterasu 24, 26–7, 38, 195
Amida 9, 92, 152
amulets *see* charms
ancestors 40–3, 44–5, 48, 50,
   105, 236
   in Agonshū 44–5, 206, 210–13
   see also memorial rites
animals, rites for 45
anshin (peace of mind) 43, 184,
   241
Asahi Beer Co. 167
Asakusa Kannon (Sensōji) 134
asceticism 108, 109–10, 111, 115,
   116–28, 132–3, 173
   see also austerities
Atlantis 234
Atsuta shrine 71
austerities 108, 121–8
   see also asceticism, *suigyō*
Awaji 36, 166, 238

babies 7, 56, 60
   see also childbirth, *miyamairi*
bathing *see* purification
Batō Kannon 192–3
belief 16, 17–18, 21, 104
Benten 151, 165
Bentenshū 222
birth *see* childbirth
Bishamonten 165, 216
Blacker, Carmen 111, 131

bodaiji (ancestral Buddhist
   temple) 83, 88
Bodhisattvas *see* Buddhas
boke fūji (prevention of
   senility) 191–2
bon see o-bon
Buddha 4, 29, 81, 215–16
Buddhas 2, 35, 77–106 *passim*,
   137–74 *passim*
   compared with
      Bodhisattvas 247
   and charms 175–93
   see also Buddhism; *see also
      under individual Buddhas*
Buddhism 3–4, 6–12, 14, 28,
   30–43, 44, 45–6, 55, 77–106,
   130–1
   legal status 85–7
   and new religions 197, 202,
      203, 208–13, 215–17
   paintings 33, 35
   relics 98, 216; *see also
      busshari*
   sects: awareness of
      distinctions 3–4, 89, 151,
      179; *see also under
      individual sects*
   and Shinto: coexistence 1–2,
      6–7, 9, 32, 38–40, 56,
      150–1, 165, 170
   statues 33, 35–7, 143–5, 146,
      172
   texts 33–5; *see also under
      individual sūtras*
   see also Buddhas, temples
bunshin (spiritual offshoot) 145,
   177
business and religion 59, 73–6,
   98, 144–5, 147, 161–4, 166–7
   see also securities companies;
      *see also under individual
      companies*
busshari (relic of the
   Buddha) 216–17, 220, 222,
   225, 230

butsudan (household Buddhist altar) 7, 53, 78, 84, 86, 90–6, 99, 103, 104, 177
  video 92
butsumetsu (death of Buddha) 30
Byakkō Shinkōkai 28, 195, 205, 229

cartoon books 136
celibacy 85
charms, amulets, talismans 11, 63–4, 65, 99, 100, 117, 120, 135, 149, 159, 171–3, 175–93, 224, 236
  see also ema, fuda, o-mamori
childbirth 59, 149–54, 189
  see also babies
children 68, 151, 152
Chinese culture 29
Chionin (Amanohashidate) 180, 181
Chionin (Kyoto) 64, 139
Chōgosonshiji (Shigisan) 139, 163–4, 169, 174, 181, 183
Chōkokuji 36
Christianity 6, 8, 14, 50–2, 86, 198, 200
  see also Jehovah's Witnesses, Jesus, Mormons, Unification Church
Christmas 51
Chūgai Nippō (religious newspaper) 46, 166
Chūgoku pilgrimage 169
clothing:
  Agonshū 222, 225–6, 230
  Buddhist 124–5
  pilgrims' 113–14, 158, 160, 162
  Shinto 65, 150–1
commercialism 136, 161
  see also tourism
companies *see* business and religion
conception *see* fertility
Confucianism 29, 30
cremation 41, 84
crops, rites relating to 57–8

Daikokuten 53, 152, 165
daimoku (Nichiren Buddhist invocation) 18
Dainichi (Cosmic/Sun Buddha) 38, 151, 215
Daisenji 187
danka (households affiliated to Buddhist temples) 86, 87, 89, 93, 102, 103, 104
Davis, Winston 5, 15, 17, 42, 49, 120, 201, 203, 204, 206
death 15–16, 34, 40, 42–4, 84–105 *passim*, 124
  see also ancestors, funerals, memorial rites
Deguchi Nao 202
dharani (words of power) 33
divination 29, 65, 129
Dōgen 81, 82, 85, 91, 92
Doi, Takako 95–6
dōiri (Buddhist ascetic rite) 125–6
dolls, rites for 46

Earhart, H. Byron 7, 199, 201
Ebisu 53, 58, 63, 165
educational success, prayers/charms for 20–1, 33, 52, 151, 176, 177, 180, 182–5, 188, 189
eels, rites for 46
Eiheiji 74
Eisai 81
ekōin see bodaiji
ema (wooden votive tablets) 65, 151–2, 153, 179–84, 185, 188, 189, 190, 192
  see also charms
Embree, John 94
emperors 26, 55, 142–3
  see also under individual names
en (affinity) 47–8, 94
Enchin 142, 145, 210
engi (foundation legends) 141–7, 149, 157, 171, 176, 210, 235
Enkyōji 143, 146, 147, 155, 157, 163
enmusubi (linking two people together as a couple) 148

En no Gyōja   117
Enryakuji   143
examinations *see* educational
    success
exorcism   123, 204, 207

faith healers   129–30
fasting   125, 127
fertility   149–50, 154–5, 181
festivals   62–8, 70–3, 77, 100, 236
    see also under individual names
films:
    Reishō o toke   44
    Yomigaeru: Tōtō   132–3, 254
fire rituals   49, 142, 204, 213, 222
    see also Agonshū, *goma,*
        hiwatari, hoshi matsuri
fishing   58
folk religion   23, 40, 127, 208,
    234
frogs   178
fuda (talismans)   160, 175–8, 182,
    184–5, 186–7, 188, 189–90
    see also charms
Fudō   52, 117, 126, 147, 177,
    216, 235
    associated with fire   118, 122
    protector of travellers   54, 151,
        191
    statue carved by Kōbō
        Daishi   144, 146, 177–8
Fugen   152
Fuji (mountain)   116
Fujii Hōen   234
Fujii Massao   72
Fujita Himiko   246
Fuku o yobu jisha jiten
    (book)   147
Fukurokuju   165
funerals   90
furusato (homeland)   71, 97, 99,
    105, 238–9, 240, 241
    see also kokoro no furusato
Fushimi Inari   71, 75, 139

Gedatsukai   7, 199, 201
genze riyaku (this-worldly
    benefits)   32–3, 69, 85, 186,
    197, 223

gifts *see* offerings
God the Parent (Tenrikyō)   202
gods *see* Buddhas, *kami*
Goi Masahisa   205
Gojō Junkyō   110, 127
gōkaku see educational success
goma   118, 119, 144, 182, 211,
    222, 230
    see also fire rituals, *hoshi
        matsuri, tsuitachi goma*
Goodwin, Janet   111
go-riyaku see riyaku, genze riyaku
graveyards   96–8, 113
    see also haka mairi
ground-breaking ceremonies
    (*jichinsai*)   39, 69
guidebooks   147
    see also manuals, religious
gyō see austerities
Gyō (documentary)   254
Gyōkyō   142, 145

Hachiman   60, 142–3, 145, 147
    see also Emperor Ōjin
Hagami Shōchō   127
haka mairi (grave visiting)   10,
    96, 98–9, 103, 239
    see also higan, o-bon
hamaya (evil-destroying
    arrows)   63, 65, 66
Hankyū Railway Co.   166
Hannya Shingyō (Heart
    Sūtra)   34, 35, 36, 121, 123,
    126, 135, 176, 184, 226
Hanshin Railway Co.   98
hara obi (sash worn by pregnant
    women)   150
Harbin, China   213
Hardacre, Helen   15, 108
Hasedera   156
hatsumōde (New Year
    shrine/temple visit)   10–11,
    12, 13, 21, 51, 62–6, 71–2,
    148, 236
healing, prayers/charms for   19,
    53, 163, 172, 173–4, 181, 185,
    203, 204–5
Heart Sūtra *see Hannya Shingyō*
Heian shrine   138

Heizei, Emperor 143
Hiei 122, 124–7, 132, 133, 143, 229, 237
higan (equinoctial grave visit) 98–9
Hirohito, Emperor 26, 30
hiwatari (fire-walking) 118, 122
Hōgonji 155
Hokutoumi (Sumō wrestler) 21
Holtom, Daniel 180
horses 179, 192–3, 243
hoshi matsuri (Star Festival) 208, 215, 218–19, 221–5, 227, 230
Hotei 165
hotoke (dead soul/Bhudda) 41
household (*ie*) 12–13, 40–1, 85
Hōzanji 147, 173, 180, 185, 190
hundred-day practice (Hiei) 124–7
    see also sennichi kaihōgyō
hyakudo mairi (circumambulation practice) 173–4, 189

Ichiōji 180
ie see household
ihai (memorial tablet) 91–2, 93–4
Ikoma 122, 123, 163–4
Imakumano 178, 192
Inai Sadao 202
Inari 38, 39–40, 60, 75, 76, 138, 140, 193
    Fushimi Inari 71, 75, 139
    Toyokawa Inari 39–40, 76
inauspicious days 29–30
innen see karma
Ise 60, 134, 140, 156, 237–8
Ishikiri shrine 53, 129, 163, 173, 181
    1983 survey of worshippers 2, 16–17
itako (blind shamanesses) 130–2
Itō Shinjō 119, 202
Iwashimazu Hachimangū 142, 147, 163
Iwayaji 155
Iyotetsu Bus Co. 162, 164

Izanagi 24–5, 26, 43, 49, 122, 241, 242
Izanami 24–5, 26, 43, 242
Izumo Kannon pilgrimage 169
Izumo shrine 148

Japan Socialist Party 95
Japan Times 99
Jayawardene, President 216
Jehovah's Witnesses 198, 199, 214, 244, 249
Jesus 28–9, 51, 197, 246
    see also Christianity
jichinsai see ground-breaking ceremonies
Jinja hohchō 237–8
jiri rita ('for self and others') 110
Jishu shrine 148, 181, 185
Jizō 37, 52, 151, 152–3, 172
jōbutsu ('becoming a Buddha') 41, 45, 46, 210, 213
Jōdo shinshū *see* Pure Land Buddhism
Jurōjin 165, 166

kaeru (frogs) 178
kagura (sacred dances) 65
kaigen (eye opening rite) 37, 144, 177
kaihōgyō see sennichi kaihōgyō
kaimyō (posthumous name) 90–1
Kamata Shigeo 42
Kamei Miyoko 195
kami 1–2, 23–7, 32, 35, 38–40, 55–76 *passim*, 168, 170, 202, 235
    definition 25
    and shrines 137–66 *passim*
    see also Shinto, shrines
kamidana (household Shinto altar) 7, 53–4, 63–4, 177
    in shops 53, 189
Kaneko Satoru 9
Kanjō 144
Kankiten 147, 180, 185
Kannon 32, 36, 147, 158, 169, 191–3, 209, 235

and Agonshū 209–10, 211, 215–16, 217
Asakusa Kannon (Sensōji) 134
Batō Kannon 192–3
Izumo Kannon pilgrimage 169
Kannongyō (sūtra) 209
Kannon Jikeikai 209
Mie Kannon 36
Ōsu Kannon temple 46
statues of 36–7, 153, 192
temples dedicated to 137, 142, 143, 145–6, 149–3, 155, 157
karma (*innen*) 47, 48, 209–10, 232
Kasuga shrine 187
Katano shrine 61–4
Kawasaki Daishi temple 191
kegare (pollution) 48
Kegonji 172
Keihan Railway Co. 54, 74, 144–5, 163, 164, 176, 177
Keizan 92
Kibun 76
Kino Kazuyoshi 238
Kinpusenji 34–5, 110, 127
Kintetsu Railway Co. 164
Kiriyama Seiyū 111, 119, 208–12, 214–26 *passim*, 228, 232
Kitamura Sayo 108, 119, 122
Kitano Tenmangū 136, 161, 189
Kiyomizudera (Kyoto) 134, 142, 145, 148, 149, 155, 174, 210
Kiyomizudera (Yashiro) 176
Kiyomizudera (Yonago) 169
Kiyoshi Kōjin shrine 178
Kiyotakisan 178
kōan (Zen riddle) 81
Kōbe festival 73
Kōbo Daishi (Kūkai) 112–14, 115–16, 140, 141, 143–4, 145, 146, 153, 163, 169, 177–8, 209, 216, 235
Kōhaku (song contest) 64
Kojiki (ancient text) 23–5, 55
Kokawadera 179, 181

kokoro no furusato (spiritual homeland) 70–1, 104–5, 123–9, 237–8, 239
Kokoro no furusato (book) 238
Kōmeitō 194
Kōmoto Mitsugu 93
Kondō Kazuo 234
Konpira 54
Korea 35
Koreans in Japan 122
Kōrien Narita-san temple 54, 74, 144, 163, 164, 169, 176
kōtsū anzen *see* travel safety
Kōya, Mount (Kōyasan) 74, 112, 140, 163, 164, 238
Kōya hijiri (mountain ascetics) 113
Kubote 128
Kūkai *see* Kōbō Daishi
Kumamoto Akira 234
Kurehayashi Shōji 70
Kyburz, Josef 192
Kyūshū-Kōbe ferry 54, 177

legal status of religion 55–6, 72–3, 85–7
lotus position 79, 126
Lotus Sūtra 18, 32, 80, 121, 123, 197, 202, 203, 211

Maeda Takashi 88
Mahāyāna Buddhism 31
Mahikari 17, 19–20, 28, 42, 49, 119–20, 195, 197, 204–5, 206–7, 242
members 199, 200, 201, 213–14
o-kiyome 49, 203, 207, 231
Mainichi newspaper 75
mantras (words of power) 33
manuals, religious 15, 32, 94, 104
marriage partners 148, 181
see also weddings
Mary (mother of Jesus) 51, 197
Matsumoto Kenichi 133
matsuri see festivals

media and religion 72, 124, 147, 218–19
see also advertisements
medical problems see healing
meditation 79, 81–3, 103–4, 105, 107
see also zazen
mediums 130–2
see also itako
Meiji, Emperor 26, 149
Meiji Jingu 26, 71
meishi (business cards) 75
Meitetsu Railway Co. 166
membership of religions (statistics) 6–9, 195–6, 199, 200–1
memorial rites 44–5, 74, 78–9, 83, 89–92, 100, 130–1, 160, 204, 206
in Agonshū 44–5, 210, 212–13, 220
for animals 45–6
for inanimate objects 46
see also ancestors
Mie Kannon 36
miko (shrine maidens) 61, 65, 67–8
mikoshi (portable shrines) 66–7, 76
Mimurotoji 156–7, 158, 159, 160
Minatogawa shrine 167
miracles 49, 205–6, 208, 234–6, 239
Misen, Mount 118
Mitsukoshi 52
Miyake Hotoshi 23, 51
miyamairi (first shrine visits) 60, 62, 71, 150
mizuko (aborted foetuses) 152–3, 179
kuyō (rites for) 45, 171, 239
Monju 148, 151, 222
Mormonism 13, 198, 200, 249
Moses 29, 51
Mouer, Ross 107
mountains 116–19, 155–6; see under name of individual mountains

Mu (lost continent) 197, 202, 234, 236
Mū (magazine) 234
Mudōji 125
muenbotoke (unaffiliated dead soul) 48
mushi kuyō (mushi okuri) (rites to drive away insects) 57–8
Myōgonji 40
Myōshinji 98, 216
Nachi 135, 137, 155
Nagamura Nichihō 123
Nakamura Hajime 133
Nakasone Yasuhiro 188
Nakayamadera 149–153, 154, 166
Nakayama Miki 194, 202
Nanda 215
Nankai Railway Co. 163, 164
Nara Great buddha 36
Nariaiji 158
Narita-san (Shinshōji) 135, 143–5, 146, 147, 148, 161, 177, 185, 187, 191
nenjū gyōji (regular yearly events) 57, 62
'new' new religions 195–233, 234, 237
see also under individual religions
new religions 8, 49, 108, 119–20, 194–233, 237
see also under individual religions
New Year 10, 63–6, 71–2, 165, 178
see also hatsumōde
newspapers see media and religion
NHK 5, 9–10, 12, 30, 182, 183, 236
Nichiren Shōshū 8–9, 80, 85, 92, 102, 123
Nihongi (ancient text) 23–5, 26
Nihon no reinōryokusha (book) 129, 132
niōmon (temple gate) 139
Nirvana Sūtra 202
Nishiyama Shigeru 14, 235
Nittaiji 136

Nostradamus 214, 215
Numata Kenya 119, 218

obi see hara obi
o-bon (festival of the dead 10,
    11, 13, 40, 51, 98, 99–101,
    103, 237
occultism 197
offerings 27, 37, 66, 94, 152
ogamiya-san (spiritual
    healers) 129
Ohnuki-Tierney, Emiko 150
Ōjin, Emperor 26, 142
    see also Hachiman
Okada Kōtama 19, 119, 202, 204
Okada Sachiko 20
Ōkawa Ryūhō 234
o-kiyome (purification) 49, 203,
    204, 207, 231
o-mamori (amulets) 175–8,
    182–4, 186–7, 188, 189–90,
    224, 235
    plastic 176
    see also charms
o-mikuji (oracle lots, divination
    slips) 29, 65
Omine-Kumano 117
Ōmi Railway Co. 166
Omura Eishō 14
oni (demons 34–5
Oomoto 19, 29, 196, 202
oracle lots *see o-mikuji*
Osorezan 130–2
Ōsu Kannon temple 46
Otokoyama 142–3, 145, 146
Ōyama Nezunomikoto
    Shinshikyōkai 195, 202, 203

pain relief *see* healing
peace 28, 213, 223, 225, 229–30
pilgrimage xii, 32, 113–16,
    157–61, 192, 231, 236, 237,
    239
    clothing worn 113–14, 158,
        160, 162
    mini 153, 168–70
    scrolls 158–9, 160
    transport used 114, 159, 161–2

see also under individual
    pilgrimages
possession (spirits) 206–7, 234
prayers 33, 94, 159, 243
    see also charms, *genze riyaku*
pregnancy *see* childbirth, fertility
priests 88–9, 171–2
    training 75, 80, 124–7
printing blocks, rites for 46
Pure Land Buddhism 9, 80, 92
purification 27, 49, 64, 67–8, 82,
    121–2, 140, 204
    of cars 185–6, 190–1
    see also o-kiyome

railways 71–2, 98, 163, 164, 166
    Keihan Railway Co. 54, 74,
        144–5, 163, 164, 176, 177
reincarnation 84
reishō (spiritual pollution) 48
Reishō o toke (Agonshū
    film) 44–5
Reiyūkai 42, 102, 197, 202,
    203–4
religion:
    and business 59, 73–6, 98,
        144–5, 147, 161–4, 166–7;
        see also securities
        companies; *see also under*
        individual companies
    folk religion 23, 40, 127, 208
        234
    legal status 55–6, 72–3, 85–7
    media and religion 72, 124,
        147, 218–19; *see also*
        advertisements
    membership of religions
        (statistics) 6–9, 195–6,
        199, 200–1
    new *see* new religions
    shūkyō: definition 13–14
    and state 55–6, 72–3, 84, 85–7
    and students 14, 20–1,
        199–200; *see also*
        educational success
Rinzai Zen 81, 91
    see also Zen
Risshakuji (Yamadera) 135

riyaku (benefits) 32–3, 36, 37, 38, 146, 147, 151, 188
  see also genze riyaku
rural depopulation *see* urbanisation
ryōen (good marriage) 148

Sahet Mahet 215
Saichō 143
Saikoku pilgrimage 143, 149, 153, 155, 156, 157–60, 169
Sakai Daigaku 42
  Sakai Yūsai 120, 126, 127
Sakanoue Tamuramaro 142, 145
sake 66, 67, 79
salt 67
samurai 206–7, 231, 234
sanmon (temple gate) 139
Sarashina Nikki (book) 36
Sasaguri pilgrimage 122
sawari (spiritual blockages) 48
school trips 135, 156
scrolls carried by pilgrims 158–9, 160
securities companies 75, 193, 243
Sefukuji 155
Seikyō Shinbun (Buddhist newspaper) 194
Seiwa, Emperor 143, 146
Sekai Kyūseikyō 19
Sekiguchi Sakae 20
sendatsu (pilgrimage leader) 115, 160
senile dementia 191–2
Senjuin 174
sennichi kaihōgyō (mountain austerity) 124–7, 128, 133, 217
Sensōji (Asakusa Kannon) 134
senzo see ancestors
sesshin (intense meditation retreats) 82–3
setsubun (spring festival) 34
seven gods of good fortune *see shichi fukujin*
shichi fukujin (seven gods of good fortune) 164–7
  pilgrimages 165–7

  see also Benten, Bishamonten, Daikokuten, Ebisu, Fukurokuju, Hotei, Jurōjin
shichigosan (7–5–3 festival) 62, 71, 150, 236
Shigisan *see* Chōgosonshiji
Shikoku 37
  pilgrimage 113–15, 155–6, 157, 162, 164, 169–70, 174, 238
Shingon Buddhism 74, 80, 112, 119, 144, 151, 209
Shinkō Jūkun (ten articles of belief) 104
Shinnyoen 18, 119, 195–6, 202, 216, 218–19, 222
Shinreikyō 195, 218
Shinshōji *see* Narita-san Shinshōji
Shinto 9, 14, 23–9, 38, 55–76
  and Buddhism, coexistence of 1–2, 6–7, 9, 32, 38–40, 56, 150–1, 165, 170
  legal status 55–6, 87
  membership 9
  and new religions 197, 202
  see also charms, festivals, *kami*, shrines
Shiseidō 75–6
Shittenōji 136
Shodōshima 36, 115–16, 154–5, 156, 162
Shōkū 143, 145, 163
shōryō nagashi (rite for the spirits of the dead) 101
Shōtoku Taishi 141, 149, 153, 174
Shōwa, Emperor *see* Hirohito, Emperor
shrines x, 1, 52–4, 60–76 *passim*, 134–67, 237–8
  and charms 175–93 *passim*
  fairs 136
  location of 137–8, 155–6
  see also kami; see also under individual shrines
Shugendō 117–19, 137, 211, 222
shugyō see austerities
shūkyō (religion), definition of 13–14
Smith, Robert 91, 93

Sōka Gakkai 8–9, 17, 92, 102, 194, 196, 200, 207, 229
and Lotus Sūtra 18, 197, 202, 203
Sonoda Minoru 68
Sōō 124
Sōtō Zen 3–4, 9, 17, 81, 85, 89, 91, 92, 102, 103–5, 130, 198, 237
temples 36, 42, 74, 78, 83
training centre 74, 78, 80
see also Zen
soul (*tama*) 40, 84
state and religion 55–6, 72–3, 84, 85–7
students and religion 14, 20–1, 199–200
see also educational success
Sugawara Michizane 25–6, 44, 242
see also Tenjin
Su-God 120, 203, 204
Sugimoto, Yoshio 107
suigyō (water austerities) 122–3
Suijin 122
Sumadera 169–70
Sumida river (Tokyo) 165
Sumiyoshi shrine 71, 147
Sumō 21
surveys on religion
Gallup 5
Ishikiri shrine (1983) 2, 16–17, 53, 129
Japan Agency for Cultural Affairs 6
Japan Ministry of Education 6
Japan Prime Minister's Office 5–6
NHK 5, 9–10, 12, 30, 182, 183, 236
Sōtō Zen 3–4, 89, 129
Yomiuri 10, 12
Susanoo 26–7
sūtras 33–5
see also Āgama sūtras, *Hannya Shingyō*, Lotus Sūtra, Nirvana Sūtra

Taira Masakado 144
Taiyō Shinjiru Piramiddo no Kai (Sun Worshipping Pyramid Society) 194–5
Takaosanji 144
Takeshita Noboru 188
talismans see charms
tama see soul
Tani Fumio 199, 200, 201, 213
Tanukidani 118
Taoism 29, 117, 142, 165
tatari (spiritual retribution) 48
telephone cards 176–7
television 64, 124, 218, 221, 226
temples x, 1, 52, 57, 64, 78–105 *passim*, 134–67, 168–74 *passim*
and charms 175–92 *passim*
fairs 136
locations 137–8, 155–6
see also under individual temples
Tendai Buddhism 80, 119, 120, 124, 229
Tengyō, Emperor 144, 146
Tenjin 26, 32, 60, 148, 180
see also Sugawara Michizane
Tenrikyō 50, 194, 197, 200, 202, 203, 220, 222, 241
Tenshō Kōtai Jingūkyō 108
thousand-day practice see *sennichi kaihōgyō*
Tōganji 36
Tōji 38, 136, 161
Tokugawa government (1600–1868) 55, 85–6, 158
torii (shrine gateway) 138–9, 174
tourism 73, 134, 155–8, 159–60, 162, 166–7
Toyokawa Inari 39–40, 76
Toyota car company 75
Toyotomi Hideyoshi 149
travel safety 148, 152, 176, 177, 185, 186, 187, 190–1
see also purification of cars
tsuitachi goma (Agonshū rite) 221, 225–7, 232

Tsutsumi Masao *see* Kiriyama
   Seiyū

UFOs 234–6
ujiko (shrine parishioners) 60, 72
Unification Church
   (Moonies) 198, 200, 249
Uno Masato 75
upāya (skilful means) 247
urbanisation 58, 69, 93, 97, 102,
   198, 200, 238–9, 240
Ushitora no Konjin 202
Utsumi Shunshō 127, 133
waterfalls 122–3, 135, 155
weddings 51

yakudoshi (unlucky
   years) 29, 62, 173
Yakuōji 173
Yakushi 32, 36, 172–3
yamabushi (mountain
   ascetics) 117–19, 120, 122,
   128, 222–5, 227, 230, 231

Yamada Ryūshin 128
Yamadera (Risshakuji) 135
Yamashina 215, 221
Yasaka shrine 139
Yasukuni shrine 56
Yomigaeru: Tōtō (film) 132–3,
   254
Yomiuri newspaper 10, 12
Yoshida Akira 167
Yoshiminedera 181
Yoshino 123, 128
yutate (hot water rite) 67–8

zazen (Zen meditation) 79, 88,
   103, 104
   see also meditation
Zen 19, 43, 74, 79–83, 103–4
   see also Rinzai Zen, Sōtō Zen
Zenkōji 188
Zōjōji 181